thought

# Without a second thought

## A MEMOIR OF LIFE IN FRANCO'S MADRID

Diane Lorz Benitez

Walrus PUBLISHING

Walrus Publishing | St. Louis, MO 63116

Walrus
PUBLISHING™

Walrus Publishing | Saint Louis, MO 63116


For information, contact:
Walrus Publishing
An imprint of Amphorae Publishing Group
*a woman- and veteran-owned business*
4168 Hartford Street, Saint Louis, MO 63116

Publisher's Note: This memoir reflects the recollections of the author.

Manufactured in the United States of America
Set in Lamar Pen, Rift, and Baskerville
Interior designed by Kristina Blank Makansi
Cover designed by Kristina Blank Makansi
Cover photo: Shutterstock

Library of Congress Control Number: 2020943940
ISBN: 9781940442440

To Ana and Alicia, the heart of the story.
And to Michael, Emmie and Sarah
so they can know how it all began.

One thing I can guarantee, Diana:
if you marry me, you will never be bored.
— Alberto Benitez, *September 1965*

*Caminante, no hay camino; se hace camino al andar.*
—Antonio Machado, *1912*

*Spain is a river of contradictions.*

A country full of normally vociferous individuals, most Spaniards chose silence rather than speak about the civil war that killed or displaced over half a million people. Even after the death of the dictator, *Generalísimo* Francisco Franco, a generation would pass before they began a dialogue to shed light on that disaster and to give it a proper burial—or at least to try. For over a decade, I swam in that river buoyed by the rich culture and the beauty of the country. I noted the scars of war that surfaced from time to time, but I didn't see the phantoms floating beneath. Neither did I feel the undercurrent of a different kind that ran in my own home. When I finally recognized it, I, too, chose silence—for a while.

I read somewhere that the light by which we see is constantly shifting. I waited to write this story until I thought the light was right.

# Chapter 1

In the summer of 1936, a baby girl napped undisturbed on a screened porch in Meadville, Pennsylvania, a peaceful college town of 25,000 souls. The only sound to ruffle the afternoon air was the occasional blast of a train whistle. An ocean away, in the historic capital spread out on Spain's central plain, a 10-year-old boy trembled in a dark basement while air raid warnings wailed outside, slicing through the heart of a city and a nation like a knife. In the years to come, their lives would come together and fall apart, forever changed by the deep scars that living through the violence and privation of war can cut into the psyche.

⁂

On July 18, 1936, Alberto Manuel Benítez Garcia sat in his room reading a Sherlock Holmes mystery, unaware that a military revolt against the government had ignited civil war. Only later that day did he learn the access roads to Madrid had been cut, trapping his eighteen-year-old sister Julina on the wrong side. She could not return from summer camp as planned, and Alberto would not see his sister again for nearly three years.

⁂

When I was seven, my mother, brother and I followed my father to his latest posting at an army base in southern California. I remember the towering palms and the smell of orange trees . I remember riding in a Jeep, and I remember our babysitter, a soldier named Skerble but whom everyone called Screwball. But most of all I remember the day my father took us to the base swimming pool. I couldn't swim a stroke, but that didn't stop me as I took a gulp of chlorine-scented air, leapt from the spot marked *9 Feet*, and surrendered to a rush of pale blue bubbles. Unlike the grey lake back home in Pennsylvania, the pool water beneath the California sun was warm and inviting. I opened my eyes, ignored the brief sting, and kicked toward the bottom looking for the two white stones my father had dropped there. The stone hunt was his idea.

"You'll be a good swimmer in no time," my father said. "And you'll never have to use water wings." That was fine with me. I didn't want to wear scratchy inflated armbands anyway.

I watched my father through the water. He sat on the bottom of the pool and made silly faces. I don't know how he held his breath for so long; I couldn't. I felt dizzy when I finally thrashed my way to the surface. But I had the stones.

"Daddy, look! I found them."

"I knew you would," he said in his chocolaty voice. He had a lovely singing voice, too, and sang songs like *Beautiful Dreamer,* and the one with my name. *Smile for me, my Diane,* he would sing—soft and reassuring. My father's eyes were darker blue than the water and his nose was flat in the middle where he broke it years before. I never knew how. When he hoisted me onto his shoulders, droplets ran along his upper arm shimmering on the words *Semper Fidelis.* It would be years before I worked out my father's journey from an eighteen-year-old Marine to a forty-year-old captain in the Army Transportation Corps, but I knew the meaning of *Semper Fidelis* ever since I was old enough to recognize letters and ask my father about them.

"Always faithful," he said with a grin. "Yep, that's me." Then his brow furrowed, and his voice took on a serious tone. "And that's the way you should be, too."

We walked to the wading pool where mother sat rubbing baby oil on my brother's back. David was three. He couldn't swim either. Mother managed an awkward sidestroke in the section marked *5 Feet* but she didn't like to get her face wet and she swam with her head held stiff above the water and her eyes squeezed shut. I felt a little sorry for her; she was kind of a fraidy-cat. Not me. I was fearless in the water—at least I thought so until the day we went to the beach for the first time.

*

The warm sand swallowed my feet with every step. My legs felt heavy like they did when I tramped through the Pennsylvania snow. I didn't mind, but I was glad when my mother stopped, looked around and called out, "How about right here?"

A few steps ahead, my father turned and lowered my brother who had been riding piggyback. "Looks good to me," he said.

Mother set down the basket that held a blanket, two striped towels and our lunch of bologna sandwiches with sweet pickles. I hoped she had packed some black olives because they were my favorite food even though I'd eaten so many the week before that I got sick.

The beach extended as far as I could see. The ocean mumbled under its breath, and figures bobbled on the water far from shore.

"Look at those people," I said. "Do they have water wings?"

My father opened the basket, took out the blanket, and then looked toward the ocean. "They're riding waves," he said. "Just wait a minute, and I'll show you how." He handed a corner of the blanket to my mother and they unfolded it, sidestepping David who was busy kicking up sand clouds.

I didn't wait. I went toward the water to get a better look. I wasn't afraid. I was never afraid; my father had seen to that. Even in the deep end of a pool I knew how to wriggle around and float on my back.

I walked to where the pale soft sand turned dark and solid; my feet no longer sank. A wave rolled in and I stood firm, giggling at the slap of water that hit my knees. The wave uncurled behind me, leaving a thin line of grey foam and a row of shiny pebbles. White seagulls soared and swooped overhead with a noise that sounded both threatening and wistful. I didn't like them. Another wave hit me, stronger this time, and I felt the sand slip out from beneath my feet. The earth churned, and my arms flailed, fingers grasping, but there was nothing there, nothing to hold on to.

"Daddy!"

I dug in my toes but couldn't keep from slipping. A force I didn't understand was dragging me out, pulling me under.

"Daddy!"

A strong hand clamped around my wrist and steadied me. "It's all right," my father said. "It's all right."

He held me tight as I regained my balance, and for the next several minutes we watched a succession of waves wrap around our ankles, wash away our footprints, then return to wherever waves come from. Gradually my father released his grip. By the end of the day, I'd lost my fear of the slipping sands. I grew to like the sensation, the tickle between my toes, but I never forgot that initial feeling—the shock of losing my footing in a place I thought was solid.

⁂

In the fall the Army transferred my father again, this time overseas. The family, now a trio, returned to Pennsylvania.

⁂

We had been home for over a year when the trunk arrived. I sat cross-legged on the kitchen floor working a metal rasp against the trunk's sturdy padlock. It was hard work for a nine-year old, and I'd been at it for what seemed a very long time. I brushed some specks of grey dust into a little pile, and continued scraping back and forth. Sometimes the tool snagged and my hand slipped.

Standing at the sink mother turned to check my progress.

"Be careful," she said.

"I will."

After drying the last of the supper dishes, mother folded the tea towel over a rod under the sink. She wore a pink striped cotton dress with short puffy sleeves. I had one just like it. Mother bought the Mother/Daughter outfits after she saw a Montgomery Ward ad in the newspaper. We wore them to the farmers' market on Saturday. People often commented on my mother's looks. Mr. Swanson, the butcher, said she looked like she just stepped out of a bandbox. I didn't know what a bandbox was, but my mother looked pleased when he said it. The bakery lady called her a fashion plate. I didn't know what that was either.

Our next-door neighbor was constantly telling me to walk straight.

"Your mother has beautiful posture," she said. "There is no reason for you to slouch."

Mother watched over my shoulder.

"Don't cut yourself," she said.

"I won't."

Mother wasn't good with tools. My father could fix anything. Mother made things look pretty. My father had a workbench in the basement, and that's how I knew about the rasp. But except for the photographs he sent, dressed in his army uniform, I couldn't recall exactly the last time I saw him. I had one of his photos on my bedroom dresser. He had written across it: *To my daughter Diane. May I always be proud of her.*

I rested my hand for a moment and rubbed the soft skin between my thumb and forefinger. My five-year old brother played with Lincoln Logs at the table. David had lost interest in my project, but I was determined to open the trunk. Mother called it a footlocker. We'd been expecting it ever since my father wrote that he was sending home souvenirs from Europe. Mother read that part of his letter out loud before she stored it in her dressing table drawer. She saved all my father's letters, just as years later, she would save all of mine.

"I wonder why your dad didn't send a key. How did he think we would open it?" She pulled out a chair and sat next to David.

"I can do it." I worked faster.

"You're just like your father inside out."

That sounded funny to me. *Inside out.* I looked up and she smiled but only for a moment.

At the time my father was somewhere between England and Japan. Mother thought he'd be home in a year.

"The war is bound to be over by then," she said.

We didn't call it World War II; it was simply the war—as though there had never been another.

The olive-colored footlocker, nearly the size of my brother, arrived with a thick paper label glued to the top: 444 Poplar St., Meadville, Penna. On the side, letters stenciled in white now read: *Major* Norbert W. Lorz, with a row of numbers under the name. I couldn't imagine what my father had sent all the way from Europe. Maybe something I could tell the nuns about at school, or show to my friend, Patty. Or maybe I'd just keep quiet, but that was hard for me to do because I'd already been places and seen things that none of my school friends knew anything about. Mother said Army Brats were lucky that way. Maybe that was the reason I skipped second grade. The nuns just moved me from first to third. Maybe travelling had made me smarter. I don't remember feeling special. I just thought that if the nuns sent me to third, well, that's where I was supposed to be. You didn't question the nuns.

In addition to California, we had lived for a year in Louisiana but between each of my father's transfers we came back to Pennsylvania. When I returned to St. Brigid's Elementary, I told my classmates about flying in a plane—in 1943 none of them had ever flown. I left out the part about throwing-up in a paper bag. I told them about the smell of red Louisiana earth after a rain, how I watched for rattlesnakes in the gully behind the apartment building we shared with other military families, and how I walked to kindergarten along a dusty road lined with drooping lilacs.

After our stay in California, I took a photograph of a giant Sequoia tree to school. And I told the class about an earthquake that shook the dishes in our dining room cupboard. Another time, since I knew the correct pronunciation of Yosemite, I shared that bit of information with Sister Anita James who kept saying *Yousamight* until I couldn't stand it any longer. She didn't seem pleased. I'd forgotten about the *Don't contradict a nun* rule.

I could describe a three-day train ride across the country in a stateroom where the beds and table and washbasin unfolded magically from the wall, and a black man in a white cap and jacket brought a tray of sandwiches to our compartment.

"Sorry, Ma'am," he'd said to my mother. "We run short of food in the dining car because we have to feed the troops first. But I'll be sure you and the children gets something to eat."

I didn't mind. Eating sandwiches on a train while the world passed by the window was more interesting than any other place I'd ever had lunch.

By the time the footlocker arrived, I knew about Nazis and Pearl Harbor. My mother didn't discuss them with me, but she listened to the radio news every evening. Afterwards, she stood at the living room window staring at the street. When I asked what she was doing, she just said, "Oh, nothing." Sometimes I found her there in the dark. Smoking a cigarette. Staring out the window. Silent.

On the rare occasion we went to a movie, the newsreel—our only view of the outside world in that pre-television era—showed bombed-out buildings and homeless children. Sometimes the theater lights came on and an usher took a collection for the March of Dimes to help people with polio. I was more afraid of polio than of bombs.

At Sunday Mass Fr. John lead the prayers for world peace and for the conversion of all non-Catholics. On school days, the nuns conducted safety drills, so in case a bomb fell on St. Brigid, we would know to lower our heads and slide under our desks.

The nuns collected clothes for war orphans, and I donated a turquoise sweater I'd outgrown. Sister told us to attach our name and address. I didn't know why until many weeks later I received an envelope from France marked *Par Avion*. The handwriting looked nothing like the Palmer Method cursive I was learning, and I didn't understand a word of the note inside. Mother sent it to Cleveland where my father's brother, the only person we knew who could translate it, taught French. He returned it with the words of a French girl thanking me for the sweater.

Besides donating clothes, we also saved metal for the war effort. I gave up my toy train and its tracks, and David and I took turns stomping on tin cans, tying them in bundles of ten to leave on the porch for a volunteer collector. Even simple things were scarce. We used stamps from ration books to buy meat, and mother cooked with something called oleo, a white glob until she mixed yellow food coloring into it and shaped it into a brick. It never fooled anyone. We knew it wasn't butter the same way we knew that Spam, in spite of the cloves and brown sugar glaze, wasn't ham. Gasoline was rationed, too, but that didn't matter to us because we didn't have a car, and even if we had had one, mother didn't know how to drive. Besides, we could walk from one end of Meadville to the other in almost no time at all.

I was aware of restrictions, but we never went hungry. Meadville was a small town surrounded by farms. On market days, local farmers sold fruits and vegetables, and the Amish ladies sold breads and cheese. When mother and her sister, who lived on the other side of our double house, couldn't buy nylon stockings, they rubbed a kind of dye on their legs and tried to paint a seam line with iodine. I knew mother could make-do in many ways but she'd never get that footlocker open on her own, and I wasn't about to wait till she recruited help.

Finally, the lock snapped. I lifted the lid and a smell I didn't recognize floated out—not unpleasant, just unfamiliar and exciting. I bent down and breathed in the scent. Then I started unpacking.

My father had enclosed a description of the souvenirs: tams, the woolen hats, he bought in Scotland as well as the fabric called Black Watch tartan. The miniature carved stone chair came from Ireland and guaranteed a happy outcome if you placed a thumb on the seat and made a wish. He sent a silver ring shaped like a buckled strap for me, some wooden games for David and a pair of antique candlesticks for my mother and also a recipe for Yorkshire pudding from an English lady we didn't know. For the next few minutes, we took turns trying on the hats and looking in the mirror. The silver ring fit my finger perfectly; mother said she would use the tartan material to make a suit for me. I liked the idea, but I'd found a greater pleasure in something else.

"Mom?"

"Yes?"

"When you write to Daddy, be sure to tell him I opened the footlocker all by myself."

⁂

My father came home safely. We moved again to a smaller town, remodeled an old house and I attended a public school for the first time. By 1950, I was a teenager in saddle shoes and a poodle skirt, a cheerleader with a flip hairdo, and I sang the lead roles in school operettas. And I followed the rules: *Obey authority. Control your emotions. Don't even think about sex!*

Once again we ate real butter and honest-to-goodness ham, and mother could buy nylon stockings. With no prior experience, she took a sales position in a small department store and was promoted to buyer less than a year later. After twenty-six years in the Army, my father went to work in a factory that made zippers. I didn't think about World War II, and my parents never discussed it. War had left my landscape unscathed, and if there were deeper scars, I couldn't see them. I didn't even know about that earlier war—the Spanish Civil War—that happened an ocean away, ripping through the country in which I would spend the most meaningful years of my life. For a very long time I didn't see the scars of that conflict either.

# Chapter 2

By the time I met Alberto Benítez, I was a twenty-two-year old assistant buyer at Halle Brothers, a prestigious department store in Cleveland, Ohio. I'd left college against my parents' wishes to look for a career in fashion retail. Alberto was a handsome thirty-two-year old civil engineer from Spain. Our initial meeting didn't bode well.

It was a Sunday morning. Charlene, a fellow Halle Brothers employee with whom I shared an apartment, had the travel section of the Cleveland Plain Dealer spread out on the living room floor. I filled my coffee mug and sat beside her. Every weekend, in addition to scanning the fashion ads, we searched the travel section for an affordable European vacation. On our current salaries, things didn't look promising, but that didn't stop us.

Charlene reached behind her and turned on the record player. A vinyl 78 dropped onto the turntable.

*Bonjour, monsieur.*
*Parlez-vous anglais?*

*Il ne parle pas anglais.*

Charlene and I had split the cost of an album titled *Speak French in 30 Days.* My roommate, a college graduate with a minor in French, was already weeks ahead of me. I lagged behind with two years of high school Spanish.

"We might as well create a little *ambiance*," Charlene said with a French pronunciation. She lit a Benson & Hedges, ran a hand through her naturally blond hair and smiled her beautiful smile.

"Fine." I said, looking at a round trip fare to Paris. "But I'm afraid this *ambiance* is as close as we'll ever get. At the rate we're saving, we'll be old and gray old by the time we can afford a ticket. *Mon Dieu,* we'll have lost all our *je ne sais quoi* by then!"

Charlene exhaled with mock *ennui*. "*Quel dommage.*"

Then the phone rang.

My roommate raised her eyebrows. I shrugged. Neither of us had a boyfriend. Romance at the moment seemed as far-off as Paris. Maybe one of my aunts was calling with an invitation to lunch. All of Charlene's family lived in West Virginia, but I had two sets of aunts and uncles in Cleveland.

"You get it," she said.

I wriggled my bottom to the little telephone stand by the dining room door. "Hello."

"Is that you, Di?"

I held the receiver away from my face and wrinkled my nose. Nobody called me Di. I detested the sound of it. I even told my mother once that I wished she had called me Diana instead of Diane. "The priest wouldn't baptize you with a pagan name," she'd replied.

That explained why my birth certificate reads *Mary* Diane. I asked mother why, since she planned to call me Diane, she hadn't registered the name as Diane Mary.

"Because I thought your signature would look elegant if you didn't use your first name at all and signed *M. Diane*."

Mother was funny that way. She used the same method with my brother whose first name was Hugh, something I didn't know until I was about eight years old because everyone called him David.

At any rate, I would tell the boy on the phone that I had been named for the Queen of Heaven and a goddess of the moon and the hunt which meant he could not take the liberty of shortening my name to Di.

Charlene cocked her head and drew a question mark in the air.

I covered the mouthpiece. "It's Tom," I said.

It was Charlene's turn to make a face.

Tom, the older brother of a co-worker, was a 6'2" civil engineer with faded orange hair and a plodding personality. When our friend said her brother would like to date one of us—it didn't seem to matter which—Charlene and I had tried to discourage the idea, but Tom didn't get the message.

His voice droned on. "I picked up my new Pontiac yesterday and thought maybe we could go for a drive along the lake. I know it's short notice. But we could have some dinner and then go dancing and…"

I tuned him out and concentrated on possible excuses: a growing pile of laundry, an impending migraine, dinner with my aunt, but his voice cut in again.

"… and he's from Spain."

"Who?" I said.

"The new guy at the office." Tom sounded irritated. "He's a little older than we are and really interesting, and he doesn't know many people yet, so ask your roommate to come with us."

*Spain!* That put a different slant on things. I turned to Charlene and smiled.

⁂

I don't know when I developed an interest in foreign places. Perhaps my father's travels influenced me, or my paternal grandfather who came from Bavaria, or my French-speaking uncle. Somehow I had the idea that everything European was better. French food, Italian shoes, Belgian chocolate, it all appealed to me. I don't know why. I just had a taste for Europe. And I was attracted to anyone with an accent.

On the bus home one evening, a young man asked me for directions. He had an accent. By the time we reached my stop I knew his name was Stefan, that he came from Romania, and I had asked him to dinner on Saturday. Another time, at a social club for international students, I danced with Saul, a Jewish boy from Hungary. He told me how he had escaped Communism by jumping from a ship in the port of Haifa and swimming to shore in Israel. Eventually he found relatives in Cleveland Heights. When Saul suggested a visit to his apartment to see his Israeli army uniform, I went. These encounters were innocent. I was intrigued, but not in love. Furthermore, my Catholic upbringing had such a stranglehold on my sexuality that anything else would have been impossible anyway. I just wanted to hear stories of a life different from mine told with a foreign accent. Sometimes, however, the accent misled me.

I thought I detected another foreign story one December evening when I left Halle's. As I waited at the bus stop, an exotic-looking sloe-eyed man in a camel's hair coat approached me.

"You wait for the Euclid bus, right? I see you here before."

I had noticed him, too, on occasion leaving an adjacent office building, a paisley scarf crossed at his throat. Where I came from men didn't wear paisley scarves. They faced winter in hunting caps with lowered earflaps. The man had nodded to me on those evenings the way one does when seeing a familiar face at a coffee shop, or a regular commuter at the bus stop.

I hunched my shoulders and stomped my feet for warmth. Behind me a red neon sign blinked *Cocktails*.

"We're freezing here," the man said. "You have a drink with me? You take the next bus?" His words hit the air in little white puffs.

"Well … okay." My fingers had turned to icicles, but I didn't accept the invitation in order to escape the cold. I went because of the accent.

We defrosted in the steamy bar in a haze of cigarette smoke and vapors from wet wool coats. I sipped something sweet and alcoholic, maybe a strawberry daiquiri—I hadn't yet discovered the glacial glamour of dry martinis.

The man spoke in a low voice with unusual inflections. I tried to imagine where he came from. English was not his mother tongue; I was sure of that. I found his speech poetic. He referred to a party where everyone had had "so much the good time." He assured me that if we continued our association we, too, would have "so much the good time." Was he German, I wondered, or Greek or Polish? Whatever he was, I needed to know so I complimented him sincerely.

"You speak English well." I said, hoping I didn't sound patronizing. "Where do you come from?"

He looked puzzled and took a sip of his drink before he said, "Pittsburgh."

No longer cold, I felt the flush rise. I don't remember how I tried to extricate myself from the *faux pas.* Whatever I said next didn't help, and Mr. Paisley Scarf and I said *adieux* a few minutes later. I never saw him again. The accent still puzzles me. On the other hand, I've never been to Pittsburgh.

⁂

Charlene didn't want to go out with Tom and said "no" at first, but I insisted.

"Never mind Tom." I said. "The Spaniard might be interesting."

*Interesting* proved an understatement.

⁂

I opened the door later that afternoon and felt a twinge of disappointment. Tom flashed an anticipatory grin too large for the occasion. In contrast, the man beside him, who barely reached his shoulder, looked serious. Tom had mentioned dancing. I didn't fancy my options.

Both men wore jackets and ties, though the dark-haired man's sport coat was cut shorter and slightly fitted, European style—I learned later that even his white shirts with the discreet monogram were custom-made in Madrid. His subtle striped silk tie contrasted markedly with Tom's shiny polyester print.

Behind the lenses of horn-rimmed glasses, the Spaniard's eyes glistened like polished chestnuts. Their boldness—like the eyes in Picasso's self-portraits—made me self-conscious. I stepped back and motioned the men inside. Charlene, who never looked self-conscious about anything, came around the corner from her bedroom.

"Hi, Tom," she said, extending her hand to his friend. "I'm Charlene."

The Spaniard didn't so much shake her hand as bend over it with a scarcely perceptible bow.

"Alberto Benítez," he said.

I offered my hand as well.

"*Con mucho gusto, Alberto,*" I said, drawing on the high school Spanish.

"Oh, I don't mind if you call me Al," he said, raising his eyes from my hand. I assumed my accent had been terrible, but he didn't look like my idea of an *Al.*

"Nice place you've got." Tom was taking inventory.

Our apartment was actually the first floor of a two-family house. We had two bedrooms, a big bathroom, a dining room, and a roomy kitchen—though for some reason the refrigerator stood on the landing of the basement stairs—a living room with a fireplace and an odd extension off the living room that we called the library because it held a set of encyclopedias. Charlene and I had shared the cost of that, too. *A* through *R* belonged to Charlene; *N* through *Z* were mine in the event we ever separated.

"So, girls," Tom said when he'd finished his assessment. "Shall we—"

"I must apologize," Alberto interrupted. "I have worn the wrong shoes for dancing. You won't mind to stop at my apartment so I can change?"

*A fabulous dancer or just picky?* I looked at his feet and immediately saw the problem; his shoe soles looked like tire tread. It would take the skill of Nijinsky and considerable strength to maneuver all that rubber across a dance floor. I loved to dance, but couldn't imagine myself in the arms of either of these men.

⁂

"Come up while I change," Alberto said as Tom pulled the Pontiac along side the curb of a west side apartment building. *How long does it take a Spaniard to change shoes?* But before I could object, Tom had opened the car door.

"Sure," he said.

The one-bedroom apartment was littered with books; unopened airmail envelopes lay on a desk and a world map was tacked to the wall of the kitchenette. A red line drawn with a felt-tipped pen ran from England to Spain and to Africa then crossed the Atlantic to Boston and Cleveland.

"Let me offer you a drink while we're here," Alberto said, taking a bottle of Johnny Walker Red from a kitchen cupboard. Plans for the evening shifted.

I asked about the map. Yes, he had worked in Africa looking for water sources in the Congo when the country was still Belgian. Underground water was his specialty. Yes, he spoke French.

"And Boston?"

"I had a scholarship for post-graduate study at MIT," Alberto said. "And that's where I fell in love." He paused and smiled. "With the United States."

For the next several minutes he extoled the teaching methods at MIT and the superior quality of everything made in the USA. "You are so efficient," he said. "Everything in this country works." As if to illustrate his point, he opened the refrigerator and held up an ice cube tray. He poured our drinks and stood leaning against the bookshelf.

"I had to return to Spain at the end of the scholarship, of course. I went to work for a company constructing an American air base outside Madrid, part of a US/Spain agreement. When that contract ended, I managed to get hired by an American company so I could return to the States. That took a couple of years, but here I am." He saluted with his glass and took a sip.

"This guy is brilliant," Tom said. "We're lucky to have him."

"Did you work in Britain as well?" I nodded at the map.

"No, but I studied English in Tunbridge Wells. You know, the town where Conan Doyle set one of his Sherlock Holmes mysteries."

I didn't know and was duly impressed. I was also struck by the Spaniard's perfect English, and his slow, careful movements, like when he placed ice in our glasses and poured the Scotch. Everything seemed so deliberate. Or maybe he was just slow. By the time he had changed his shoes, it was too late for dancing. We settled for dinner but, given all that followed, I find it odd that I can't remember what or where we ate the first time I met the man from Madrid.

"Please." Charlene said once we were home. "Don't ask me to do this again. Tom is as interesting as dishwater and the Spaniard is too intense for me. I'll leave the Europeans to you."

"I don't think we have to worry about that," I said with a laugh. What did I have in common with a man of the Spaniard's background? As nearly as I could figure, he was ten years older, and I couldn't imagine he'd be interested in me, so when the phone rang when I came home from work the next evening, I was surprised to hear that Spanish accented perfect English asking for me.

"Good evening. This is Alberto Benítez, may I please speak with Diana?"

*Diana!* I heard everything I ever wanted wrapped up in the way he said my name. *Dee ah nah,* each vowel heavy with promise. I was sure, however, that he had made a mistake. Sunday's excursion hadn't been a date in the strict sense of the word, but Alberto and Charlene had sat together in the back seat in the new Pontiac and Charlene had been better at conversation than I. I assumed Alberto had confused our names and really wanted to talk with the charming blond. I felt obliged to tell him.

"Oh, Alberto, I think you mean Charlene. She spoke with you most of the evening. I'm the dark-haired one."

"I know perfectly well who you are, Diana, and I am calling to ask for the pleasure of your company at dinner on Wednesday next."

*The pleasure of your company on Wednesday next. My goodness!*

This time I went not only because of the accent, but because Alberto Benítez struck me as the most fascinating man on the planet. That next Wednesday was the first of many dinners, and I sometimes wondered what the sophisticated European saw in me with my small-town background and incomplete education. It never crossed my mind that I was as exotic to Alberto as he was to me. And I couldn't have imagined things would turn out as they did.

# Chapter 3

We had been married for two months in March, 1966. For the second Thursday in a row, Alberto's parents invited me for *merienda,* a little snack usually served around seven in the evening. Spaniards never ate dinner before 9:30 or 10:00, and the early evening nibble kept one going till then. In the case of my in-laws, *merienda* consisted of tea and cookies. I wondered if Thursday tea would develop into an institution like the Sunday family lunch. I wished my husband had come along to make conversation easier, but Alberto's office at the Ministry of Public Works followed the typical Spanish schedule from10 a.m. to 2 p.m. and 4 p.m. to 8 p.m. At the moment, he was busy with a highway inventory recently instigated by the Franco regime.

"Yes, Franco is a dictator," Alberto told me shortly after we met. "But he is a benevolent one."

I knew the meaning of benevolent.

"And besides," Alberto added, "Spain has exactly the government she deserves. *Dios mio!* We Spaniards are such a disorganized lot we couldn't possibly govern ourselves. Oh, yes, we are brilliant. We make wonderful plans. But after we take the first step, we don't know where the hell to put the next one. We need a strong leader."

I wasn't concerned about the government, but without my husband to act as periodic interpreter, I braced myself for the problematic dialogue ahead with an absent-minded mother-in-law and a father-in-law who grew more hard of hearing by the day.

I had taken the number 14 bus that stops in front of *Paseo del Prado 24,* a building that faced the Botanical Gardens. Midway between the Prado Museum and the Atocha train station, it fell within walking distance to the college of engineers where my father-in-law taught for many years. He said they lived in the best part of the city, and I'm sure that was true when they moved there over a quarter of a century earlier. Now, the neighborhood felt congested and gritty. A steady stream of diesel-fueled taxis en route to the train station polluted the air. My throat felt scratchy the moment I stepped from the bus.

I pushed open the ironbound glass door to number 24 and entered the lobby of a building I judged to be mid-nineteenth century.

"*Buenas Tardes,*" the *portero* said. The combination doorman/superintendent, also mid-nineteenth century I thought, rose from behind a wooden desk and shambled to open the elevator gate. I felt the familiar trepidation. Resembling a wrought iron birdcage, the elevator looked too delicate for heavy lifting. Through the filigree of twisted metal, I could see the cables and smell the grease, and hear what sounded like protest when the cage stuttered upwards. No one ever used the elevator to go down. I tried once, before I knew about the *up only* law. The *portero* caught me and shouted the way people do when they think you don't understand the language, as though volume were an aide to comprehension.

"*Arriba, sí. Abajo, jamás!*" Up, yes. Down, never!

I assumed the limited service had something to do with the elevator's age, but I commented later to Alberto about the *portero's* surly attitude.

"He's like that to everyone," my husband said. "Has been for years."

"I'd think he'd be a bit more polite, at least to the people who pay his salary and provide his housing. He has a little apartment in the back of the building, right?"

"Yes."

"Doesn't anyone complain? What do your parents say?"

"Everyone knows he's a grouchy old man now but they ignore it because of the way he behaved during the war."

The war that no one ever discussed popped up now in a conversation about doormen. Strange.

"Imagine," Alberto continued. "He'd already been the *portero* for some years when the siege of Madrid began and he knew everything there was to know about the building including its inhabitants and their activities. When he had a chance to warn someone of a possible raid by Franco's men, he did. If he had an opportunity to hide someone in one of the vacant flats, he did. I think there are probably people living there today who owe their life to him. I'm not positive, but I think so. And that is something you don't forget."

"Your parents?" I wondered if, aside from the bombing, they had felt threatened because of their political beliefs—or if anyone even knew what they were.

"No. My father managed a cement plant. No one bothered him. We nearly starved to death, but that's another story."

*

The elevator clunked and rattled. Six floors later it jerked to a stop. I stepped out in front of dark green double doors and pressed the brass button.

An ear-piercing *brrrrring* ricocheted around the stairwell. My father-in-law had adjusted the volume to accommodate his hearing loss, an alteration I'm not sure the neighbors appreciated. I felt certain the sound carried to the occupants three floors below and that at least half the building knew every time *Los Benítez* had guests.

Normally, Modesta, the live-in maid answered the bell. But on Thursdays and Sundays the *muchachas,* as they were called, had the afternoon off. I don't know why all the maids in Madrid had the same afternoon off but they did. (Like the *up only* elevator, this was another custom I didn't quite understand.) On Thursday afternoons, hundreds of girls, dressed in their best, window-shopped along the *Gran Via,* sauntered in *Retiro* Park or flirted with soldiers at a neighborhood dance. On Sunday the scene repeated itself. Today, instead of Modesta, *Don* Manuel—even his children used the formal *Don* when speaking about, and often to, their father—would open the door himself. I waited.

A thud of heavy deadbolt came first, followed by a rattle of chain, then the scratching sound as my father-in-law turned the key in his vintage but robust security system. The door hinges squealed, the weighty panel swung open to reveal the frail eighty-year-old man smiling at me. He walked slowly now, but still stood straight and his eyes, the brilliant blue of cornflowers, sparkled, alert and engaged. With his narrow chin, prominent ears and marked receding hairline, he resembled the American dancer Fred Astaire, albeit with ill-fitting dentures.

*Don* Manuel wore his usual at-home attire: felt slippers, black trousers, white shirt, dark tie, and a baggy, grey cardigan with pockets.

"*Hola, hijita.*" Hello, little daughter.

I leaned forward. A few grey whiskers brushed my skin as he kissed me on each cheek. He rarely addressed me by name, calling me instead *hija,* daughter, or sometimes *hijita,* little daughter. The little had nothing to do with my size. The Spanish diminutive, *ita,* signified affection, and I sensed his fondness not only in his greeting, but in the gentle way he took my coat and placed it on the velvet settee in the entry hall. Separated by generation, culture and language, the Benítez family and I had all the ingredients for a difficult relationship, yet the opposite was true. To me they showed only an open mind and a warm heart.

"*Ha llegado Diana,*" Diana's here, *Don* Manuel called as we entered the living room. The way he said it *llegada* sounded like *shaygahda;* after sixty years in Madrid, he still sounded Andalusian.

"My father never lost his uncultivated rural accent," Alberto had said. "He gives away his origins the moment he opens his mouth."

We passed through the French doors to the living room where my mother-in-law, Julia, sat at the *mesa camilla,* a round table with a floor-length skirt that concealed a heating device called a *brasero.* In rural villages the *brasero* consisted of a shallow metal basin in which the villagers ignited a slow-burning fuel such as almond shells, often the only heat in the house. Madrid and the urban areas had central heating but some households kept a *brasero*, I think, just to create a cozy spot before the central heating came on for the season, or for the days it failed, which it often did in the old buildings. Here, an electric unit had long since replaced the almond shells.

My mother-in-law hunched over the table squinting at the cultural section of the previous Sunday's newspaper; her glasses lay to one side. She wore a tailored beige blouse and a pleated green skirt. Her only jewelry was a narrow gold wedding band and a gold bow-shaped brooch at her throat. The skirt, I imagined, she had made herself. Alberto had told me his mother as a young woman had studied *corte y confección,* the comprehensive courses of pattern and dressmaking. She would not have thought of a career; this was simply a facet of an accomplished housewife. Married women of her class and generation rarely held jobs; however, she had written, illustrated, and published two books on doll making. The piano on the far wall was another example of her talent, although I wondered how long it had been since she touched the keys. She had studied for years at the music academy, but the one time I asked her to play—after Sunday lunch early in our friendship—she claimed she had no sheet music and couldn't play from memory. I couldn't imagine her as the vital, talented woman my husband had described.

Julia looked up as we entered the room and seemed puzzled for a moment before a smile of recognition crossed her pleasant face. She seemed easily confused these days. Aside from her pure white hair like a puff of meringue, there was nothing remarkable about her. Now her hair glistened in the light from what Alberto's nine-year old niece called *el asador de sesos*, the brain baker. The brain baker was one of *Don* Manuel's inventions.

Frustrated by the erratic nature of central heating and the limited output from the *brasero*, my father-in-law had undertaken to remedy the situation. He could not regulate a uniform temperature throughout the flat, but he had managed to create a strategic pocket of intense heat with a device of his own design.

Once upon a time a ceiling lamp hung over the table in front of the sofa. It must have been pleasant to read there, but *Don* Manuel had removed the light bulbs and replaced them with heating elements. Instead of a soft reading light falling from beneath a maroon shade the size of a bushel basket, a chandelier consisting of four hot coils radiated above the heads of those seated there. While the old couple basked in the glow of their electric halos, the rest of the family worried about spontaneous cranial combustion.

If my in-laws had been alone that Thursday, they would have had tea at the table beneath the brain baker. Instead we went to the dining room. Modesta had laid one end of the long table with a linen cloth, cups and saucers, and a metal tray that held an assortment of cookies still in their paper wrappers. I already knew I didn't like them.

Spanish *galletas*, with the texture of cardboard and an aroma reminiscent of sawdust, had nothing in common with the tender Toll House cookies that came from my mother's oven. A slather of strawberry jam might have rendered them palatable but my father-in-law never bought strawberry jam because, he said, the tiny seeds worked their way under his dentures.

I sat opposite him and watched the fragile figure take charge of the teapot, a metal urn that resembled a vintage coffee percolator—minus the lid. Modesta had left the container filled with water. While Julia smiled passively—sometimes I wondered if she, too, had lost her hearing—my father-in-law immersed a wand-like element into the water. I had never seen one. Next, he inserted the prongs of the element's frayed electric cord into an orange industrial-grade extension cable that ran along the top of a carved oak sideboard. An oil painting of St. John the Evangelist hung on the wall above it.

Several years earlier my mother-in-law, with a special license granted to art students, had copied the painting from the original *El Greco* that hung in the Prado Museum. The religious image did not reflect the beliefs of the Benítez family. (As far as I could tell, I was the only person, aside from *Don* Manuel's sister, Anita, who attended Mass on a regular basis.) And, though it may have been beautifully rendered, I didn't care for the art.

In the painting St. John, wearing an acid-green robe and a faded red cloak, holds a golden chalice in his right hand and points to it with his left. A winged dragon stretches open-mouthed above the rim alluding to poison and to the story that John was given venom to drink to prove his faith in God. In the gospel according to Mark, "These signs will accompany those who have believed: In My name they will pick up serpents, and if they drink any poison, it will not hurt them…."

The saint had a ghastly complexion and unnaturally long fingers. Behind him swirled a mass of dark grey clouds. Even without the rising serpent, the painting struck me as an odd theme for a dining room.

On the wall to St. John's right was a round white porcelain outlet typical in buildings of that age. As *Don* Manuel plugged in the extension cord, I braced myself for another common feature—the blown fuse. That day, though, the lights remained steady but the proximity of electricity to water and the slight tremble of my father-in-law's hand still made me uneasy.

The pot coughed then settled into a steady gurgle. Meanwhile, the normally abstemious man uncorked a bottle of *anís,* a sweet, licorice-flavored liqueur.

"It comes from my village in *Córdoba.*" He grinned with pride the same way he did when he told me that he and Picasso were born in the same year and only eighty miles apart.

*Don* Manuel fussed with the bubbling pot and then, as he filled my cup, extolled the flavor of *anís* as a sweetener for tea. I shook my head when he offered me the bottle. A faintly medicinal vapor rose when he added a teaspoon of the liqueur to his own cup and he inhaled deeply before taking a sip. A moment later, he urged me to take a second cookie. This was the *Don* Manuel I saw, considerate toward me and indulgent with his grandchildren. He had, however, a less attractive side.

By the time I met my father-in-law, a civil engineer, he had retired from teaching at the College of Engineers and from his directorship of a large cement company, a position he held before and during the years of the civil war. Among his many achievements, he had translated technical books from German and had developed a system of sliding molds used to construct storage silos. He kept a warehouse on the edge of town and still leased out his equipment from time to time. I'd heard him discussing his patents with Alberto. The discussions invariably resulted in argument. In spite of our brief shared history, I knew my father-in-law's story well—at least I knew my husband's version.

⁕

Manuel Benitez Ramirez was born in 1888 in the southern province of Córdoba, the oldest of seven children. His parents owned a small general store, and both culturally and economically lived in narrow circumstances. From the outset, Manuel's unique intelligence set him apart from his siblings—to the degree that his parents made a huge financial sacrifice to further his education by sending him to live with an uncle in a town large enough to have the equivalent of a high school. When he graduated with outstanding grades, his parents asked him what he would like to study next.

I can't vouch for the accuracy of the anecdote, but the story that runs through the family says that when Manuel heard civil engineering was the most grueling of all professions and required six years of study, he said, "Then I will be a civil engineer." So, at the age of sixteen, the skinny, timid village boy went to Madrid with only an old bicycle and the meager allowance of one hundred pesetas a month that his parents managed to scrape together.

"My life was brutally difficult," he told his son many years later.

He lived in a wretched rooming house studying eleven hours a day six days a week. On Sundays he sometimes crossed the city on his bicycle to the home of an uncle, a tailor with a shop on *Calle Mayor.* The uncle, in turn, had in-laws who lived on the edge of Madrid. In their house on *Suero de Quiñones* Manuel met Julia, the thirteen-year-old girl he would later marry.

Julia Garcia Lorenzana was the daughter of a cavalry colonel, veteran of the war in Cuba (the Spanish/American war in which Teddy Roosevelt fought with his Rough Riders). She took painting classes, studied piano and was, as Alberto put it, "in a class above that of the poor provincial student. I don't know what my mother found attractive in him," Alberto said. "I doubt Manuel Benitez had ever attended a concert in his life."

I think she must have seen that what the village boy lacked in social refinement he compensated with intellectual aptitude. He graduated with honors from one of the most arduous preparatory academies in Madrid, and completed his training at the College of Engineers. By the time they married, Manuel had his career firmly in place, which meant taking his bride to live in a godforsaken village near a cement plant. But eventually, it brought him prestige and financial security. It also brought the stomach ulcers that would plague him the rest of his life.

When their daughter was born in 1917, they named her Julia after her mother and called her Julina to avoid confusion. Eight years later, they named their newborn son Alberto. According to my husband, he was named for Albert Einstein.

During those years, they lived in a large flat on *Zurbano* Street. Manuel traveled often to the cement plants he managed, and Alberto recalled summer vacations on the beaches near the coastal town of *Zumaya* where his father's company provided a house for the family. He also remembered his father's strictness regarding education and, especially in Alberto's case, just which path that education would take. Julina was free to follow language arts and library science at the university. Alberto had no choice.

"There was no question about my future," Alberto said. "If I had wanted to be anything other than a civil engineer, I would have been stuffed like a parrot and perched on the piano. On a professional level, *Don* Manuel was much admired—as a father he behaved like a tyrant."

*

In 1936, however, Manuel's plans for his children's education were supplanted by worries for the physical survival of his wife and son. Julina had found refuge in the home of an uncle in a relatively safe area of the country, but shortly after war broke out, Franco initiated the siege of Madrid. For the next three years the city's population struggled under the most reduced circumstances. Amid air raids and fighting in the streets, they searched for food and a way to keep warm in the icy Madrid winters.

"What impressed me most," Alberto said, "was the intelligence and the tenacity of my father in trying to cover the basic needs of our family."

In spite of the absence of coal and electricity, Manuel managed to resolve the energy issue for his household. He found the solution in petrol, the only resource still available. Somehow he availed himself of two portable kilns from a ceramics factory. He converted the little ovens from electricity to gasoline. In order to do that, he required some delicate instruments to adapt the small burner inside the ovens. He took his ten-year-old son to visit the neighborhood clockmaker and found the tools he needed among a store of watch faces and clock springs. Flushed with success, he bought additional kilns and placed them throughout the house for heat. But the most important use, according to Alberto, was in the kitchen to cook. Alberto relinquished pieces from his Mecano set so his father could make a spit.

"On the rare occasion, we had anything to put on the spit, it was my boring job to turn it by hand. But how my father found food is another example of his ingenuity."

Like coal and electricity in the beleaguered city, any animal fat such as bacon or butter was impossible to find, as well as olive or other vegetable oil. The human body, however, requires fat and Manuel began to investigate the possibilities of sebum, the hard, solid fat extracted from herbivorous animals. When melted, it is used to make candles and soap.

Again, Manuel took his son with him when he went to a soap factory where they sold sebum in square, thick blocks. He bought fifty blocks, carried them home and dumped them on the kitchen table. At least they could use it for frying or to rub on bread.

"Of course, it tasted awful," Alberto recalled. "but at least it wasn't toxic."

In those days, Spain did not produce bottled soft drinks, so people made *refrescos* at home with a flavored syrup and seltzer water. Sugar, of course, was as scarce as everything else during the war, but Manuel found the answer to that shortage in one of the few shops still in operation with an inventory of syrups. When the shop owner asked what flavor Manuel wanted, my father-in-law replied that the flavor didn't matter; he would take the entire supply. Next he visited a pharmacy to buy *Pastillas de Leche de Burra,* donkey's milk tablets, a kind of lozenge, reputedly full of vitamins, taken as a cough remedy and sold by weight.

"How many grams would you like, sir?" the pharmacist said.

"All that you have."

"But sir, I have fifteen kilos!"

"Then I'll take the fifteen kilos."

"And that," Alberto said, "was how, even on the worst days of the war, we managed breakfast. The menu consisted of donkey's milk tablets dissolved in boiled barley water sweetened with gooseberry syrup. On good days we dipped in slices of coarse bread previously fried in God knows what, and ate it amid the fumes from the gasoline engine.

It was no wonder now that the old man took such pleasure in his tea and cookies.

⁂

At the tea table *Don* Manuel, in his deafness, shouted with a force that shook the sugar bowl, and I felt particularly self-conscious bellowing back with imperfect grammar. I loved to speak Spanish, but I was not fluent. A few days earlier I had told my sister-in-law that I was embarrassed by these blunders. I used the word *embarazada.* Who wouldn't? *Embarazada* surely meant embarrassed. I thought the meaning was clear until Julina pointed out that *embarazada* meant *pregnant* which, at the time, I most definitely was not.

During these attempts at communication, my mother-in-law sipped her tea, a vague expression on her face. When her husband asked her to pass the cookie tray, she looked confused. At the end of an hour, I was exhausted. Even asking about their health had proved problematic. I wanted nothing more than to say *adios* and flee. And, if this is to be a weekly event, I wanted to vary the venue. I suggested tea at our apartment the following week. In this way, I said, they could see Alberto when he came home from the office. *And I will find some tasty tea cookies*, though I don't say that out loud.

⁂

"How was *merienda?*" Alberto asked later that evening.

"I'm glad your parents like me," I said, "but your father gave more information than I wanted when I asked how he was feeling today."

"What do you mean?"

"He told me he was *constipado*. And he said it so loudly I'm sure the neighbors heard." In my mind the word *constipado* needed no translation.

Alberto smiled. "My father was sneezing and coughing today, right?"

"How did you know?"

He pulled a *Kent* from the white pack on the coffee table. "C*onstipado* doesn't mean what you think. It means he has a cold."

"Then what does *estoy resfriado* mean?" I thought I knew the expressions for having a cold.

"It means, *I have a cold.*"

"So what does *estoy acatarrado* mean?"

"It means *I have a cold.*"

"And if I say *yo tengo un catarro?*"

Alberto exhaled slowly. He hesitated as though searching for the right words and squared his shoulders the way he did when about to offer what he called one of his pearls of wisdom. He lowered his voice. "Diana, ours is a very rich language." He paused for dramatic effect—he liked doing that—and then said, "It means *I have a cold.*"

As an afterthought, he added, "And so does *estoy constipado.*"

Fascinating! The only way I knew how to say *I have a cold* in English was … I have a cold.

⁂

Our doorbell rang the following Thursday at 6:45 p.m. Alberto was at the office. A bit early for my in-laws, I thought, but there they were when I opened the door, all smiles and kisses. *Don* Manuel seemed unusually pleased. They had arrived in record time. *Good*, I assumed they had taken a taxi. Nobody thought my father-in-law should still be driving. Even if he had been robust with perfect hearing, the traffic codes in force when he learned to drive over half a century earlier no longer applied. Nevertheless, he insisted he managed as well as the next driver and continued to urge his aged Mercedes through Madrid's ever-increasing traffic. Oblivious to traffic lights, signs and the general alarm of pedestrians, he forged ahead like the Spanish version of Mr. Magoo. One experience with his eccentric driving sufficed for me. He totally disregarded the lines on the pavement; white, yellow, broken or solid, they were all the same to him. And because of his hearing loss, the warning horns of other motorists didn't faze him.

I asked if the cab driver had any difficulty in finding our address; we lived on a short street in a new neighborhood that was sometimes difficult to find. But they hadn't taken a cab. *Don* Manuel had driven himself. He expressed surprise that more people didn't use the new lane that ran the length of the *Generalísimo*, the avenue named for Franco that was Madrid's main north-south thoroughfare. He had popped right into that empty *carril* in front of the Prado Museum and headed north. He said the light traffic had surprised him. It took a minute for me to realize why, and when I did, I couldn't wait to tell Alberto that his father had discovered the *Bus Only* lane and appropriated it for his personal use.

⁂

Alberto came home late, just as his parents were getting on the elevator. They exchanged brief kisses in the hall and said they would see each other on Sunday, as usual. As soon as Alberto had shed his jacket and mixed a martini, I repeated his father's latest adventure. My husband lit a cigarette, laughed and shrugged his shoulders. I didn't repeat the comment his father had made earlier.

I had filled the cups, passed a platter of delicate tea cakes from *Mallorca*, the best pastry shop in town, and had barely pulled out my chair when my father-in-law said he was pleased that Alberto had married me. I thought he approved of the tea cakes. But before I could reply, he said he hoped I would use my influence to curtail Alberto's drinking.

"*¿Perdón?*" I couldn't think of anything else to say. I felt a flush of anger. *This is not a comment you should make to me. Tell your son directly.* And "*usar tu influencia*" sounded manipulative. *Why me? Do it yourself if you are concerned. Or have you already* *tried?* But I didn't say any of that. Furthermore, I didn't agree.

My husband drank more than any person I knew, but I had never seen him tipsy, much less drunk. I said so. *Don* Manuel shook his head. "*Mi hijo bebe demasiado,*" he insisted, and the way he said it didn't invite discussion. I didn't understand why he thought his son drank too much aside from the fact that he himself didn't drink at all except for the drops of *anís* in his tea. I always had wine at the Sunday lunches. Did he think I also drank too much? I looked for my mother-in-law's reaction, but she busied herself selecting a pastry and seemed not to have heard. *Poor old dears,* I thought. *What do they know?*

In retrospect, what did I?

# Chapter 4

Our apartment was only a few minutes from Alberto's office at the Ministry of Public Works. He always came home for the typical three-hour lunch break—a Spanish custom about which I still had misgivings. But one day, shortly after we had moved in, I was glad he didn't have to rush back to work. I'm not sure Spaniards even had a word for *rush.*

"Don't trip over the crate," I said as Alberto entered our minuscule front hall a few minutes after two, his usual time.

A wooden box partially blocked the door to the living room.

"What is it?" he said as he removed his jacket and loosened his tie.

"Judging from the return address, it's another wedding gift from your relations in Córdoba. The *portero* brought it up around noon."

I made a face when I said *portero* because I didn't like our doorman and, from the way he behaved, he didn't care for me either.

Mario was the *portero's* name. He wore a dark blue uniform with brass buttons and a cap with a shiny visor. He could have passed for a captain on a cruise ship. He spent a lot of time outside leaning against the building smoking. He rolled his own *Ducados,* made with foul-smelling cheap black tobacco, and when he wasn't smoking, he was kicking a soccer ball along the street with the neighborhood boys. Mario smiled and tipped his cap to the other residents, but when I passed, he busied himself lighting a cigarette or shuffled the mail. With the other ladies, he jumped to attention and offered to carry their packages, but he never saw me unless I was with Alberto. Maybe he didn't like Americans, or foreigners in general, or my accent.

Alberto eyed the crate. "No doubt another typical artifact."

I patted his cheek.

"Sorry."

I should have been more specific the day I gushed to my mother-in-law that I absolutely adored Spanish arts and crafts. The dear woman had shared the news with every Benítez from Madrid to Córdoba. A few days earlier we had received *algo típico* from an uncle in Rute—a three-foot tall metal sculpture of *Don Quixote* complete with *Rocinante*, his horse, and a four-foot lance that came in three sections. At the moment, that iconic knight was tilting at my raincoat in the back of the bedroom closet. I meant no disrespect to the uncle or to *Quixote,* but, well, when I said typical, I was thinking of antique hand fans or table linens embroidered by cloistered nuns.

As Alberto worked to pry open the crate with a screwdriver, we speculated on the contents. Then *pop!* The top came off. Surely something precious rested under all the layers of paper. My husband ripped aside the final sheet.

"Oh, my Lord," I said. "If you'll pardon the expression."

Alberto made a noise that sounded like *ouff.*

Facing us was a three by four-foot depiction of the Lord's Last Supper embossed on a sheet of copper surrounded by a carved wooden frame. The central figure raised a hand in blessing while thirteen somber countenances stared at us, and twelve burnished halos (Judas didn't have one) caught the afternoon sunlight.

"Did he think we had a private a chapel?" Alberto said.

"I don't know," I said. "But I have the perfect place for it."

I ignored my husband's look of alarm and motioned him to pick up one end while I lifted the other and moved backwards toward the bedroom.

"Not over our marriage bed!" Alberto refused to take another step. He used the Spanish words *cama matrimonial,* another term that had come as a revelation.

I had expected an American-size double bed, but a *cama matrimonial* was actually two twin beds attached to a single headboard, each with its own mattress and sheets. The arrangement struck me as somewhat problematic and extremely *un*-matrimonial.

"Don't worry," I said, tugging my reluctant husband through the doorway while he still held his end of the sacred shipment. I elbowed open the closet door and shouldered aside my black cocktail dress. In unison we lowered the

Lord and his followers to the floor and leaned them against *Quixote's* horse.

"Just for the time being," I said. But I was already thinking I had resolved the matter of the *portero's* Christmas gift.

# Chapter 5

I liked our neighborhood of narrow streets, patterned sidewalks and blocks of apartments each with an individual personality. We lived on the top floor of a fourteen-story building. A sleek marble lobby with a pair of black leather sofas, a wall of metal mailboxes and a built-in desk for the *portero* took up the ground floor. By contrast, directly across from our front door, three small shops occupied the street level of an apartment building half as tall as ours. Between two other buildings, overlooked by balconies and flower boxes with trailing geraniums, four iron benches edged a green plot not much larger than a tennis court. An old man in a black beret, his cane leaning against his knee, read the paper there on sunny mornings. In the afternoons, mothers often congregated with baby carriages—great domed contraptions outfitted with lace-trimmed pillows and embroidered sheets. The women knitted and chatted while their infants napped in luxury. I was learning that Spanish children, especially babies, were cherished and coddled and dressed and decorated in a way I had never seen. The air around the little park was fresh, far different from the congestion of *La Puerta del Sol,* the Gate of the Sun, in the heart of the city eight miles and at least two centuries away.

*Sol,* as most people called it, was the historical center of Madrid. It had a *Times Square, New York* air about it—only older—with neighborhood street names that reflected their past: *Calle de Bordadores* and *Arco de Cuchilleros* named for embroiderers and knife makers, and *Plaza de la Paja,* straw square, that I imagined had once been a straw-strewn market place. Unique shops specialized in hand fans or walking sticks and umbrellas. Others sold only religious vestments and First Communion dresses. Or buttons. It was *the* place to shop for mantillas and castanets or to snack on ham and chorizo in one of the *tapas* bars.

"Try not to look like a tourist, and hang on to your purse when you go to *Sol,*" Alberto had warned me. "The place is infamous."

I knew he was thinking of the *gitanos,* the gypsies. The name came from the word *Egypt.* Spanish gypsies spoke a language called *caló* and were synonymous with Flamenco music. Lola Flores, one of the most flamboyant entertainers of the day, was nicknamed *La Faraona,* Lady Pharaoh. Gypsy men with equally colorful monikers often made a living in the bullrings as *toreros.* I had never seen a Flamenco production or a bullfight. I would have gone to either at least once, but I had married a man who said, "Bullfighting is *not* the national sport, it is a national shame!" And he thought Flamenco was for foreigners. The only gypsy I knew sold flowers on the steps of the market.

"Buy my fresh carnations," she would say in a singsong voice. "Come on, sweetheart, they're cheap today because you are so beautiful."

We both knew she exaggerated. If I didn't buy—although I usually did—she would say, "At least give me a few pesetas for breakfast. I haven't eaten today." And we both knew that was an exaggeration, too. Still, I found something appealing about her good-natured impertinence. Once, when she gave me her "no breakfast" story, I went to the market and came back with a bottle of milk and two sweet rolls. "Thanks, blue eyes," she said. She made me laugh. The gypsies at *Sol* that Alberto cautioned me about were something else.

I couldn't pick them out at first, but I soon learned to spot them. Silent as shadows they slipped through the crowds, their eyes alert for a pocket to pick. They preyed on tourists. Undetected, they committed their thievery right under the noses of the *Guardia Civil* who stood at the entrance to the Ministry of the Interior. Franco's Civil Guard, in their distinctive olive-green uniforms, polished boots and black patent leather hats, were as common as signposts. They patrolled country roads on horseback or stood sentry in front of official buildings.

The three-story red brick building that commanded one side of *La Puerta de Sol*, was built in 1768 as the main post office. In the nineteenth century, it was converted to the Ministry. The day I went to renew my residency permit (before the local authorities issued me a Spanish passport insisting my marriage to *Señor* Benitez automatically made me Spanish, too), I didn't know the building also served as headquarters for Franco's Security Police and a prison for political dissidents. The section I visited looked like any other dimly lit government office, and I went about my business unaware of its grisly activities. How could I have known about the mysterious so-called suicides, the university boy who threw himself from a window with his hands and feet bound, or an old man who refused to even walk by the building because, he said, he could still hear screams? No one talked about this dark side of the regime. The war that had ended nearly thirty years earlier had nothing to do with me, and the generation that had suffered most remained silent, willing to ignore or deny their history. Even Alberto, who had told me about his harrowing escape from Madrid, seemed philosophical about the aftermath.

Franco still controlled the press and his military parades reminded us regularly that his regime had provided over a quarter of a century of peace. It never occurred to me to ask the price. The United States saw in Franco a strong anti-communist ally, and the two countries formed agreements that allowed the construction of three US military bases on Spanish soil. All I saw was a country that appeared to have come to terms with its Civil War.

I slipped happily into the world of my husband's family and into his circle of friends, a generation of educated people building Franco's new Spain. My husband designed and implemented Franco's infrastructure with enthusiasm. The only unrest I saw was blamed on Basque separatists and in that case, as Alberto pointed out, we needed Franco to squash them and hold the country together. If there was another side to the regime, I couldn't see it—just as I hadn't seen the gypsies. No one spoke about torture or reprisals or common graves—not even in whispers.

Years later, long after Franco's death and interment in *El Valle de los Caídos,* The Valley of the Fallen, I found an answer to my un-asked question in a Spanish newspaper. *We were tired,* the journalist wrote. *We exchanged everything for peace and security and white bread. And we lived in exile in our own country.*

⁂

I didn't go to *Sol* often. I didn't like the crowds and the traffic jams and, besides, I had everything I needed in my own neighborhood north of *Bernabeu* soccer stadium.

A fishmonger and a vegetable vendor had shops on my street—actually nothing more than shallow stalls—where the activity was as new to me as the size of the baby carriages. I watched the fish man fillet a sole with only a few swipes of his thin blade. *Swish! Swish!* And he laid the strips of white flesh on a piece of thick paper and asked if I wanted the bones for stock. I was always surprised that the vegetable seller never charged for parsley. When I needed some to garnish the fish, he would reach into a basket, pull out a fistful of sweet smelling herb, tuck it beside my other vegetables, and wrap the lot in a cone of newspaper.

At the end of the block an arrogant French butcher sold the best veal in town and priced it accordingly. *Salón Parra*, the beauty shop, sat on the corner one building away. We had a neighborhood bar, too—just a counter with a few stools in a cramped space—that served coffee and soft drinks and *tapas.* The bar served alcohol too, but here, unlike in bars in the States, a child could sip a Coke next to an adult who drank a beer. I don't know what the laws were regarding alcohol and age, only that multigenerational drinkers gathered together under one roof and consumed their beverage of choice.

Next to the bar, in a shop not much larger than a confessional, I bought my household cleaning supplies—envelopes of *Blanco de España*, a magical, acrid powder that whitened the grout between tiles, and *estropajos,* wads of vegetable fibers to scour everything from pots to floors. Just inside the door, a skinny girl in a grey smock hunched over a tube-like apparatus and repaired nylon stockings with an electric needle. For a few pesetas she mended the runs so they didn't show and returned the stockings in a little tissue paper pouch.

From our balcony, I could watch the neighborhood activity, its rhythm as predictable as the tides. On weekdays a wave of children and *muchachas* came first; girls and boys in school uniforms, the younger children grasped by the hand of a maid in a white apron. After delivering the children to the bus or walking them to school, the maid returned to the home of her employers and emerged a few minutes later with a grocery list and a mesh shopping bag. Not every home had a refrigerator—ours was so small it barely held a liter of milk and six eggs—so I shopped daily, too. And I enjoyed it. I liked the marketplace chatter and seeing new foods, like the mottled green *chirimoya* fruit that looked like an egg from a giant prehistoric chicken. Most foods were sold by weight. I observed other shoppers negotiate the metric system with ease while I struggled to make it relevant to my own needs. *So that's what 100 grams of ham looks like.*

The briefcase brigade rode the next swell in the morning. Every person on the Iberian Peninsula seemed to carry some version of a *maletín de ejecutivo,* the executive satchel. Not limited to diplomats and senior managers as I previously thought, or to executives as the name implied, the Spanish briefcase was universal. I saw it carried by students, professors, bill collectors, priests, bus drivers, civil engineers, of course, and even nuns. Our *portero* carried one for the simplest of errands. Anyone with a piece of paper and a bit of business sallied forth in the morning with his *maletín*.

My father-in-law never left home without his own battered, brown briefcase. He brought it when he came to tea though it held only his keys. On Sundays he carried it to the pastry shop (his weekly routine) and filled it with a dozen meringues for dessert. Once, the only time he ever agreed to lunch with us in a restaurant, he brought his aged accessory along.

We sat under a shade tree on the restaurant's patio. *Don* Manuel placed his briefcase under a chair. The waiter passed around menus and asked if we wanted bread—restaurants charged for each serving. Before anyone could reply, my father-in-law reached under his chair.

"No, no," he said. "We've brought our own."

With that, he plopped a baguette on the table—or rather two pieces of the long loaf because he had cut it in half to fit in his case.

"*Por Dios, Padre!*" Alberto hissed.

Unlike his father, Alberto didn't count every peseta. But my infamously tight-fisted father-in-law looked not the least self-conscious. On the other hand, Alberto had not suffered the meagerness of his father's student years, or struggled for food during the war in quite the same way. In that light, why would *Don* Manuel pay for individual *panecillos* when for the same price he could buy a loaf that sufficed for the entire table? And what better transport than his briefcase?

As the flow of children and maids and men with briefcases receded, the neighborhood traffic settled to a ripple until a returning surge at 2:00 p.m. brought everyone home for lunch (except for the children, who ate at school). The shopkeepers lowered their shutters and the streets fell silent. At 5:00 the procession began again—more or less. The shops re-opened and the briefcases returned to work until the official closing time of 8:00 or 9:00 p.m. depending on the business. The only schedule I related to was that of the school children who went from 9:00 a.m. to 5:00 p.m.

"You know," I said to Alberto, "if businesses didn't close in the middle of the day we would have only two daily rush hours instead of four."

My husband studied traffic patterns for a living. I'm sure he realized that, but I said it anyway.

"*Querida,*" he said. "I can widen highways, build dams and design bridges, but I don't think even I can influence my compatriots to forego the siesta."

I busied myself easily in the morning. I even grew accustomed to lunch at 2:30. But the closure of the entire country for three or four hours every afternoon felt unnatural.

No one I knew actually took a nap, except for Alberto's father. I'm not sure he slept, but he took a book to bed every afternoon with instructions to the maid not to disturb him before 5:00. Alberto relaxed easily after lunch with a brandy and the newspaper until time to return to the office. I fidgeted.

Compared to the weekday surges, Sunday was a trickle. Only the bread and pastry shops opened for a few hours in the morning. Bells called the faithful to Mass. I went alone to the 10:00 a.m. service. Alberto slept. I would ply him later with a glass of *Tang* and a pot of coffee until he grudgingly came to life. Then, fully hydrated and caffeinated, he took me to share in another Spanish tradition, The Sunday Family Lunch.

# Chapter 6

On that sweltering August day, I would have preferred to eat in the countryside under a grape arbor at *El Mesón* rather than at my in-law's apartment. *El Mesón* was a nineteenth century farmhouse that had operated as a restaurant—except for a time during the Spanish Civil War—since 1932, and I adored the place.

"I knew you'd like it," Alberto said the first time he took me for dinner. "It's full of all those typical artifacts you're so crazy about."

"Sometimes I think I'm more Spanish than you are," I said.

The menu featured seasonal foods—fat white asparagus with mayonnaise, omelets of baby fava beans with garlic shoots, salads dressed simply with olive oil and vinegar—and the *asados*, the roast suckling pig and lamb, for which the restaurant was known. I felt particularly comfortable eating under exposed beams, surrounded by white walls hung with heavy ceramic plates and copper pots. Two life-sized pigskins hung on the wall in the cobblestoned entry, a reminder of the time when they served to store oil but now were used only for decoration. In winter we sat at a wooden table snugged beside one of the fireplaces at either end of the long, barn-like room. In summer we sat outside. From the shade of the *parra*, we watched the color of the surrounding fields change with the breeze from tan to gold and back again. Bands of scarlet poppies fluttered beside the road. Some managed their way through the gravel of the courtyard where we parked the car. I picked half a dozen of the seemingly hearty flowers one afternoon but they fainted moments later and by the time we arrived home no amount of water could revive them. The other summer attraction of *El Mesón* was the temperature, always several degrees cooler than Madrid's, and on that particular August afternoon I longed for any place with a temperature less than ninety degrees Fahrenheit. Instead, because it was Sunday, we drove to Alberto's parents' house for the typical family lunch.

I stewed inside our air-condition-less *Seat* as we drove along the *Generalissimo.* A popular refrain described Madrid's climate as *six months of winter and three months of hell.* The refrain didn't mention the other three months, and at the moment I wondered how long hell would last. I looked at my husband.

"How can you stand it?"

He never left home without a sweater and he drove in the heat that day with a navy wool pullover draped across his shoulders.

"It is still possible to catch a cold," he said. "And I don't want a draft on my neck."

As far as Alberto was concerned, the hotter, the better, but I thought the only good thing about Madrid in summer was the lack of traffic.

Regardless of type of employment or length thereof, everyone had a month's vacation, typically August, and from the look of the semi-deserted streets, eighty percent of Madrid had left for cooler climes. The other twenty percent comprised people like Alberto's parents who never went anywhere now. His sister Julina and family would leave in a few days for *San Vicente,* a northern fishing village that had been their vacation retreat for years. Alberto and I hadn't yet decided what to do.

As the clock chimed three, we entered the dining room where Alberto's parents, his sister, Julina, her husband, Luis, and their children, Isabel, age 9 and César, age 4 waited. Slanted shutters redirected the bright sun, a water pitcher perspired on the linen-covered table and deep soup plates promised a chilled *gazpacho.* The oscillating fan *Don* Manuel had placed on the floor ruffled the tablecloth and he kept adjusting it to avoid any direct draft. He, too, wore a sweater. Our cast of characters, with varying degrees of charm and idiosyncrasy took their places and played what had now become their predictable roles.

My mother-in-law sat at the head of the table and Luis took a chair at the foot. The seating arrangement had nothing to do with protocol; we had simply fallen into this pattern.

I sat between *Don* Manuel and Alberto with our backs to the sideboard and St. John the Evangelist looking over our shoulders. My impeccable sister-in-law—I never saw

Julina with a hair out of place— sat between her children. Physically, Julina resembled Elizabeth II of England—full bust, narrow hips and dark hair worn in a short bouffant. When I first met her, I had thought she was formal and serious, unlike Alberto who teased easily with everyone. Maybe that was just the librarian side of her. Julina worked at the library associated with the US embassy. Occasionally, after my morning errands, I stopped at the library to chat and during those visits, I had found a trusted and affectionate friend.

Julina sometimes asked me to take care of the children when a school holiday coincided with their *muchacha's* day-off and Julina had to work. She tried once to teach me to knit, arming me with fat number nine needles and a skein of bulky yarn, but after observing my initial attempts, she shrugged.

"You look like some kind of contortionist, my dear sister."

We decided to call each other *dear sister* because neither of us had a real one. We laughed easily together, but her manner at the lunch table was decidedly reserved.

She treated her parents with detached respect, considerate but cool, and I thought I knew why. For ten years *Don* Manuel had opposed the marriage of his only daughter to Luis, a teacher and a playwright with an uncertain financial future. He thought she should marry an engineer. Couples generally did not marry until they could afford to buy a flat and, when they did, they lived in it for the rest of their lives. Renting apartments and the fluid lifestyle of Americans was not part of the Spanish culture.

So for many years, Julina lived in her parents' house—as did all unmarried Spanish women, and even most men—until finally, either because Luis had earned a prestigious award for one of his plays or because of time itself, *Don* Manuel provided the down payment for a flat. But it came with a stipulation. As Alberto would say later, "My father never does anything without having a string attached."

In this case, the string was that the title remain in *Don* Manuel's name until Julina and Luis paid off the mortgage. The result was that for twelve years my dear sister-in-law and her husband furnished and paid the mortgage on a flat that was theirs in every way except name.

I asked Julina once if her mother ever interceded on her behalf. I knew the older woman shared an interest with Luis in art and music, and thought perhaps she had seen him as a more attractive son-in-law. Julina shook her head.

"The only time I tried to confide in my mother, she stopped me and said that whatever I told her she would have to repeat to my father."

Alberto, too, had called his father a tyrant but that was difficult to believe as I watched the elderly man pour *Fanta* for his granddaughter, Isabel.

Isabel wore a red-trimmed navy jumper and white crocheted socks, an outfit her grandmother had made—including the socks. The little girl had a turned up nose and a mass of dark springy curls. She regarded me with a mixture of curiosity and possessiveness and waited for my inevitable grammatical mistake. When I made one and looked toward her, she corrected it.

Julina frowned at her daughter. *"No seas impertinente, hija."*

"She's not impertinent," I said. "She's a good teacher." I felt no shame in taking instruction from this patient nine-year old.

A moment later, Isabel whispered something to her father who looked at me, smiled and nodded.

"What did I do now?" I asked.

"Nothing." Luis said with a smile. "She thinks you look like Mary Poppins."

I pretended to open an umbrella. Luis lowered his glasses, and studied me in mock earnestness for a moment. Then turned toward his daughter.

"*Exactamente!*"

The dark glasses and mustache, accessories I would not have liked on anyone else, suited Luis. They made him look like the artist and writer that he was, though he earned his living in an advertising agency. He had received the *Lope de Vega* award and the *Calderón de la Barca* prize for two of his plays, and his collections of short stories brought critical, though not financial, success. He blamed the government for suppressing his work. From what I understood, his writing was not blatantly anti-Franco, but his opinions about the current regime were thinly veiled and, although not banned, he found it difficult to publish his stories or produce his plays. But nearly a decade had passed since Luis had won the awards. I didn't see or feel the same restrictions in the 1960s that he had experienced in the 1950s.

Alberto told me the censors had relaxed in recent years. "Things often slip through the cracks now," he said.

Nonetheless, if *Time* ran a story the Franco establishment

didn't like, they pulled it from the newsstands. *Playboy* and magazines of a sexual nature were banned entirely. The same restraints applied to movies. Luis said that during their summer vacation in northern Spain, he and Julina sometimes took a taxi (they didn't own a car) across the French border to see a film prohibited in Spain. I understood his frustration, but only to a degree. Spain, under what my husband emphasized as a *benevolent* dictatorship, didn't suffer drug problems or street crime or political demonstrations or a population of gun owners gone wild. In my own country we had assassinated our president, killed our foremost Civil Rights leader and murdered a prominent activist. The struggle for racial equality erupted in violence and we railed against a war in Vietnam. I felt safer in Spain. The possibility of a gypsy pickpocket seemed a minor inconvenience.

The conversation at table was superficial and polite—temporarily.

César wiggled on his chair. His grandmother quieted him.

Luis lifted his water glass (he rarely drank alcohol) toward me. He'd settled his glasses back on his nose.

"Cheers, sister-in-law," he said, and I felt the bond of friendship tighten.

"Maybe now?" I whispered to my husband. It seemed like a good moment to tell them our news.

Alberto shook his head. "Wait till coffee."

My father-in-law sawed a baguette, handed out fat chunks of bread and scanned the table to be certain we all had something to drink. Normally he tapped a button on the wall just below St. John that rang a bell in the kitchen signaling Modesta to bring the first course. Instead, he reached inside his sweater pocket, cleared his throat and, with a little flourish, lifted a silvery object to his lips. Every eye was on him.

"*Padre,* what…?" Alberto's next words were drowned out by two shrill blasts from a police whistle.

My mother-in-law raised a hand to her ear and seemed confused; Julina looked embarrassed. The children convulsed in laughter. Luis remained stone-faced but his moustache twitched and when I looked at Alberto, he was dabbing his eyes with a napkin. I wasn't sure how to react. I took a sip of wine.

Breathless from his effort, *Don* Manuel explained that he was still working to repair the bell that had broken earlier in the week. In the meantime, he thought he had found an effective substitute. No one disagreed. A moment later we heard the squeaky wheels of the teacart as Modesta pushed it along the book-lined corridor from the kitchen.

Modesta, dressed for Sunday in a black uniform with white collar and cuffs, parked her trolley at the end of the sideboard and lifted an ironstone soup tureen to the table where saucers of garnishes waited for the gazpacho—chopped cucumbers and tomatoes, minced onion and miniature croutons. Modesta had been with the family nearly fifteen years. Although she and Alberto were the same age, forty, her maternal manner, especially with my mother-in-law, and her matronly figure made her look much older. In spite of our married status, she still called Julina and me *Señorita;* the only *Señora* in the house was *Doña* Julia.

Alberto said once that the only thing he missed while he lived in the States was a good gazpacho. By now, I knew what he meant. I could have eaten that refreshing soup for the rest of the meal, but *Don* Manuel blew his whistle again and the second course arrived.

Modesta placed a white platter in front of Julina; my mother-in-law had yielded the serving responsibility to her daughter. The platter held three tiers of *tortilla*, an egg concoction that, except for its shape, had nothing in common with the Mexican dish of the same name. The Spanish *tortilla* is an omelet. The most common one, my favorite, was made with sautéed potatoes and onions. However, that day's version came stacked like a layer cake: first a *tortilla de patata,* then one of spinach and, finally, a top one of baby shrimp. Julina stood and, as we passed our plates to her, she sliced carefully, served each of us a wedge and pointed with her knife to a sauceboat that held the garlic-laced mayonnaise meant to dribble alongside. I did more than dribble. A few minutes later, we wiped our plates with knobs of bread and waited for another blast of the police whistle.

Then came *besugo,* a fish large enough to feed ten. I was learning the Spanish names for fish I didn't even know in English, in this case, sea bream. *El besugo* laid on its side, stuffed with a mixture of sautéed vegetables and garlic, bathed in white wine, head still attached. A slice of lemon covered the eye or the spot where the eye used to be. I didn't want to think about it. Julina took up the fish knife and serving fork and skillfully removed the bones before motioning for our plates again. Then it started.

Alberto asked his father about the current state of affairs with a particular client. I already knew something about the contentious transaction and that Alberto, while not directly involved, took the side of the client. Although retired, *Don* Manuel occasionally leased out the machinery he had developed for use in building silos. Alberto called the method ingenious and profitable. He took me once to the small warehouse where his father stored the equipment in a jumble of pipes and hydraulic jacks. "My father could make millions," he'd said, "if he would just get organized, but he won't pay for a foreman, and he spends most of his energy now in legal battles over patent rights."

So when Alberto asked the question, I knew disagreement was on the way. They argued about everything. The previous week Alberto had challenged his father to a duel. Who could solve a problem faster, Alberto with his pocket calculator or *Don* Manuel with a slide rule? I nudged my husband under the table. Why raise a prickly subject now? He paid no attention. Before long they were shouting—the father because he was angry, and the son because the father couldn't hear. The rest of us concentrated on the *besugo.* The men fell silent only when Modesta appeared to ask if we were ready for dessert.

The ice cream had a calming effect. The children gave their orders to *Don* Manuel, whose turn it was to serve.

*"Abuelito, abuelito,"* they said, *"un poquito más!"* Grandpa, grandpa, a little bit more!

My father-in-law sliced a portion of ice cream from a tri-colored block—each child indicating with his fingers how much he would like—then layered it between two thin wafers. The adults, too, placed their order for a made-to-measure sandwich, except for Alberto and me. I passed on the ice cream but nibbled a wafer. Alberto opened the sideboard and took out a bottle of brandy. Then, we moved to the *salon* where Modesta had laid out the coffee service on a round table in front of the sofa. Julina began to pour.

"Now?" I said to Alberto.

He nodded.

"But you tell them." Now that the moment had arrived, I felt suddenly shy.

He didn't. He leaned against the piano and said, "Diana has an announcement."

I felt the way I did when we went to a restaurant in the early days when he pretended he couldn't speak Spanish and made me order. He would look at the waiter and say in English, "The lady speaks Spanish, I don't." And he wouldn't back down. Or when he double-parked in front of the drug store one day when we were on a road trip and asked me to buy shaving supplies.

"I don't know what those things are called," I protested.

"Well, this is the best way for you to find out. I'll be waiting right here." He laughed and reached across me to open the door. "Who loves you more than I do?"

"You have an odd way of showing it," I said, and noted that he seemed to find some pleasure in my discomfort.

And now he said I had an *announcement,* which sounded so dramatic. I didn't like the way everyone paused to look at me. And couldn't he have said *we?* After all, the news wasn't mine alone. But I looked around the room and said, "Well, we are going to have a baby."

There were little gasps and pleasant *ahs* and smiles and congratulations all around. Only nine-year-old Isabel looked as though she wanted to ask me something but didn't quite know what.

"You must go to Varela," Julina said immediately. "He's a wonderful obstetrician. Luis has known the family for years."

"And I'll make the *canastilla,*" my mother-in-law said. "You tell me when you are ready and we will go to the shop together."

I knew what she meant. The *canastilla* was nothing more than a large wicker basket reminiscent of the kind my mother used for laundry, but here the basket was lined with quilted satins, trimmed with ruffles and fitted with a mattress and handmade sheets. For the first few months, newborn babies slept in something that looked like an illustration from a fairy tale. I loved the idea and said so. Julina and her mother chatted about fabrics and layettes, but the two people who seemed the most pleased at the news were Isabel and *Don* Manuel, who patted my arm before leaving for his *siesta.*

"*Cuídate, hija.*" he said. Take care of yourself, daughter.

I looked toward my husband, but he was absorbed with his calculator.

Julina caught my glance.

"Was your brother always like this?" I said.

"Don't say I didn't warn you," she said.

We spoke lightly, but the truth was she *had* warned me. *She just doesn't know him like I do,* I thought at the time, and I had brushed aside her skepticism.

# Chapter 7

It was nearly midnight. The brass lamp on an end table, a wedding gift, cast light over Alberto's shoulder. He sat in the green chair reading an article he had written for the *Ministry of Public Works Review*. This was the second time one of his pieces had been published, and while I understood and shared his pride, I wondered how many times he could re-read it.

The chair, part of the apartment's furnishings, looked like leather but was actually plastic. It had a matching sofa. The coffee table didn't match anything but my artistic brother-in-law had made a colorful collage that we slipped under the glass. It created a conversation piece at the same time it covered the scratches. I had decorated the sideboard and bookshelf with a few other wedding gifts—ceramic jars, a pewter pitcher, along with the ivory carvings Alberto brought from the time he worked in the Congo. We were both eager for the completion of our own flat, still under construction, but in the meantime, the little rental apartment suited us. The apartment had once been twice the size until an ambitious landlord closed off a portion to create another unit. As a result, we had a sealed door in the middle of our living room wall. I hung a tapestry to disguise it but it didn't block out sound and whenever Alberto sneezed, a voice from the other side said *Bless You!*

As we did every couple of weeks, we had gone to dinner with Julina and Luis. While all of us preferred an early meal, it was after 9:00 p.m. when we sat down at a favorite seafood restaurant, and nearly an hour and a half later when we said good night.

"I'm going to take a shower," I said, after we arrived home. "I smell like fish and garlic."

"Okay," Alberto said. He opened the liquor cabinet, poured a small glass of brandy, picked up the *Review* and settled in the chair.

At supper, I'd devoured a first course of *angulas,* baby eels served in a shallow clay dish with sizzling olive oil, garlic and a sliver of red pepper. White and not more than an inch long they looked like broken spaghetti. Except for two black dots the size of pin pricks, which I supposed were eyes, you couldn't tell head from tail, and one ate them whole with a small wooden fork. The fork kept the *angulas* from slipping off and also from burning your mouth with hot oil. But as Julina said, "Careful as one tries to be, there's always a droplet running down your chin."

Clearly my tastes were changing. I now ate barnacles and octopus and squid. A saucer of sizzling baby eels—a sight that once would have turned my stomach—had become a favorite appetizer, though its lingering aroma had not.

I stood in the shower and as the warm water washed away the smells of supper, I remembered our talk at the table.

"So," Luis had asked me. "How are you getting along with Carmen Laforet?"

"I love her! Thank you very much."

Luis had recently loaned me *Nada,* Laforet's novel set in post Civil War Barcelona and written when the author was only twenty-three. Luis had a knack for suggesting literature that fell within my grasp both linguistically and culturally.

"Diana loves all your suggestions," Alberto said. He exaggerated the word *all.*

"Not quite," I said thinking perhaps the moment of confession had arrived.

"Really?" Luis pretended to be hurt. "Not *all?*"

"I'm sorry to say, brother-in-law, that there is one area where I can't share your enthusiasm. I haven't admitted it till now for fear of sounding like a heretic."

"The Inquisition has been gone for some time," he said. "I think you're safe." He smiled and broke off a piece of bread.

The previous Sunday Luis and my mother-in-law had discussed a particular El Greco painting. I had only seen *The Burial of the Count of Orgaz* in a reproduction, but I found it as odd and gloomy as the St. John over the sideboard. And yet who was I to have an opinion about an artist so revered and so quintessentially Spanish? I took a deep breath.

"I don't like El Greco." I expected a clap of thunder, or at least a little gasp from my fellow diners. Nothing happened, so I went on. "I mean, I *want* to like him, but I don't."

Not appreciating the Spanish icon made me feel—I don't know—as though I lacked some fundamental sensibility. Maybe Luis would give me some insight—how and what to look for in the art I didn't understand. But he barely reacted. He just pushed some bread crumbs to one side and said, "You're young yet; you will."

I didn't ask at what point the age of enlightenment would set in. I had just turned thirty. I had all the time in the world, and I wasn't going any place.

⁂

Refreshed from the shower and a splash of lavender water, I sat on the arm of the green chair a few minutes later and ran my finger along the back of Alberto's neck. I wore a pale blue nightgown. Alberto raised his eyes from the page for a moment, patted my knee and continued to read. Slowly, he lifted the hem of my nightgown and I felt his hand along the inside of my thigh. His right hand still held the Ministry of Public Works Review. He managed to turn a page with his thumb while his left hand continued to move under the gauzy blue fabric.

"I'm going to bed." My lips brushed his ear. "Are you coming?"

"You go ahead. I'll be there in a minute."

I turned the bedside lamp to its dimmest setting, arranged the sheet to cover my feet which were often cold, and lay facing my husband's side of the bed. I had left the bedroom door ajar. Alberto's shadow momentarily cut the shaft of light. I thought he was coming to bed until I heard the click of the liquor cabinet door. I pulled the sheet up to my neck, turned off the light and thought of Ivan. I didn't want to think about Ivan. No, that's not true. I very much wanted to remember him.

Ivan was married. He had finally found a nice Jewish girl he could introduce to his mother. But when I met him at a holiday party in Cleveland, before Alberto, he was a twenty-six- year old bachelor. I had just turned twenty-one.

Ivan had worn a red, V-neck cashmere sweater over a white T-shirt, and grey flannel slacks. He looked comfortable, the kind of person at ease with himself. He wrote copy for an advertising agency, he told me, and played racket ball several times a week. Perhaps that's why he looked healthy and energetic. He was also very funny, complaining about his tendency to early baldness and his mother who kept trying to find him a wife. And when someone started to sing Christmas carols, Ivan knew all the words—an unusual accomplishment, I thought, considering his background. He loved Italian food, too, which explained why, a week later, Charlene and I made spaghetti and meatballs for Ivan and two of his friends, an attorney and a wannabe writer, also Jewish.

"You know this isn't going anywhere," Charlene said after the boys left that night, and I knew exactly what she meant. Charlene was a strict Lutheran, and I was a practicing Catholic. We could laugh with the boys over a plate of pasta. We just couldn't/wouldn't/shouldn't get serious, much less marry. We all knew that.

But Ivan hadn't wanted a lifetime commitment when he invited me to a movie one Saturday. I refused at first when he suggested the French film, *And God Created Woman* with Brigit Bardot.

"Oh, Ivan, I don't know if that is the kind of movie for me."

That Bardot appeared topless in the film caused scandal in the United States of the 1950s. The Legion of Decency, a Catholic organization, had banned it completely.

"Diane, one little movie isn't going to ruin your life," Ivan said.

Well, I thought, I could always go to confession the following week. I can't remember the film and barely recall the drink we had afterwards at a neighborhood bar, but eventually we ended up at my apartment with Sarah Vaughn singing from the record player in the living room while Ivan and I drank coffee in the kitchen. I don't know why we were standing or even what we were talking about when Ivan took the cup from my hand and set it beside his on the counter. He smiled, put his hands on my shoulders and leaned forward.

Boys had kissed me before—not many. I may have even kissed them back. Or thought I did. I never got too involved because extreme kissing fell in the same category as banned movies. But what other boys had done and what Ivan was doing was the difference between plain vanilla ice cream and a hot fudge sundae. His hands moved from my shoulders to my waist. I relaxed against the oven door, never mind the knobs poking my spine. This time there was no doubt I was kissing back.

Sarah Vaughn had sung her way from a wistful *Little Girl Blue* to the final song on the album, *It Never Entered My Mind.*

The kitchen air felt warm and dreamy and Ivan's voice, when he whispered in my ear, was intimate and earnest.

"What would the nuns at your Catholic school say if they could see you now?"

"They probably thought it was just a matter of time," I mumbled into his neck.

With our arms clasped around each other, I felt the laugher ripple through our bodies, but when he stepped back, Ivan's face had gone serious.

"It's up to you, Diane."

I understood his meaning. As much as I longed for the kissing and whatever might follow, and for the music to continue, the only sound I heard was the automatic shut-off switch of the record player.

"I can't, Ivan. I just can't"

"Then I'd better go."

"Yes, go."

*

I was already asleep when Alberto finally came to bed.

# Chapter 8

"Alberto."

No answer.

"Alberto, it's nine o'clock."

Silence.

I stood by the bed wide-awake and fully dressed while my husband lay coma-like with the sheet pulled up to his chin.

"Alberto, last night you asked me to get you up. Remember? Your coffee's ready."

I opened the shutter with one hand and jiggled the sheet with the other.

Alberto opened one eye and groaned. "Please, will you turn off the light?"

"I can't. It's daylight, and you have a meeting."

For a man who loved his work as much as my husband professed, he certainly took his time getting to it.

I shook the sheet again and this time Alberto roused himself and slouched toward the bathroom, moaning all the while.

In the kitchen I arranged the coffee pot, a cup, a plate of *magdalenas* and a glass of Tang on a green plastic tray. The Tang was further proof of my husband's love for most things American. I didn't understand how he preferred a neon-colored artificial powdered drink to the natural juice of Spanish oranges, but he did. I set the tray on the dining table and followed the sound of a buzzing razor.

"I'm leaving now," I called to the back of his head at the sink. "I'll see you at lunch."

Alberto knew I planned to visit the Prado Museum that morning. Intrigued by Luis's remark about El Greco—that with age I would come to appreciate his art—I wanted to spend some time in the museum that had a room full of El Greco paintings.

"No, wait for me," Alberto said. "We'll go out together. The museum won't be open yet anyway, it's too early."

"I know, but the bus will take a while. And I want to be home again before it gets too hot."

"Just wait a few minutes. I'm almost ready."

So, I waited. I ate another *magdalena* to pass the time—though I'd already had breakfast—then I filled a sprinkling can and went to the balcony to water whatever was growing in the flowerpots left by previous occupants. I didn't know the name of the plants, but I was gratified that a few sickly leaves had thrived under my care. In a short time three clumps of bright green foliage had grown as high as my knee. If the growth spurt continued, I would soon need larger pots.

I lowered the watering can and stood motionless as a brown and yellow butterfly hovered over a pointy-edged leaf. A moment later it moved to the balcony railing, paused as though considering its options and then flew off. Maybe it went to look for Teresa, the Italian seamstress who had worked with me in Cleveland.

"We're married twenty-five years," she told me one lunch hour, "and I still get butterflies in my stomach every time Sal walks through the door."

I stepped back to the dining table. There were no butterflies in my stomach.

Weeks later I would find out from Julina, the plants were called *ortigas*, stinging nettles.

"It's a miracle you're not covered with a rash," she had said.

But the morning I waited for my husband, I didn't know the flourishing vegetation was toxic.

"Which one?" Alberto said. He had draped two neckties across the back of a chair and stood with his glass of *Tang* in one hand and a cup of coffee in the other. In general, he preferred standing to sitting. I had asked him about that once.

"In my student days I spent so many hours at a desk or a draft board that I feel much more comfortable standing."

By now I was used to his pacing with a glass in his hand.

I held the ties up side by side.

"The striped one," I said.

Still holding the cup and the glass, Alberto stretched his arms wide.

"Knot it for me, please, *querida.*"

"Oh, for heaven's sake! Shall I tuck in your shirt too?"

"Well, you can if you want to." He grinned and winked.

That was the last thing I wanted. I passed the tie under Alberto's collar, looped the silk a couple of times and slid the knot to his throat. Resentment made my hands shake. Why didn't I just pick up my purse and leave for the museum? Because I didn't want a scene. Another woman may have been pleased or flattered. I felt manipulated.

We left the apartment together, took the elevator to the lobby and nodded *Buenos Dias* to the *portero,* who was waving a feather duster at the mail boxes. A few moments later I wiggled my hand good-bye as Alberto pulled away in the car, and then walked a block in the opposite direction to the bus stop. I paused to look in the window of a children's boutique, thinking, not for the first time, that Spain had the most beautiful baby clothes I had ever seen: girls' dresses with smocked tops that looked like honeycomb and was called *nido de abeja,* bee's nest; double-breasted velvet-collared coats for boys; and white lace christening gowns with long trains. I appreciated their beauty but turned away with misgivings about their practicality.

⁂

The number 14 bus, the same one I took to Alberto's parents' flat, stopped near *El Museo del Prado*, The Museum of the Meadow. Constructed in 1745 as the Natural History Cabinet, the building opened as a public art museum in1819. Flanked by the Hotel Ritz and the Botanical Gardens, with the stately church of *Los Geronimos* rising behind it, the museum now faced a busy boulevard.

Any meadow creatures that had lived here in the past had given way to a trail of taxis and a river of impatient *Madrileños* beeping the horns of their look-alike *Seats,* the only nationally produced car at the time.

At the base of the wide stone steps leading to the museum's entrance, a street vendor attached postcards and bullfight posters to the side panels of his portable booth. On a bench nearby, a young woman sat painting miniature watercolors of *Old Madrid.* A display of her work lay on a canvas sheet at her feet, ready for tourists. And at the top of the stairs, a middle-aged woman with a scarf wrapped round her neck, in spite of the summer heat, sat in a cubicle dispensing *entradas.*

"*Buenos Dias,*" I said slipping some pesetas under the glass panel.

"*Una?*" she asked.

"*Sí, una.*"

I took the ticket, passed a pair of guards at the doorway and entered the rotunda that anchored one end of the building. The museum's main hall lay in front of me. I could have crossed the rotunda in just a few paces had the path been clear, but it wasn't. A giant bronze sculpture dominated the space.

On an earlier visit, a guide had explained the larger-than-life statue. Over eight feet tall with a lance in his hand, King Carlos V towered victorious over Fury sprawled at his feet. Following a sixteenth century convention, the artist had clothed His Majesty in the garb and armor of a Roman warrior. Dressed in this fashion, the broad-shouldered, muscular figure could not fail to impress.

"And imagine this," the guide had said. "All his clothes come off! Beneath the tunic we have a perfectly sculpted male nude."

I had looked for indications of how the bronze attire might be removed, a tiny hinge or a clasp. The seamless finish gave no clue. I took the guide's word, but I had gone away wondering less about *how* the clothes came off and more about *why.* And *when.*

I skirted the sculpture and entered a wide corridor as long as a city block. Paintings of battles, saints and rulers stretched for centuries on either side of the main hall; stories punctuated with blood, religious ecstasy, and dynastic power. I had no frame of reference for the stories. My experience with history paintings began and ended with *Washington Crossing the Delaware.* As for the religious figures, the images in my girlhood church seemed, by comparison, happier in their holiness. The word *gloomy* crossed my mind as I walked along the corridor, followed by *daunting* when I considered the museum's size.

I passed rows of royal portraits, formal faces in heavy gilt frames. How long, I wondered, before I could put all those kings in order? There were several Felipes: Felipe I, called *The Fair* because he was handsome, Felipe II, nicknamed *The Prudent,* Felipe III, *The Pious,* Felipe IV, *The Great* and Felipe V, knows as *The Spirited.* There were also four kings called Carlos, several Fernandos and a pair of queens named Isabel. And if I were going to begin at the beginning, I would have to start with *Pelayo* from the year 718. Definitely daunting.

Individual galleries branched off the main corridor and I looked for one labeled *El Greco* or Doménikos

Theotokópoulos, as the artist was known in his native Greece.

Sitting on a stool just inside the doorway, the customary gallery attendant wore a wrinkled blue jacket and an expression that said, *Don't ask.* I tightened my lips, assumed an attitude of self-confidence that I didn't actually possess and stepped into the world of *El Greco*, hoping for enlightenment.

I recognized St. John at once. He held his gold chalice with the green dragon just as he did on my mother-in-law's wall, though here he seemed larger. Paintings of other religious figures hung on red wine-colored walls. Haloed and ashen-faced saints raised their eyes to heaven with a holy fervor that looked decidedly uncomfortable. Their elongated bodies stretched upward toward swirling grey clouds while their faded robes twisted around them like flames in a draft.

I felt peculiar. I had wanted to be moved and inspired, but instead all I felt was clammy. I tried to shake an increasing queasiness, but it followed me around the gallery.

Of all the faces on the walls, the lone secular exception was a portrait titled simply *Caballero Desconocido,* Unknown Gentleman. He looked straight at me, a serious countenance from the sixteenth century, set off by a white ruff against a somber background devoid of details. His expression was neutral except for the challenge in his eyes. *What are you doing here?* they demanded. Again I felt the surge of discomfort, this time accompanied by shortness of breath. I turned away from the *Unknown Gentleman* and nearly collided with an equally unknown saint. That's when I saw the black spots.

At first I thought the dots were flaws on the canvas. I squinted for a better look, but the spots moved and floated beyond the frame. I closed my eyes for a moment and when I opened them again, the red walls moved, too, undulating in slow motion. I wished I hadn't eaten the second *magdalena* at breakfast. I felt hot and cold at the same time, and so weak that I feared falling against one of the priceless paintings—or worse. Had anyone ever thrown-up in the Prado?

"*Por favor,*" I said to the gallery attendant, waving a limp hand toward the stool.

Perhaps he would relinquish his seat until I felt stable. Through a twirl of dots, I saw his lips form words, but the only sound that reached my ear was a soft moan from the back of my throat as what must have been the ghost of *El Greco* pushed me toward the exit.

Outside, I leaned against the railing until the spots disappeared, but I couldn't bear the thought of a crowded bus home. Grateful for a taxi at the corner, I sagged into the worn seat, trying not to inhale the air that reeked of cigarette smoke.

"*Juan Ramón Jiménez 2,*" I mumbled, fumbling for the handkerchief I had sprayed that morning with *Alvarez Gómez* citrus cologne. I hadn't imagined I would be using the lemony fragrance as an antidote for morning sickness. In fact, I was so newly pregnant that I hadn't thought much about morning sickness at all, and the little I'd heard hadn't mentioned spots. I lowered the window and looked at my watch. My visit with *El Greco* had lasted barely half an hour—not long enough to develop an appreciation and, oddly, the painting that stayed in my mind wasn't an *El Greco* at all but a *Murillo* I'd seen along the way.

*The Holy Family of the Little Bird* the label read. The only way I knew it was the Holy Family was because the label said so. The figures had no religious attributions and wore clothing contemporary to the seventeenth century when Esteban Murillo painted them. They show a tender domestic scene in which St. Joseph occupies most of the picture plane as he supports the Child Jesus who appears as a toddler. The Child holds a bird in his right hand. Mary, the mother, winds wool off to the left side with what looks like a basket of laundry at her feet. Both parents have their eyes on the Child. Countless paintings focus on the Madonna and Child, but this one features a gentle father. The supernatural is combined with a charming moment of daily life—a sweet message easier to read than *El Greco's.*

It was shortly after noon when I arrived home, still two hours before Alberto would come for lunch. The nausea returned as soon as I opened the door to an apartment nearly as hot as the street below. I kicked off my shoes, shuffled to the bathroom, opened the spigot marked *F—F* for *fria,* for cold—and held my wrists under the stream of water.

The mirror above the sink reflected a pasty face surrounded by lime green wall tiles. I didn't look well in green, never had. With the back of my hand I brushed a strand of hair from my forehead or maybe I was trying to brush away the thought inside. I studied my reflection and as the water changed from cool to cold the thought came alive. *What have I done? What on earth have I done?*

I don't know why the realization came to me that particular day and not some other, but there it was in its chilling ugliness. I didn't love my husband. Maybe I never had.

I closed the faucet and shivered, but not with cold, with shame. I looked in the mirror again, watched my eyes fill with tears and heard the sound of my own voice. "I'm sorry little baby. I am so sorry." I was saying the words out loud. In that moment, standing with my unborn child, all I felt was guilt.

With a towel to my face I sat on the edge of the bed and the question changed. *What have I done?* became *what will I do?* I knew the answer at once. *Nothing*. If you were raised the way I was, there was nothing you *could* do.

I was Catholic. I had vowed, "till death do us part" in a church known for its rigid stance regarding marriage. I couldn't show up seven months later, pregnant, and say, *I seem to have made a mistake.* I couldn't admit that mistake to anyone.

My relationship with Alberto had always been a challenge and anything but a straight line. I had been so excited by the promise of an exotic new world and so busy trying to live up to what I thought he wanted that I had pushed aside the matter of the missing butterflies in my stomach.

I had thought the butterflies would come with time. They hadn't. And now I realized they had never been there at all. So I prayed I could keep their absence secret. If no one knew, I could still be a good wife and a good mother, couldn't I? Of course I would stay, and I would keep silent.

*Now I lay me down to sleep.*
*I pray the Lord my soul to keep.*
*If I should die before I wake,*
*I pray the Lord my soul to take.*
*God bless Mommy, God bless Daddy,*
*And make Diane a good girl.*
Diane Lorz
Meadville, PA. 1940

# Chapter 9

*September 1965.* Alberto hadn't proposed, exactly. I mean, he didn't take my hand across a candle-lit table at a romantic restaurant and say *Will you marry me?* Instead, we were standing beside his car in the parking lot of the Madrid airport. He had placed my suitcase in the trunk, turned and said, "Don't you think we've fooled around long enough?"

As nearly as I can recall, I answered, "Probably."

We had not seen each other in three years, not since my first visit to Spain, the visit I had hoped would last forever. That time, with a one-way passage to *Algeciras,* a port I had only recently learned to pronounce, I had waved farewell to the Statue of Liberty and sailed away in a fog of romance. The visit had ended in disappointment. This time, things would be different.

*

Five years earlier, after we first met back in Cleveland, we had dated for several months. Alberto didn't talk of love or a future together, but when his company sent him to Venezuela for a special project, he returned with a gift of a delicate gold and pearl pin with matching earrings, and later, from a trip to Mexico, he gave me two heavy silver bracelets. Even without words his intentions seemed more than casual.

I was excited when he said he would like to meet my parents. I phoned home to ask if I could bring a Spaniard to lunch on Sunday.

"Yes, of course," Mother said. "But what do Spaniards eat?" She seemed more interested in the menu than in my relationship with the man in question.

On a cloudless May morning, Alberto and I drove the ninety-five miles from Cleveland to my parents' home in Saegertown. I was taking the world traveler to a Pennsylvania hamlet of less than 400 households and a lunch of stuffed pork chops. I was anxious, but that disappeared when I saw how easily Alberto engaged with my father. They were interested in each other, and easily shared stories. Alberto had anecdotes about his work as a civil engineer in Africa and my father told stories about his own travels during WWII and his days as a young man helping to build roads in Haiti.

Alberto complimented mother's pork chops, but the thing that impressed him most was my father's workshop in the basement and a photograph of the hunting cabin he had built in the foothills of the Allegheny Mountains. By the time we said good-by, the only person still ill at ease was my mother. I could tell. She had made little attempt at conversation and as we were leaving had barely smiled when Alberto said he hoped I had her recipe for pork chops.

Alberto took my hand in the car. "I like your parents," he said. "And I would very much like to have a workshop like your father's some day."

"Really?" This was a side of Alberto I hadn't visualized.

"It is so quintessentially American," he said. "We don't have a do-it-yourself mentality in Spain. We don't have your fabulous do-it-yourself stores. If something needs a repair, Spaniards call in the specialist—everyone except my father."

Alberto released my hand and reached for a cigarette.

"But it's just a question of time," he said. "It might take a decade, but everything you have in the United States will reach Spain—eventually."

I didn't know then the country he compared to the United States still suffered the effects of global isolation and the aftermath of its Civil War twenty years earlier. I didn't know that American cigarettes were so rare and expensive that they were sold individually, just one or two, not a pack, or that an attendant stood at the entrance to the restroom in the movie theater and asked, before you entered, if you wanted toilet paper. If you said yes, she tore what she considered an adequate amount from a roll she kept in a basket, then extended her hand for a tip. I didn't know the Spanish version of toilet tissue had the same color and texture as 80-grit sandpaper. I didn't know that 45% of the country was devoted to agriculture or fishing and that 15% of its population was illiterate. I didn't know about a class system as rigid as Catholicism, or that it was the state religion. And I could not have imagined how easily I would adjust to all of that, or how I would see it all change. On that Spring afternoon, as we drove back to Cleveland, I was just relieved the lunch had been a success.

Alberto and I continued to date, a non-sexual, non-committed relationship. He went to Madrid for a brief vacation and brought me a brooch and bracelet. I had never seen anything like them.

"It's *damascene,"* he said. "The Moors brought the gold and silver inlay technique to the Iberian Peninsula in the eighth century. These pieces were made in Toledo."

Before Alberto, no man had ever given me jewelry. I loved the attention. Alberto obviously had some feeling for me, but I wasn't sure what or how deep or for how long. I didn't know what lay behind the gestures. He never said more than, "I hope you like it," or "I was thinking about you." Not until several months after the lunch with my parents. I sat in his car waiting for him to turn the key in the ignition and take me home. We had had an after-work dinner at a downtown Cleveland restaurant—something we did often—but instead of starting the car, he put his arms around me and said, "I love you." Then, because I was glad he did and because an answer seemed expected, I said, "I love you, too." I had never said that to anyone and no one, not even my parents, had ever said those words to me.

I waited for the swell of violins and the swoosh of butterflies in my stomach, even just the brush of a single wing tip. Nothing. This wasn't like the movies. But it had to be right. This man I admired, this man who had everything I wanted said he loved me. Of course I loved him in return.

Then, one evening, after a supper of Alberto's attempt at paella in his apartment, he showed me a letter from his father. Franco's Minister of Public Works had invited several engineers from the US Bureau of Public Roads to develop a program to modernize Spain's highways. Alberto's fluency in English and experience in the United States made him a perfect fit for the project.

"My father thinks I could find a position on that team at the Ministry."

I knew how much Alberto loved his profession. I admired that. His enthusiasm was infectious, and I listened with interest when he talked about highways and bridges. But I also knew how much he enjoyed living in the United States.

"How would you feel about returning to Madrid?" I said.

"I haven't decided yet."

I cleared the remains of supper. Alberto re-corked the bottle of red wine. Normally, we talked easily but conversation had stalled. I looked at my watch.

"It's a work day tomorrow," I said.

A few minutes later, Alberto opened the car door for me, ready to take me home. He put the key in the ignition, took it out again.

"But I don't want to lose you," he said. "How would you adjust to Spain if we married? You have never been out of the States."

He hadn't proposed marriage exactly, but at least his intention was clear. Of course, I would have preferred the proposal—an impassioned *I can't live without you. Come with me, all will be well.* But his concern was well founded. I didn't even have a passport. My knowledge of the language was based on two years of high school Spanish and the only things I knew about Spanish culture were what Alberto told me. However, what I lacked in experience and common sense, I made up for with optimism and faith.

"I guess there's only one way to find out," I said.

*Logical,* I thought. *Go to Spain; see for yourself.* I didn't want to lose him either.

My parents didn't try to stop me. I suppose they realized any protests would fall on deaf ears. They hadn't been able to keep me in college and now, after living on my own for four years, they might have thought I was old enough to know what I was doing.

"Be safe," they said. "Take care of yourself. Write often."

I resigned from my job, sold my furniture, and closed my bank account. In September 1960, I bought a one-way passage on the *S.S. Constitution* and sailed with Alberto to a country controlled by a dictator. With the superficial deliberation of a twenty-four-year old, I never gave it a second thought.

⁂

The fading Polaroid photo shows us seated on a banquette in the ship's lounge. Outside the frame, multinational travelers smoke and drink at low tables around the room. A four-piece orchestra plays dance music. When the ship lists, the seated passengers reach to steady their glasses. Dancers skid to the edge of the floor, laughing. The musicians play on. I sit, in a silver lamé sheath, between Alberto and the round-faced Spanish olive exporter who has joined us. We smile for the camera with raised cocktail glasses. Two empty ones sit in front of Alberto. I see them in the photo. At the time I was too excited to notice.

⁂

For the next eighteen months I did *see for myself.* Nothing about Spain reminded me of the United States. I expected and looked forward to the historical and geographical differences and was willing to adapt to a change in diet. I enjoyed the linguistic challenges, and Alberto proved an ideal professor. He augmented my vocabulary, improved my grammar and explained the pervasive class distinction. "I exemplify an education that fostered elitism," he said. He didn't approve. "In many ways I prefer the American way of life. I like its directness." The Spain Alberto introduced to me was anything but direct. To me, the entire country, regardless of class, felt constrained by a multilayered code of behavior. And social upward mobility (a term I learned much later) under Franco's regime was nearly impossible.

⁂

So-called *nice girls* didn't live alone or even share apartments, so, with the help of Alberto's sister Julina, I rented a room near the United States Embassy in the elegant flat of a widow. Julina also introduced me to a friend who ran a school for English speaking children. I exaggerated my résumé to qualify as the new fourth grade teacher and later I found a second job working afternoons for a couture house, dealing with their American clients. These were *acceptable* occupations; working in a department store where I had several years of experience was not appropriate for a young woman of my class—perhaps I should say of Alberto's class—though until then I had never given much thought to my own.

Alberto and I met every evening for dinner; sometimes with his friends or co-workers, other times I cooked at his apartment near *Plaza de Castilla.* The apartment had caused raised eyebrows in his family. Normally, even men well into their thirties still lived with their parents. Why wouldn't they? Especially in Alberto's case, where his parents had an ample flat and two maids and he never had to worry about meals, and where his laundry was delivered fresh and ironed to his dresser drawers. *Don* Manuel fussed about what people would say regarding his son's "unnatural" living arrangement. Alberto's friends looked at him with a mixture of awe and envy.

"I've lived too long in the States," he said. "I'll never live under my father's roof again."

Sundays he took me to his parents' house for lunch, and I saw Spanish family life from the inside. For the most part, I liked it or thought I could get used to it. But I didn't see a husband.

The Ministry valued Alberto's experience in the States. He wrote articles for the *Revista de Obras Públicas* and was enthusiastic about his prospects. I only wished he had made clear they included me. We didn't fight. I didn't offer ultimatums. But after a year and a half I felt that life in Madrid was not for me—not in a country where my business background didn't count for much, and not as a single woman. And I wasn't the only one to think so.

Maria Fe, my landlady, and I usually ate lunch in the formal dining room. Juana, the maid, stood by the sideboard silent as the other furniture but ready to pass the soup tureen or the fish platter when *la señora* raised her hand. I received a unique education at that table. Maria Fe looked formidable. She wore her steel-colored hair short and her clothes simply cut. Her only accessory was a single strand of pearls. I couldn't imagine Maria Fe with a hearty laugh. But in spite of her stern exterior she was, like Alberto's sister, a thoughtful friend.

On a particular day she offered advice about grocery shopping. "Don't ever send the maid to market. Always go yourself."

I must have looked surprised.

"If you send a maid for a chicken, she will come back with a chicken. But what if a fish is a better buy? You see what I mean?"

I nodded.

Then she looked at me with her unsettling gaze and said, "You don't belong here. You should go home."

I was stunned. What on earth had prompted that?

"Alberto doesn't treat you properly," she said before I could respond.

What could Maria Fe know about Alberto Benitez? She had met him only twice.

"Don't ask me how I know," she said touching her head. "My grey hairs tell me. He isn't right for you."

Maria's opinion aside, I was coming to the same conclusion.

⁂

My trip to Spain ended almost the way it had begun, in Alberto's car after dinner at a favorite restaurant.

Alberto pulled to the curb in front of Maria's building. There were few cars on *Lopez de Hoyos* in those days and at that late hour only the *sereno,* the neighborhood night watchman, paced the dimly lit street making his rounds. He checked the locks on the shuttered shops and shook the gates of the apartment buildings. A metal ring of skeleton keys hung from his belt and clinked with every step. Later he would open the gate for me and I would tip him a five-peseta coin. But first…

Alberto reached to kiss me goodnight. I pushed him away.

"What's the matter? The *sereno* isn't looking."

"It's not the *sereno,* Alberto."

"Then what…?"

"I've decided to go back to the States." I hadn't prepared a farewell speech beyond those words.

He sat back, saying nothing.

"I need a real job, Alberto. And a real apartment. I can't live like this."

I had left a career in the States and an independent life. I had taken a risk when I came to Spain and I didn't regret it, but I couldn't live in a rented room with an uncertain future. I felt I was living in shadow. If Alberto had asked me to marry him in that moment, I would have said *yes.* But he didn't.

"I'll miss you," was all he said.

*

I returned to the department store in Cleveland. A short time later, thanks to a phone call from a friend, I moved to San Francisco to work as a department manager for *I.Magnin*, the most prestigious chain of specialty stores on the West Coast. Madrid had been an education—sometimes prickly—in language and culture. San Francisco was an instant fit. I found an apartment in a charming Victorian house on a hill in Pacific Heights. Some evenings I went to a café on Union Street to listen to folk music and later walked home to the sound of foghorns mixed with the memory of a Bob Dylan song. I wrote to Alberto about biking in the park and taking a cable car to work. He told me about his work. We stayed in touch. Why not? We had parted in disappointment, not anger.

On sheer airmail stationery we penned our superficial news. From time to time we exchanged a gift—I sent Alberto a wooden monkey (I don't remember why) and he sent me a fur-lined shepherd's hat because, he wrote, he remembered my enthusiasm for typical, traditional artifacts. Our letters took 5 to 7 days to arrive; a transatlantic phone call was an expense reserved for emergencies. I never knew anyone who made one. I wonder how today's technology would have affected our lives. Would we have emailed daily? Or FaceTimed? Would I have texted to tell him I was going to buy a car? As it was, I put that information in a postscript on a letter that didn't have much in it except a description of fog floating over Golden Gate Bridge. *PS, I think I'll buy a Volkswagen.*

Two weeks later, Alberto's letter arrived. "Don't waste money on a car. Come to Spain on your vacation."

I bought a round trip ticket.

⁂

We drove directly to Alberto's apartment. Once, in accordance with the prevailing morality and an effort to preserve my good, Catholic girl image, I would have booked a single room in a hotel. But, technically speaking, I could no longer claim to *be* a good, Catholic girl. I had lost that title some time earlier. Now, no one even mentioned a hotel.

Sometime later we sat at a table that folded from a wall of bookshelves in the cluttered space that served as Alberto's living/dining room. We had ordered lunch brought up from the café downstairs. Alberto pushed aside the plates and breadcrumbs and poured himself a brandy before unrolling a sheet of architectural drawings.

"I've bought a flat," he said. "It won't be finished for a year or so and it's not large, but it has 3 bedrooms plus a maid's room and I can afford it without too much stress. What do you think?"

*Cuesta del Zarzal.* We would live on a street called *Bramble Bush Hill.* It sounded rural and romantic. I traced the rooms with my finger trying to convert square meters to square feet. The flat looked fine on paper. Only months later, when construction had advanced to a point where I could actually pace-off the rooms, we saw that in order to accommodate a dining table we would have to eliminate a wall. That's how we lost the third bedroom.

The following hours blended from one to the next in a blur of excitement and jet lag. I'd had breakfast in San Francisco and then, *poof!* I was drinking tea in Madrid with my future in-laws. A lot had happened since breakfast.

*Paseo del Prado* hadn't changed. Alberto's parents hugged and kissed me like an old friend. They asked the usual: *How was your trip? How long will you stay?* And then ushered us to the table. Alberto waited until his father ceased fussing with the teapot before he said, "How do you feel about having an *Americana* in the family?" I don't think the question came as a surprise. His mother reached for my hand across the table and his father grinned. *"Bien,"* he said. *"Muy bien."* I felt the way I always had in the Benitez family, secure and accepted.

We sent a telegram to my parents to announce our engagement and the following day they replied. *Congratulations. Please get married at home. Love Mother and Dad.*

"I don't mind to get married in Pennsylvania," Alberto said.

*Fine with us,* we cabled back. We'd work out the details later.

Alberto had taken a week's vacation but wanted to finish some details at the ministry before we left on a road trip north. While he went to his office, I visited Julina at the library associated with the United States embassy where she had worked for several years.

"My favorite *Americana!*" She kissed my cheeks. "How long can you stay?"

"Well, I'm going to marry your brother so I guess we could say *permanently.*"

Julina stepped back. Her smile faded.

"Are you sure, Diana? Alberto is a difficult man."

I couldn't take her seriously. Some classic sibling difference, I thought. Yes, Alberto had more self-confidence than anyone I had ever known. And he admitted to being a bit of an elitist. But if that was what she meant by difficult, I could handle it.

"He can't be *that* bad," I said.

Julina shrugged. Her smile returned.

"Well, come for a drink this evening," she said.

⁂

Luis opened the door.

"Welcome to the family!" he said.

My future-brother-in-law had a limited English vocabulary, but he used it with wit and dexterity. The first time he surprised me with a few words, I said I hadn't realized he spoke English.

"Oh, *jes*," he replied. "And I can also tell you the *deefairent* parts of the body!"

I laughed till my eyes watered, never imagining that the phrase would work its way through two more generations. Years later, during an unlikely lull in conversation at some family gathering, a voice would pipe up and fill the void with *Oh, jes, and I can also tell you the deefairent parts of the body.*

The evening of our engagement, however, after kissing me and shaking Alberto's hand, Luis led us to the living room where a bowl of almonds and a bottle of red vermouth sat on the rustic coffee table. Isabel, now eight years old, lifted her face for a kiss then turned to scold her four-year old brother, César, who was somersaulting across the room dangerously close to the antique table Luis used as a desk. A moment later, Julina came down the hall with a tray of sliced chorizo, olives and cubes of tortilla. Everything felt warm and familiar. Except for the age of the children, nothing had changed.

We arranged ourselves around the little table. Julina and I shared the sofa. Alberto sat in one of two wing chairs, while Luis sat in the other with Isabel trying to squeeze in beside him. Julina and Luis didn't usually drink alcohol but eventually everyone, including the children, had a glass of something—an orange *Fanta,* a non-alcoholic beer or chilled vermouth with a slice of lemon.

"Cheers!" Luis said, raising his glass as Julina lifted a tissue-wrapped package from the table and handed it to me.

"It's from all of us," she said. "But Luis picked it out. We hope you like it."

I unwrapped a necklace. Three red enamel squares hung like a Calder mobile from a silver wire that circled the neck. I liked it. It was simple and unusual and, although I couldn't know it at the time, the necklace was just the beginning. For all the years to follow—for birthdays and

Christmases it would always be *Luis picked it out for you*—a book or a piece of ceramic and, when we moved into our new flat, a still-life water color that we hung on the dining room wall. And always, sitting at Julina and Luis's coffee table with Mendelssohn on the record player, the children correcting my grammar, I felt nourished far beyond the almonds and the olives.

The following day, Alberto and I drove to a resort on the Costa Brava. Alberto revealed the landscape for me, like turning the pages of a book. Where I saw only mounds and valleys, Alberto saw Moorish remnants and ancient riverbeds. In the time before Alberto and his band of engineers had improved the roads, a journey held adventure at every turn. Once, on a deserted mountain, Alberto stopped at the side of the road where a rudimentary hand-painted sign read *AGUA POTABLE,* drinking water. I saw nothing to indicate a rest stop, but Alberto got out of the car and pointed to a clear stream of water running from a pipe stuck in the side of the mountain. A tin cup hung from a chain attached to the pipe.

"Is this really safe?" I asked.

"Of course," Alberto said. He splashed his face, filled the cup, drank and then handed the cup to me.

"Go ahead," he said.

I don't know what bothered me more: drinking unfiltered, chemical free water direct from the source or using a cup that had been touched by Lord knows how many lips. If Alberto had not been watching, I don't know if I would have brought the cup to my mouth. But he was. And I did. And all I remember was how cold it was.

Now, on this Costa Brava trip, we had traveled for several miles looking for a place to have lunch. We passed villages, but in the 1960s village population was shrinking. Young people looked for work in the cities and rural life was often reduced to a community of six or seven families, none with a restaurant.

I was scanning the map on my lap for a town that might be more than a cluster of stone dwellings when I felt the car turn onto a bumpy road.

"What are you doing?" I said as Alberto shifted the *Seat* from fourth to third.

The only signs of human life on the hilltop were a small house and a rudimentary barn. Alberto didn't answer for a moment and stopped near the open barn door.

"I'm starving," he said and got out of the car.

In the doorway, a wrinkled-faced man who could not have stood more than five feet tall watched motionless. Immediately, I thought of the Spanish war and what Alberto had told me.

"The children born and reared during the 1930s never thrived," he said. "We were all mal-nourished."

I had seen that for myself. Alberto had reached 5'7", but his cousins, born a decade later when food was more abundant, were all nearly six feet tall. Still, Alberto seemed to tower over the rustic figure in the doorway who wore a black beret, the type the Spaniards call a *boina,* a white collarless shirt and shapeless brown corduroy pants that looked to be a one-size-fits-all variety. What I could see of his weathered face and exposed forearms appeared to be brown corduroy, too. The men exchanged a few words then disappeared into the barn. When they emerged a few minutes later, Alberto motioned for me to join them.

"We can eat here," he said.

"Here?" I looked around.

At that moment Alberto chose to speak English.

"Yes, the old guy says he has food."

The farmer looked at me quizzically, then beckoned me to the barn. To one side, just past the door, stood a small wooden cask. He lifted the lid with a tentative smile alternately tapping his chest and pointing to the barrel. Inside, lay the glistening river trout he had pickled himself, and for a moment a whiff of pungent brine replaced the aroma of grain and livestock.

"*Muy bonito,*" I said.

The farmer's smile broadened. Before I could say more than *very pretty,* he had pulled a pair of sawhorses from a corner, set a plank upon them, and then dashed up the rise to his house. He returned with a chair dangling from the crook of each elbow and his wife a few steps behind. I knew the woman was his wife because of her dress—long-sleeved, calf-length and black—the traditional mark of a married woman in rural society. One expects cultural differences between countries, but even in Spain itself the contrast between city and village was extreme. As I stood before the farmer's wife in my pale beige hip-huggers with the flared cuffs and a sleeveless top that opened in front to what I hoped was a tantalizing inch above my bra, the difference must have seemed extraterrestrial to her.

The woman carried a tray with plates and cutlery, a bottle of wine and half a round of coarse country bread.

She set the makeshift table with a white cloth while her husband talked trout. When she finished, she turned to us.

"*Huevos fritos?*"

"*Perfecto!*" Alberto and I answered in enthusiastic unison because, though it sounds quite simple, an egg fried Spanish style is a wonderful thing. There is magic in the olive oil. Slipped into a skillet of near-boiling oil, the egg white shudders and bubbles. As the cook gently bastes the egg's center, the white forms a lacy halo around the yolk. Sometimes the white gets crisp on the edge. I always ate that part first and then, after piercing the yolk with the crust, soaked it up with a chunk of bread. Salty, hot, golden and delicious.

⁂

"How did you manage that?" I said to Alberto an hour later as we carried on to the coast.

We'd had first course, second course, bread and wine plus a slice of pale green football shaped fruit called *melón*. Never mind the wine could have doubled as paint thinner.

"Well, when I asked *el viejo* if he knew of a restaurant somewhere, he said he had never heard of one but, if we were really hungry, he could probably feed us. You saw, he rather insisted."

"Talk about Spanish hospitality! And he didn't want to take any money. I'm glad you found a way."

"We probably made his day. He'll be talking about this for ages. I'm sure he never had an *Americana* eating trout in his barn before."

I laughed. "That was a first for me too."

⁂

By September the summer tourists had departed the Costa Brava. Our semi-deserted hotel sat among pines overlooking the sea. It could have been perfect. Except for a few Germans, we had the pool to ourselves and lunch on the sunny patio seemed a good idea.

"We should order the mussels," Alberto said. "This is the region for them."

"Okay." I liked just about anything that came from the ocean.

"*Y un tinto de la casa,*" he said to the waiter.

"A glass, sir?"

"A bottle."

It all went down so easily but the combination nearly killed me. The seafood, the wine and the sun on my head produced a thirty-six hour-long migraine, and any hope for a romantic interlude vanished. Alberto slept while I threw up in the bathroom, or he read on the terrace while I napped in the darkened room. I can't even remember how or when we planned a wedding. But somehow, by the time we returned to Madrid, we had set a date for the New Year, January 1966.

I phoned my parents in Pennsylvania as soon as I returned to San Francisco.

"I'll work through the Christmas season," I told them. "It's the busiest time of year for the store and I don't want to leave on short notice. Besides, I don't know how long it takes to reserve the church."

I needn't have worried about the church. No bride in her right mind schedules a mid-winter wedding in Pennsylvania.

We would be married in the parish where I had been baptized, made my first communion and been confirmed. Father Cannon agreed to officiate—the same priest who had handed out report cards at St. Bridget's grade school. My Catholic life was well documented; Alberto's less so.

Alberto had gone through the same religious formation though no one in his family took it seriously. They were not unusual. Everyone professed to be Catholic—after all it was the state religion. Whether they attended Mass, except for weddings and funerals, was another matter and, while Alberto had been reared as Catholic, producing the evidence proved problematic. A photograph of a little boy wearing a white sailor suit with short pants and carrying a rosary was the only indication Alberto's mother found of his first communion. As for a confirmation certificate:

"Those records are gone." Alberto wrote. "The church was burned during the Civil War."

I don't remember how we overcame that detail but somehow we pulled together a wedding even though the event coordinator (my mother) lived in Pennsylvania, the groom was at home in Madrid and the bride had a job in San Francisco. I had never dreamed of a lavish production so a small gathering suited me. My closest Cleveland relations, two mutual friends of Alberto's and mine from our Cleveland days and a professor/friend of Alberto's from MIT braved a winter storm to attend. The photographer captured us as we left the church. Alberto holds my elbow as we negotiate the icy steps. I wear a street-length white brocade dress, a fur jacket and boots. The sky has turned blue.

"Oh, look!" I said a moment later. "The sun's come out. I think it's an omen." Then I clutched my short veil to keep it from sailing off in the wind.

# Chapter 10

I've always thought my real life began in the mid 1960s. At the age of thirty I was living my exciting European dream. I was captivated by Spain and fascinated by a language that, in some strange way, spoke to me more deeply than my native tongue, with words layered in history and meaning, and a husband who explained them. Maybe the dream wasn't perfect, but it was close enough.

*

"Should I tell them I'm pregnant? I don't want to mislead anyone," I said.

We had just finished lunch in our apartment. Alberto drew light circles on the tablecloth with the foot of his brandy glass as we mulled over this latest turn of events. Several weeks earlier, when we discussed my looking for a job, it had seemed like a good idea. I hadn't known then that I was pregnant and now I had second thoughts.

Alberto had encouraged me. I had not married a stereotypical Latin male who thought a woman should stay at home. In fact, I didn't even know any men like that, and all my Spanish girlfriends worked. Paloma, an attorney, worked in her father's patent office, Cristina was an airline attendant and both Blanca and Milali worked in a ministry office. I liked the idea of contributing to our income. Though not vital, it would help when the time came to decorate our new flat— if and when that time ever came. I prayed we could move before the baby's birth.

"The contractor says not to worry." I had said at one point.

Alberto looked over the top of his glasses.

"Diana, someone telling you not to worry, is precisely when you should begin to worry."

I didn't want to just sit around worrying, so I answered an ad in the *ABC*, the Madrid newspaper whose name was nothing more than the first three letters of the alphabet. *English-speaking salesgirl needed. Mitzou* was a chic boutique on *Calle Serrano,* a street lined with jewelers and high-fashion shops. I had walked there often, stopping for a coffee or a glass of *tinto* at one of the sidewalk cafes. I hadn't shopped in *Mitzou* myself, but I was confident of one thing; I knew how to sell expensive clothes. After an interview with the French couple who owned the shop, (*Mitzou* was the woman's name) they thought so, too, and offered me the job. That was just a few days before I learned that I was pregnant. Now what should I do?

"I'll just have to quit in a few months," I said. "Is that fair?"

"Take the job," Alberto said. "You have nothing to lose. Wait a while to tell them you're expecting. If they want you to work part-time after the baby is born, you can think about it then. In the meantime, this is a good experience for you."

I went to work at a time when the dollar was strong and American businesses and tourists were finding Spain a very welcoming country. Language schools filled with Spaniards who wanted to learn English. The international film industry flourished due to cheap labor and a favorable climate. The sunny landscape of *Andalucia* made an ideal setting for American Westerns. A vibrant expatriate community lived the good life they found easily available—the cheap labor, both domestic and industrial, good food, luxury products like *Mallorca* pearls and *Lladró* porcelains, fine leathers for which *Mitzou* was renowned, and sun. My new employers catered to this discerning international clientele. I thought I'd found my niche. Sometimes I don't see the warning signs.

For my first day at the shop, I chose a simple brown linen dress and a small gold brooch shaped like a quill with a line of diamonds along the spine. The brooch had been a wedding gift from Alberto's mother and I wore it often because it made me feel good. That is to say, it *usually* made me feel good.

Mitzou, her puff of red hair floating in the air, gave me a cursory tour of the shop in which everything from the furniture to the walls was upholstered in striped grey silk. She introduced me to a pair of Spanish salesgirls who stood with crossed arms glaring at me with the same hostility I had previously sensed in Mario the *portero.* Then she motioned me to her office, a jumble of suede and leather swatches and sketches of mini skirts and gaucho pants.

"Please, remove that brooch," she said.

"Pardon?" I thought for a moment she wanted to inspect it.

"You must be careful. Don't wear anything you value because it might disappear."

"You mean…?"

"I don't know how, but you will lose it," she said.

*And welcome to my shop,* I thought as I pinned the brooch to my bra strap under my dress. I couldn't wait to tell Alberto about the nest of vipers I had fallen into.

My first mistake had been wanting to look good. I made the second by behaving like an American. I had been taught to look busy. On a slow day with no customers, you still had to look busy. You rearranged the stock, you fluffed the merchandise, you did something—anything. You didn't adopt the bad-attitude, crossed-arms stance. But, since my new employers kept their precious leathers behind the upholstered cupboard doors, I didn't have much to rearrange except for a few handbags on a glass table. That didn't take long and I moved on to the cupboards. I needed to know the contents in case a customer arrived. Until now the vipers had ignored me. I didn't hear viper number one slither up behind my back.

*"Que haces?"* she hissed.

What was I doing? I tried to explain. I wanted to see the merchandize and get an idea of size ranges. Then viper number two materialized, snapped the doors shut and told me to open them only when a customer asked for something specific. *How would a customer even know what…* but the vipers had returned to their corner; Mitzou had disappeared. I looked at my watch—three and a half hours till lunch.

Four weeks later I was still complaining to my husband.

"I don't know how much longer I can tolerate that place. I can't trust the vipers and Mitzou is kinda nuts. This afternoon she came out of the office singing *We all live in a yellow submarine* in English with her French accent. And there were customers in the shop."

"Then leave," Alberto said. "You don't need to have a nervous breakdown over this."

"No, I'll stay a little longer."

My clothes still fit and I didn't look pregnant. And I enjoyed the customers. I sold leather jackets to the American TV actor Bill Cosby and suede coats to the wife of the famous writer James Michener who was in Spain doing research for his book *Iberia.* Released a short time later, the book became an international best seller. So, I thought I would continue to enjoy the customers and wait till the end of the month to resign. That didn't work.

Viper number one may have appeared disinterested as she leaned in her usual position against the wall, but I'm convinced her eyes never blinked. Some people possess an uncanny knack for eliciting information from even the most guarded souls. People like me who don't think fast on their feet make easy targets. When the viper slid up beside me one day and said, "When is your baby due?" I just blurted out, "In March."

"How did you know?" I said when I realized what I had revealed. My skirt didn't show a bulge.

"Oh, I can always tell," she said, and I thought she sneered. I knew she would tell the shop owners at the first opportunity but I beat her to it. I told Mitzou that Alberto, an over-protective husband, wanted me to stay at home to await the birth of our first child. All I felt at this slight exaggeration of the truth was relief. I couldn't wait to leave.

"You understand, *Madame,*" I said.

"But of course. Stay well. *Merci beaucoup y adios.*"

Now I turned my attention to baby clothes and diapers (we made our own from soft cotton and I hemmed mine by hand), and studying for a Spanish driver's license. My international permit had expired. None of this seemed particularly challenging.

I knew I would have to study the Spanish traffic laws and signals. After that, I thought I would need just a brief visit to Madrid's department of motor vehicles. I had forgotten that the word *brief* couldn't be applied to the Spanish department of anything.

"I'll have my secretary set up an appointment for you at one of the driving academies," Alberto said.

"But I've been driving since I was sixteen." Did I really have to go to class?

"Everyone has to take classes on how to handle a car. Then you take two tests, one written and one practical. The written test comes first. If you pass that, you will be notified a month later. You will be able to take the practical test then."

"A month? You have to wait a whole month!"

The written component worried me. Some unfamiliar technical term could trip me up. But I couldn't foresee any difficulty with the actual driving. With fourteen years of experience, I didn't need classes.

"Can't we just get the text book of traffic laws? I'll study that. If I can pass the written test, I'm not worried about the driving part."

That's what we did. In the evenings after dinner, Alberto tutored me until I felt confident enough to take the test. One didn't just show up at the license bureau and ask for the exam. Like everything else in this country, it required a great deal of paperwork, a lot of waiting in line, and a visit to an *estanco*. Usually a minuscule space the size of a confessional, these licensed establishments sold only postage stamps, tobacco and the official *estampillas*. Invariably, a woman stood behind the counter.

"A war widow," Alberto told me. "Franco granted *estanco* licenses to women who lost a husband in the Civil War. A kind of compensation for a fallen warrior."

For a few *pesetas* I bought the *estampillas* and delivered them to the proper authorities. Why couldn't they sell the little stamps at the same location that required them?

"Spain is different," Alberto said, quoting from the current tourist slogan.

I passed the written exam on the first try. Alberto took me to dinner to celebrate. I could relax now and breeze through the actual driving test. I would be the first woman in the Benitez family and the first woman in our group of friends to drive.

A month later (I had to wait my turn), I went to the official testing site prepared to drive our little *Seat* around the prescribed course. When I dressed that morning I could no longer fasten the waistband of my skirt. I would need maternity clothes soon. I closed the skirt with a safety pin and went to meet the driving test man. What is the opposite of mutual attraction?

He wiggled his skinny bottom into the passenger side and took my paperwork. After checking that all the *estampillas* were in order, he shrugged his shoulders as though saying *This is going to be a waste of time, and women shouldn't be driving anyway.* The smell of cigarette smoke made my stomach lurch. In a patronizing tone he instructed me to drive straight ahead, stop at a yellow line and wait for him there. Then he slid out. He didn't say there would be *two* yellow lines painted on the pavement. I arrived at the first one, looked in the rearview mirror and noticed another car nearly touching my bumper. I passed the first yellow line to allow him more room and stopped just before crossing the second one. The passenger door flew open. The Test Man shouted in what I thought was a jubilant voice, *"Suspendida!"*

"Suspended? How did that happen?" Alberto said when I told him.

"I guess I can't follow directions. I failed the damn test because I crossed a line. It had nothing to do with driving. And now I have to wait another thirty days before I can try again."

A month later I arrived to retake the test wearing a black turtleneck sweater and a somber grey maternity jumper. I looked like a pregnant existentialist. The same smelly Test

Man took his place beside me. I knew now that I would stop at the first yellow line and made clear I understood the instruction. After stopping at the yellow line, I should wait for his signal to turn left.

"*Muy bien,*" Test Man said sounding less than convinced and eyeing my stomach.

I don't know why he couldn't stay in the car with me, but he popped out again. I advanced with caution to the first yellow line and stopped. I waited. I looked around. Test Man had disappeared. Maybe I should not have looked in the rearview mirror. My father taught me to drive in a 1949 Ford station wagon. He thought looking in the rearview mirror was a good idea.

"Check your rearview mirror often," he said.

So I did. I saw three cars behind me. They're waiting for me to move on, I thought. I'm holding things up. I did what any accommodating person would do; I turned left. I'd barely shifted to neutral again when Test Man pressed his face against the windshield.

"*Suspendida!*" He looked as though he'd just won the lottery. Nothing I said could change his mind. He had told me to wait and I had paid no attention.

"This is ridiculous," Alberto said. "I'll call someone in the license department and pull a few strings."

Madrid had reached over two million inhabitants, yet in many ways it remained a small town of tight connections. I didn't want that. I was embarrassed enough. I didn't want our friends to think the only way I could acquire a driver's license was through my husband's contacts. I returned to the scene of my transgression four weeks later.

I had to push the car seat back several notches in order to fit behind the steering wheel. I wondered if my nemesis would be there and, if so, would he have any compassion for a woman in my condition? I saw the answer when he smiled a yellow smile, and said something like, *Oh, it's you again.*

I threw my inflated self on whatever remnant of Spanish gallantry the Test Man possessed. After all, I had the honor of the Benitez family to uphold and a string of Spanish girlfriends to inspire. I needed that driver's license! This would have to be my final performance, I said, because in another month I would be too large for the driver's seat. With eyelash-fluttering false modesty and the best Castilian accent I could muster, I swore not to cross any line or negotiate any turn without his explicit permission.

"Well?" Alberto said when I picked him up from the office later.

"I did it. I'm legal."

# Chapter 11

Early in our marriage Alberto began what would become a custom, one that pleased me very much. Often, just before leaving the office he would phone me to ask if he could bring a coworker home for a drink before lunch. Since the lunch hour extended from two till five, we had plenty of time for a pre-meal *aperativo.* I never minded. Other times he called at the end of the workday with the same request. Could he bring someone—a colleague, a friend—home with him?

"Of course," I would say, then set out a bowl of olives and fill the ice bucket.

I sensed Alberto felt proud of his American wife and wanted to show off a bit. Fine with me. I enjoyed pouring a cocktail for his co-workers (none of them drank more than a weak gin and tonic), who seemed as eager to explain Spain's idiosyncrasies to me as I was eager to learn. Sometimes the engineer—they were all engineers—was planning a trip to the States and wanted to practice English. At other times he might be *de Rodriguez.*

"Can I bring Ramón for a drink after work?" Alberto said one spring day. "He's *de Rodriguez.*"

"Who?" I said. The only Ramón I knew didn't have *Rodriguez* as his last name.

That was how I learned that *Rodriguez* was as commonplace as *Smith* and typically used as an alias—the clichéd Mr. and Mrs. Smith on a hotel registry, for example. The expression *de Rodriguez* applied to any married man who was on his own for a few days—an American would have said *batching it.* In Ramón's case, Milali, his wife, had gone to the mountains for a few days with her sister. At times like these, his friends stepped in to make sure he didn't feel abandoned. According to ancient Spanish custom, man should not eat or drink alone.

I liked these affable men, and when I met their wives, I liked them, too. I found myself with a group of ready-made friends—several couples united by a desire to improve their bridge game and eat good food. We took turns hosting an evening of canapés and cards. Sometimes we picnicked in the country. I bought a grill. American-style barbecue equipment, the kind on legs with a hood and a cache of accessories, hadn't arrived in Spain, yet. What I bought looked like an oven rack.

We would drive to a spot in the country (I never saw any designated picnic areas), look for a hillside not already claimed by sheep and set up our kitchen. All we needed were twigs and bits of wood to make a fire, and four good-sized rocks to support the oven rack. Even though the cook had to work in a squat or on his knees, the oven rack served us well. The rest was easy.

We spread our assortment of olives and cheese on a plastic sheet on the ground and propped the wine bottles in the shade of an aromatic juniper bush. We sipped a red *vino de Valdepeñas* and nibbled bits of well-cured *Manchego* on baguette until our fire reached the proper intensity for my specialty, *chuletas de cordero.* Modesty aside, my baby lamb chops had reached celebrity status. After spending the previous night in a bath of olive oil, red wine, garlic and oregano—I mean the chops— they would hit the hot rack and sizzle as their herby smoke mixed with the scent of juniper. The results were toothsome morsels as addictive as popcorn. When only charred bits remained on the rack, when the bottles lay drained on their side, we went to the village for dessert. There was always a village.

My memory runs the *pueblos* together, at least the ones we visited on picnic days. And as sure as there was a village, there was a *plaza mayor,* the village square that centered community life. On one side stood a seventeenth or eighteenth century church that still tolled the Angelus, and facing it across the dusty square stood a tavern. Except for a bin near the door that held frozen ice cream bars, it looked the same as it had 300 years earlier, or so I imagined. We would crowd at a wooden bar eating ice cream, drinking chicory-laced coffee or sipping brandy. Above a shelf that held an assortment of liquors hung the inevitable framed photograph of Franco in military uniform. Round-faced and balding, he wore a smaller version of the mustache favored by Adolph Hitler. A crucifix hangs beside him.

A crucifix in a bar surprised me the first time I saw one, but I got used to it, just as I grew accustomed to Franco's face in church. In the vestibule, a plaque beside Franco's likeness declared that under the auspices of *Su Excelencia Generalísimo* Francisco Franco, the main altar had been restored. Or, thanks to the patronage of our Illustrious *Caudillo* the stained glass windows now glowed with their former splendor. Franco's foes during the Civil War had destroyed countless churches and convents. The great commander had set out to repair the damage and he made certain his stamp was on the improvements.

Once, on one of our village trips, Alberto stopped in front of a church squinting up at the bell tower.

"What are you looking at?" I said, pretty sure he wasn't experiencing a spiritual moment.

"Bullet holes," he said.

Twenty-seven years after the conflict ceased, the scars of war were still visible.

Had I lived in the early years of Franco's regime, I would have felt restrictions. I would have noticed absent friends. But at the moment, we lived a comfortable life. I felt secure. The economy was growing and, as Alberto would say of his countrymen, "*La raza mejora.*" The race is improving. I think of us as a bridge generation; a group of thirty and forty-year olds that spanned the years between a dying dictatorship and what would eventually become a modern monarchy.

All our friends were married, except for Blanca and Jorge, and even they walked down the aisle soon after we met. I should say soon after *I* met them; Alberto had known them for years. I remember the first time Alberto introduced me to Blanca.

"She owns half the province of Murcia," he had said.

Blanca looked at me and shook her head.

"That's a slight exaggeration."

Alberto had made the remark because Blanca was a countess. Three other friends had titles, too, but none of them ever spoke about them or acted differently from anyone else. It seemed to me they wanted to downplay their ancestry. They weren't snobs. They all held jobs, and I never felt out of place in their company. I don't know why Alberto liked to tease them.

Another time, Cristina and Fernando (Fernando held a title, too, Marquis of something or other) told us they planned to spend part of their vacation near the Bay of Biscay.

"Can you imagine, Diana?" Alberto said. "They have a summer palace in San Sebastián."

"Oh, but it's a very *small* palace," Fernando said. He, too, shook his head.

I didn't know the degree of truth in Alberto's remarks. I didn't care. The only reason I knew some of my new friends had titles was because Alberto had told me. And the only outward sign was the flash of an heirloom bracelet or ring when one of the women dealt cards on the green felt table cover.

Blanca and Jorge invited us to their wedding. They were married in *Los Jerónimos El Real,* the church where the aristocracy and high society had been celebrating their unions since the 1500s. I looked forward to the event.

"Will the women wear *mantillas?*" I asked my husband as he zipped the back of my grey knit dress the morning of the wedding.

The photos of society weddings in the magazines I read at the beauty shop showed women with five-inch tortoise combs in their hair over which they draped a shoulder length lace veil. I sometimes saw an older woman wearing a *mantilla*, minus the comb, at Sunday mass.

"Maybe the bride and groom's mother," Alberto said. "No one in my family, except possibly my aunts in Cordoba, has worn a *mantilla* for years."

I had wondered about *mantillas* and whether or not Blanca would wear a vintage gown, maybe the one her mother had worn. But it was the groom's attire that stole the show.

Jorge was a civil engineer. Civil engineers wore uniforms on formal occasions. Alberto was proud of his own, although so far in our married life he'd had no opportunity to wear it and it hung under plastic in the back of the closet. Alberto's uniform looked much like a navy-blue double-breasted suit with brass buttons. Jorge wore the deluxe model.

Jorge awaited his bride at the top of the aisle. Sunlight streamed through the stained glass windows, glinted on the trim of his uniform and cast him in a golden glow. The groom stood barely 5'5" tall. Every inch of him was full of charm and wit, but on his wedding day he was more uniform than anything else.

On his shoulders Jorge wore broad gold epaulets with fringe. They added width to his frame, which in Jorge's case was not a propitious direction. A taller man could have worn them well, but on Jorge the epaulets looked like gilded airplane wings. I imagined a strong updraft bearing him aloft to join the carved seraphim that circled the altar.

The uniform also included a gold sash, a five-inch wide swath that circled his waist twice and finished with a knot at the hip. The tails reached his knees and ended with another band of fringe.

I had a background in fashion. I found all this interesting—not only the garments themselves, but also who wore them and why. Before Alberto and Spain, the only civil engineer uniform I had seen consisted of a pocket protector. What would an American engineer think of all this gold and fringe? And I hadn't seen the half of it.

Jorge's hand fell to his hip. For a moment I thought he was adjusting the sash. Then I saw it.

"A sword?" I whispered to Alberto.

"It's part of the formal uniform." Alberto sounded irritated.

I didn't want to laugh, but I couldn't shake the images that kept coming to mind. Jorge looked fully prepared to breach the communion rail and lead a charge against the clergy. I worried about the sword, though, as it was nearly as long as the man who wore it. I feared any sudden movement on Jorge's part would entangle the dangling steel with the trailing sash and that Jorge would end up head over heels splayed beneath the pulpit. And then what would happen to the hat?

Of course, he had a hat. You can't have an outfit like that without a matching hat. I guessed that the sword had come from Toledo, a city famous for blades since the time of the Moors. But the hat was decidedly French. Spanish civil engineers were preserving the *bicorne*, a style left over from the unfortunate reign of Joseph Bonaparte a hundred and sixty years earlier when Napoleon attempted to impose his dynastic ambitions on the Iberian Peninsula. The profile resembled an elongated semi circle with a duckbill at each end. Outlined with gold cord, the hat looked heavy, but Jorge managed to balance it on the inside of his left arm as his bride approached. Then he set it aside for the ceremony. Blanca looked lovely and calm, but I was so struck by the groom's attire that I never could remember the gown she wore.

When we were planning our own wedding, Alberto had written to ask if he should wear his uniform. Even though, at that time, I had never seen one, I wrote back saying I thought a uniform from a foreign country might be misunderstood in my parents' small community. Later I could only imagine what my father—the ex WWII major—would have thought at the sight of his only daughter riding off into the sunset with a man in a gold trimmed suit, wearing a sword and a Napoleonic hat.

# Chapter 12

We knew nothing about babies. Alberto *was* the baby in his family, and I had never even been near a newborn except for my brother who arrived when I was four and, frankly, didn't interest me much. My father told me that mother had gone away for a couple of days to "get" the baby. For all I knew she had gone to the corner grocery.

At age thirty I was equally ill informed regarding pregnancy. None of my close American co-workers had been married. I had never had a pregnant girlfriend. The lack of direct exposure to the maternity world came as an advantage. Since I had no pre-conceived (pardon the expression) ideas, I felt no apprehension. Having a baby was just part of married life. I almost said part of the plan, but my husband and I didn't have a plan—exactly.

Before we were married, Alberto and I had talked about having children. The discussion lasted less than three minutes and, as was so often the case, took place after dinner while Alberto sipped a brandy.

"Do you want to have children?" Alberto said.

"Yes, of course."

"How many?"

"More than one. But not more than two."

"Our children would grow up totally bi-lingual," he said. "But I must insist on one thing and that is that they don't speak some horrible mishmash. They use either English or Spanish correctly but they don't mix the two."

I agreed.

"But I'll never be a typical *petit bourgeois* father."

"In what respect?" I said.

"What I mean," he said, "is that I'm not the kind of man to push a baby buggy in the park."

I agreed. If my children grew up moving confidently between the United States and Europe with the higher education that Alberto fostered and provided, I could at least push the carriage.

⁕

My sister-in-law, Julina, had introduced me to the obstetrician Dr. Varela. I felt at ease with him immediately. He had beautiful manners and managed to look distinguished in a white lab coat, and he was just enough older than I was to inspire confidence. Julina also encouraged me to enroll in a series of classes called *Preparación al Parto,* Preparation for Childbirth. The technique of Dr. Aguirre de Carcer was new in the 1960s and considered revolutionary. I wonder that Franco didn't restrict those classes, too, as he tried to control every system of contraception. The Francoist ideology worked hand in hand with the teachings of the Catholic Church.

In the penal code of 1941, two years after Franco's rise to power, articles 343 and 416 forbade the distribution of any medicine, substance, object, instrument, apparatus, means or procedure that would interfere with procreation. A prison sentence or fines were levied against persons found guilty. When the birth control pill arrived nearly 40 years later, the code included a fine of up to $15,000 for anyone who prescribed or sold it. For fear of reprisals some pharmacists refused to even stock it. With my understanding doctor, though, and a girlfriend who told me how, I found a way around the law. Forbidden as a means of birth control, the pill could be prescribed as a remedy for hormonal disorders or acne. Getting around the Church wasn't so easy.

I tried once to confess. The priest said he would offer absolution only after I had read a particular book. I never read the book. I never went back. But that's another story.

⁂

I went to the first *Parto* session alone. I looked around the lecture hall of the small modern clinic and noted the age of some of the women. Spanish women (all apparently good Catholics) frequently had children well into their forties, but some in this group looked well beyond forty. Dr. Aguirre approached the lectern. He, too, surveyed the scene.

"I must inform you, ladies," he said. "This class is for pregnant women only. When you come next week, please,

friend's example, give birth with freshly coiffed hair and painted nails.

"What should I do?" Alberto was half dressed and pacing a hole in the flooring. "Should I call my parents?

"No, not yet." *What on earth could they do?*

"What about Julina?"

"Don't call *any*body," I said. "Just put the suitcase (I had to provide my own baby clothes and diapers) in the car and wait for me here. I'll be back in an hour." And I walked the half block to *Salon Parra* as fast as I could.

The shampoo girl leaned over my shoulder.

"When is you baby due, *señora?"* she said.

"Around noon, I think, so let's skip the scalp massage today."

I don't normally like being the center of attention, but I found the general reaction in the salon rather enjoyable. As I left the shop a short time later, I overheard the shampoo girl say to the manicurist, *"Es Americana."* She's American.

⁂

Victoria, the midwife, was waiting at the hospital. Dr. Varela would arrive shortly. In the meantime, I inhaled and exhaled the long cleansing breaths I had learned in class and willed my body to relax. *I can do this. There's nothing to it. I'm in control.* Alberto fidgeted, excused himself often to smoke in the corridor and wondered aloud if he had time to go out for lunch. *Lunch? Why wasn't he counting?* According to the Aguirre method the husband was supposed to be timing contractions. At the moment my husband, the mathematical whiz, couldn't even count. *Never mind. I'll do it myself. Inhale. There's nothing to it. Exhale. There's nothing to it.* When the orderly wheeled my bed to the delivery room I waved to Alberto. I was still in control.

The lovely Victoria stroked my arm. The charming doctor, with whom I was falling in love, murmured something reassuring. Then the lights went out.

I heard voices in the dark. Someone was calling my name. *Diana*? Had Alberto come to the delivery room? Spanish fathers didn't enter the delivery room. *Señora?* I was shivering. Someone placed a blanket over me.

"What?" My voice sounded odd.

Gradually the lights came on again, but not the overhead ones of the delivery room. I was in my room. Alberto and the doctor stood at one side of the bed, the midwife was on the other.

"You have a daughter," Victoria said.

"Already?" I was trying to understand. "I had the baby?"

"You did," the midwife said, "and you are both fine."

"But…" I remembered nothing.

"The doctor saw that your little girl had the umbilical cord wrapped around her neck so to make the delivery safer and easier for both of you, we administered some anesthetic."

Alberto nodded. "That was the best thing to do."

So that was it. When Victoria had placed a mask over my face I thought it dispensed oxygen. I inhaled willingly and with that gasp all the preparations for a natural, drug free delivery vanished. I slept through the main event and had no memory of it. The Aguirre classes hadn't mentioned that possibility. I felt a tinge of disappointment.

Dr. Varela leaned forward and touched my face. He trailed his fingers softly across the bridge of my nose and under my eyes. *I am definitely in love with this man.*

"Does it hurt?" he said.

"No. Why?" What a strange question.

"You have some bruises on your face," he said. "I am very sorry for that. It's never happened before."

He turned to Alberto.

"Your wife fought the anesthetic." He looked at me again. "You don't remember trying to remove the mask? Did we hurt you?"

I shook my head. I didn't remember anything.

"Where is she?" I said. I hadn't noticed the tiny crib.

The midwife lifted the baby to my arms. And then a strange thing happened. A jolt of emotion unlike any I had ever known ran through me. With the clarity of lightning, a thought flashed in my mind. *I will claw the life from anyone who ever tries to harm this child.* I felt no remorse for this murderous notion, only surprise at the vehemence and unexpectedness of it. Then a second thing happened. Maybe it didn't actually happen, but I remember it just the same. My daughter opened her eyes. They glistened like black olives in a fair face tinged with pink. She looked directly at me. I know she focused, and she laughed as though we shared a secret.

A short time later a nurse came for Ana—we would name our daughter Ana Cristina, a name easy to say in both English and Spanish and, coincidentally, the name of Alberto's favorite aunt whom we had asked to be godmother. The nurse asked for the diapers I had been instructed to supply, and told me to get some rest. At *San Francisco de Assis* hospital newborns slept in a nursery. The mother saw her baby at mealtimes or when visitors came to inspect the recent arrival. During the intervals, the new mother could doze in a blessed silence that, in many cases, she would not know again for years. Ana and I thrived under this system. She came to the room periodically to nurse. We chatted for a while and when the conversation bored her, I called for the nurse and my baby returned to her companions in the nursery.

The Benítez family visited in shifts, my girlfriends brought flowers and Alberto came at lunchtime and after work in the evening. On the second night he phoned from the café in the lobby and asked if I wanted anything.

"A martini sounds good," I said. He appeared a few minutes later with a plastic cup and two olives on a pick. I had been joking but should have realized that if there were a way to bring gin to the maternity ward, Alberto would find it. I took a sip and gave the rest to my husband. I had already had a beer at lunch. Everyday at 2PM, an aide brought a tray with a three course meal plus a mini brown bottle of *Mahou.*

"It has good nutrition for new mothers," the nurse said.

I never cared for beer, but as long as the bar was open, a little red wine might be nice.

"Oh, no, *señora.* It must be the beer."

Perhaps the lunchtime libations had accounted for Milali's relaxed state when I visited her. I am sure they contributed to mine. I enjoyed my days at *San Francisco* and no one seemed in a hurry to see me leave.

I whiled away the hours cooing to my baby and trying to memorize *Baby and Child Care* by the famous American pediatrician, Dr. Spock, whose body of advice centered on trusting one's instincts and using common sense. I didn't have more than a smattering of either when it came to babies, and the one instinct I did have had involved homicide at the mere thought of any danger to my child. I spent five days like this—cooing, napping, reading, drinking beer and eating the bonbons Alberto's office sent.

The relaxed dress code was another feature I enjoyed at *San Francisco*. I was not forced to wear a hospital gown. Gown my foot! I knew about gowns, and an oversized bib did not constitute a gown. At *San Francisco* a woman could wear her own nighties. Surely Ana would have approved of mine. One was a pale blue nylon affair with a white lace bodice, another looked like a Greek toga with a floppy pink bow on the shoulder. All things considered, my reaction to the doctor's news when he told me I could go home might have been understandable.

"You may leave tomorrow morning," he said on day five. I looked at his smiling face and burst into tears.

"But all is well, *señora,*" he said casting the midwife a questioning glance. She appeared equally perplexed. A moment earlier we had been eating chocolates and now I was wiping tears with the bow of my nightgown. What had come over me? First, thoughts of murder and now hysterics, clearly I was not the woman I once was. I asked for one more day. I couldn't face leaving the comfort and security of *San Francisco de Assis* for the great unknown. My beloved doctor said yes. By the following afternoon I had collected myself. I left the hospital dry-eyed, but then I had to worry about Alberto, who had worked himself into a tizzy.

The thought of driving the car with a new baby in it had reduced him to a chain-smoking bundle of nerves. Our car didn't have seat belts, but then neither did anyone else's, and we didn't have a car seat for the baby. I held Ana in my arms as we crossed Madrid at a snail's pace. Alberto sat rigid with a vice-like grip on the steering wheel that he didn't relax until he parked in front of our apartment. His new-father nerves returned a few days later, a Saturday.

"Maybe we could go to *El Meson* for lunch," Alberto said.

We hadn't taken the baby out, yet, and I found the idea of lunch in the country very appealing. I had a baby-carrier by then.

"Perfect," I said.

We got as far as the *Plaza de Castilla* five blocks away when Alberto, instead of taking the second exit, circled the plaza and headed home.

"I just can't do it," he said.

The sleeping infant had sapped all Alberto's confidence. He thought the slightest bump in the road spelled disaster and he drove at a dangerously slow speed. I didn't volunteer to take his place because I didn't think I would be much better.

The following day, Sunday, we made it to the family lunch, though it took us a very long time.

*

When I saw Dr. Varela for a final post-baby visit, I asked for his bill. He said he didn't have one. I thought at first he meant that he would mail it. "*Ah, no,*" he said. He believed his family had never adequately thanked my brother-in-law for saving their art collection during the Civil War. He hoped delivering our baby would show his gratitude.

"That war ended thirty years ago," I said to Alberto. "Can you imagine? And if he felt he owed anyone anything it would be to Luis, not to me."

Alberto nodded. "We'll have to find a way to thank him, something more than a note with flowers."

In the end it was Luis who told me that Dr. Varela collected a particular style of antique porcelain. I hunted the shops until I found an early nineteenth century *Sargadelos* platter. But as we said in the note, it couldn't begin to express our thanks. Then, just when I thought having a baby couldn't get any better, it did.

Alberto's insurance plan from the Ministry covered maternity costs. Nonetheless, I had to take the hospital bills to the insurance company myself. The wrinkled man in a wrinkled suit behind the window adjusted his glasses, looked at the documents carefully and found them in order. Then he looked again and asked if I had actually spent six days in the hospital. I had. He reached for his pocket calculator, tapped in some numbers, opened a drawer and slid 3,000 pesetas in my direction.

Why? "*No comprendo,*" I said.

The wrinkled man leaned closer to the glass and told me

that the length of my stay at *San Francisco* indicated some slight complication, some little difficulty, and I was entitled to compensation.

"What a country this is," I said to my husband that evening. "I had a baby and made $50.00 in the process."

Alberto shrugged. "We live in a paternalistic society."

Feeding the baby proved more problematic than anything else. I hadn't been very successful at nursing, so now the baby drank from a bottle. Feeding Ana meant preparing a German formula that our pediatrician, a man of inflexible persuasions, had recommended. I began by sterilizing four glass bottles and rubber nipples in the pot I normally used for spaghetti. In those days, I boiled and sterilized anything that came near my baby's face. I measured the powdered formula and stirred it into boiling water, but no matter how energetically I whisked, the concoction always turned lumpy. I had to pour it through a sieve also previously boiled to within an inch of its life. Alberto tried to help. In our cramped kitchen, in the ghastly light of a fluorescent tube that ran across the ceiling, we extracted boiled bottles from the steaming pot with disinfected tongs, trying not to scald ourselves in the process. If by accident the tongs or the sieve touched the counter top, we boiled them again. We boiled the funnel too which, of course, we needed to pour the formula into the bottles but we had to pinch the tip because it was too wide for the neck of the bottle. The boiling, the stirring, the re-boiling, the pinching, the pouring, the process was endless. We no sooner finished with one batch than it was time to start another. I had resigned myself to a few sleepless nights with a crying baby, but Ana rarely cried and she slept on schedule. It was her diet that was doing me in.

The pediatrician scowled when I asked if I could make a batch of formula large enough for two or three days. We had a refrigerator, which not everyone had, and with half a dozen bottles of formula there would be little room for anything else. The doctor continued to frown. That was the problem with foreign women, he said—always looking to do things the easy way. And why did I think God put breasts on women in the first place? It wasn't a question; it was an accusation. And no, I could not make the formula in larger amounts.

In addition to the labor-intensive food plan, the pediatrician provided a booklet in which to chart Ana's weight. That made sense—to a degree—but he insisted I weigh the baby after every meal. Each visit to the pediatrician left me further demoralized. I phoned Milali.

"*Totalmente absurdo!*" she said when I described the German formula and the after-meal weigh-ins. Immediately she gave me the name of a Spanish formula that mixed easily with bottled water, told me to take the scale back to the pharmacy where I had rented it, and, above all, change doctors. I did. We all thrived. And then Aurora came to us. But before Aurora there had been Petra.

# Chapter 13

Everyone I knew had a *muchacha,* a live-in maid; Alberto's parents had two. In our apartment, we barely had room for the baby much less an additional adult, so I hired an *asistenta,* a woman who came for a few hours three times a week to clean and do laundry. Of course, I could have done it all myself, but I was expected not to. Domestic help was a thread in the fabric of Spanish life and, from what I saw, was likely to remain so. I lived in a class society. It wasn't that Alberto and I were wealthy (US standards would have called us middle class), but in a country where a middle class was just emerging, we were vastly different from a population to whom education had been denied or restricted, opportunities virtually non-existent, and where the conditions of one's birth set the future in stone.

Thousands of village girls came to the city looking for work and an escape from life in a thatched roof house with no plumbing and a future raising pigs and threshing wheat. Some villages still used a public fountain for their water supply. Rural education covered only the bare basics. Spain still had large impoverished provinces. Badajoz and Zamora, for example, lands that once provided conquistadores to the New World, now sent their girls to the city as maids. Or, as I saw on a road trip with Alberto to Galicia, the women stayed home and struggled in the fields behind a plow and a team of oxen.

"Where are the men?" I asked Alberto.

After a pause, he said, "Gone. The ones who haven't migrated to South America are fishing off the coast."

⁂

The girls who came to the city arrived with no skills and often, as in the case of my *asistenta,* could barely read or write. Petra was her name, the feminine of Peter, the rock. Rough and reliable, the middle-aged married woman lived up to her name, and whatever she lacked in education and refinement, she compensated for with good humor and practicality.

Petra, I learned, was determined to put a shine on everything. The first morning she came to work for us she cast an appraising eye around the apartment and suggested a particular cream to remove a stain from the marble-topped table in the hall. Squinting at the patina on an antique copper pitcher, she seemed about to offer a remedy for that, too, and looked skeptical when I said it was part of the pitcher's charm. She told me which soaps to buy and advised me not to waste money on aluminum scouring pads. She preferred the traditional ones made from plant fibers. In addition to household advice, Petra provided me an education in linguistics and folklore. I only learned about Petra's limited reading ability the day I gave her a shopping list.

"Oh, just tell me what you want, *señorita,*" she had said. "I don't read well but I have a good memory."

I was still pregnant when Petra first came and she fussed over me as the baby's birth neared.

"Maybe you should stay home today," she said one morning. "The streets are icy. You don't want to fall."

It didn't often snow in Madrid, but a winter rain could freeze on the sidewalks. I had good boots and went out anyway. Petra was still clucking when I returned. When Ana was born she clucked over her, too, but in a way I couldn't always appreciate. Between her accent (heaven knows what she thought of mine) and her confounding vocabulary, I often needed Alberto to translate. Petra came three mornings a week. Invariably, by the time my husband came home for lunch, I had a question.

"Why would Petra say that?" I said to Alberto who had just finished a plate of fat white asparagus with Petra's garlic-laced mayonnaise.

I had seen her earlier leaning over Ana's basket. "*Bruja, bruja, bruja,*" she mumbled.

"Doesn't *bruja* mean witch?" I said.

"Theoretically," Alberto said. "But a witch doesn't have to be bad, if that's what you're thinking. You might also say *enchantress* or *sorceress.*"

I was glad I'd held my tongue that morning. Once before I had nearly fired her for a similar misunderstanding.

"She told me to shut-up!" I said to Alberto. He just smiled and put a sugar cube in his coffee. By now he was used to my lunchtime Petra stories. "I know she isn't refined," I said. "That's not her fault. But I'm not going to tolerate her speaking to me like that! All I did was ask if her cold was better."

"What exactly did she say?" Alberto was still smiling.

"She said, '*cállese!*' I know that means *shut-up*. Right?"

"Theoretically." (If he said *theoretically* one more time, I was going to scream!) "But in common usage it means something like *oh, don't mention that* or *let's not talk about it*. It doesn't carry a rude connotation."

So Petra continued to cluck and confuse until the time came for us to move to our new flat. She understood that we now had room for a full-time *muchacha*. I hoped to find a woman as kind and thorough and reliable as Petra had been, and someone with the same maternal instincts she had shown to me when I was pregnant and later to Baby Ana. She seemed a natural-born mother. I wasn't like that. While I wanted children, I hadn't felt driven by a deep maternal urge until I actually held my own child. I remembered the fierce primal emotion that ran through me the first time I looked in my baby's eyes. Now, I wanted that kind of mature woman to be part of our household.

It turns out, I found someone very different.

Modesta, the *muchacha* who worked for Alberto's parents, arranged for a girl to come to our apartment on her afternoon off for an interview. Modesta didn't actually know the girl. She had a friend who had a friend who had a brother who had a sister who was looking to change employers. That's how the system worked.

Alberto had returned to the office. I was alone and a little nervous. I had interviewed salespeople in my previous life. But the requisites for selling clothes in the U.S. and those for housekeeping in Spain were very different. The well-intentioned warnings from my girlfriend, Paloma, ran through my head. Did the *muchacha* come from a *pueblo* whose accent defied dialogue? Would she play the radio soap operas so loudly while she ironed that you couldn't hear yourself think, and did she take the transistor from room to room while she moped and mopped in time to love songs by Julio Iglesias? Could you read her handwriting on a message? Could she even read? Would you always have to straighten the pictures after she dusted? Would she burn holes in your favorite tablecloths or put bleach in a load of laundry that contained a red towel? Worse yet in Paloma's eyes, were the girls who, uninvited, drank your Coca Cola. I didn't doubt Paloma's experiences, but the questions uppermost in my mind, as I waited that Thursday afternoon were: Why did she want to leave her present employers, and did she like babies?

*"Buenas Tardes, soy Aurora,"* I am Aurora, she said when I opened the door a few minutes after five. I had known Petra, the rock, and now I was meeting Aurora, the dawn.

Aurora/Dawn made me think of a small-town librarian and my third-grade teacher, Sister Maryann. She had very short dark hair and wore no makeup. Her white blouse with a lace-edged collar was tucked neatly into a straight navy skirt. She wore sensible black pumps and carried a black leather purse with a handle. I asked her to sit, but her back never touched the chair and she didn't cross her legs. Aurora answered my questions in a straightforward manner, and I needn't have worried about her accent. She sounded like most *Madrileños*, except for the way she rolled the *ll*, which was a pleasant sound and might have been typical of *Sigüenza* where she grew up. I'm sure she had never seen an American before.

I couldn't blame Aurora for wanting to change employers. She worked in a house of five unruly children where the *señora* delegated everything—childcare, cooking, and cleaning—to this young girl. *Señora* also had breakfast in bed. Aurora told me these things in a matter-of-fact voice. She didn't complain; she stated the facts. She was just as forthright when she said she didn't know much about babies. There we had something in common.

Aurora was the youngest in her family, she told me. She had two older brothers. The only babies she knew about were the chicks and piglets she had raised on her parents' farm. That was more experience than I had. All I had was a copy of Dr. Spock's *Baby and Child Care*. I took her to the bedroom where Ana lay napping in the blue wicker basket. Aurora leaned over the baby and touched her cheek. *"Ahh,"* she said, and Ana smiled in her sleep. I took it as a sign.

We agreed on a salary of 3,000 pesetas a month—the equivalent of $50.00 at the time, and slightly more than the going rate. I would supply Aurora's uniforms—pastel stripes for the morning and black with white collars and cuffs for evening. We made plans to visit the new flat together. I was eager to show Aurora her bedroom and bath. I knew what a typical maid's room looked like. In Maria's house and in my in-law's house, the rooms were airless, dark, cheerless quarters in the rear of the flat. Our new building was unusual because the kitchen faced the street. Both the kitchen and the maid's room next to it were filled with light. In the older buildings the service areas faced a dingy interior well full of stale kitchen smells. I was as excited to decorate our kitchen and Aurora's room, as I was to hang pictures above the baby's bed. I thought Aurora would be happy with us. And I certainly didn't expect breakfast in bed.

*

"You did what?" Alberto said when he came home that evening. "You hired a seventeen-year-old to take care of your baby!"

"I just like her," I said. "She seems serious."

"You're entrusting your new home to a teen-ager?" He opened the bar and reached for the gin.

"Listen, Alberto, she's been taking care of a house with five children plus their spoiled parents. I think she can manage things for us."

I had no doubts about Aurora. In spite of all our differences, I felt we had already connected somehow. But my husband … Why did he say *your* baby, and *your* house? Should it not be *our?* I had noticed Alberto's choice of pronoun at other times, too. *Your* in-laws he said rather than *my* parents. While I felt part of a family circle, my husband seemed to stand half removed at the edge. I didn't ask why. I couldn't. And I didn't try to draw him in. I couldn't do that either. I didn't even want to.

# Chapter 14

I stepped back and admired the built-in bookcase for the millionth time—waist high cabinets topped with marble slabs—shelves to the ceiling. Our *estantería* covered the entire wall from one side of the living room to the other. When I touched a button beside the door, the bookcase glowed in soft indirect lighting. My husband and I had nearly come to blows over its design. In the end we had compromised. Alberto chose the spot for a custom-made bar—glass shelves behind a locked door, and I chose the colors—beige marble cabinet tops and cream woodwork. Now, looking at the wall, I felt a surge of satisfaction. It was perfect.

We had finally moved to our brand new flat with our six-month old baby and an equally brand new *muchacha.* In our eagerness to leave the crowded apartment, we took up residence with barely more than the bookcase and beds. The rest of our furnishings, a sofa and chairs, sat in an upholsterer's shop on the other side of town while in our basement storage room a vintage table and chairs waited for me to rejuvenate them with steel wool and furniture polish. We hadn't bought the furniture, but had salvaged it from a cellar under the Ministry of Public Works.

The Ministry was being modernized in more ways than one. Technology was coming from the U.S. (Alberto's experience was part of it), and the physical appearance of the Ministry was changing as well. The soft sofas, the ample armchairs, and the wooden tables that once equipped the Ministry offices were being replaced with black leather furniture and chrome fixtures.

"And we have cubicles now, just like in the States," Alberto said with a grin. The transformation thrilled him. I groaned.

Among other responsibilities, Alberto now dealt with finding room for an IBM tabulating machine in the office's new configuration, and he needed somewhere to house what had become outdated paraphernalia. That was why he had the keys to the Ministry's underground storerooms.

"We can have a look tomorrow," Alberto said, handing a beer to Ramón, who had come home with him after work. He seemed to include me in the "we," and I looked to Ramón for confirmation.

"The *jefe* told us to make room anyway we could and if we saw anything in storage that we could use for ourselves we could take it. Milali has to work but the three of us could go. We might find—I don't know—something. Do you want to come?"

*Nobody kept an inventory of ministerial property? Was this even legal?*

"Sure," I said.

We met the following day in the Ministry cafeteria shortly after 2:00 p.m., the beginning of the lunch hour. We ate wedges of *tortilla* and slivers of ham at a long wooden bar in a space with all the warmth of a train station. The building, with its row of arcades along the *Avenida de la Castellana*, was called *Los Nuevos Ministerios*, the New Ministries. The plans for the building had been approved under the Republic sometime in the 1930s, before Franco came to power, but the governmental complex was still called *New* more than thirty years later. In a country that counted its history by centuries, a thirty-year period must have seemed insignificant.

We finished what Spaniards called an *aperativo* (I could have called it lunch) and made our way to the cellar. The stone staircase that led to the upper floors was wide enough for a parade marching six abreast. But we didn't take the steps; we went behind them to an elevator. Alberto jiggled the keys and said something I couldn't hear to a uniformed janitor who pushed the down button and looked at me as though he knew I didn't belong there. A few moments later, the three of us stood in the tentative glow of a bare ceiling bulb in the musty subterranean storage space. Rows of cracked leather sofas, wooden benches, desk lamps with frayed cords, and elaborate brass floor fans stretched out before us. A veil of grey dust blurred their edges. The air smelled of mold and what I later learned was the horsehair used to stuff the upholstered pieces.

"*Dios mio!*" Alberto said. "This stuff hasn't seen the light of day since the abdication of Alfonso XIII in 1931."

Ramón was already sniffing out possibilities. It didn't take him long. He stopped beside a red velvet loveseat. (Red loveseats in the Ministry offices?)

"My wife would love this," he said. "It just needs a little cleaning." He brushed his hand along the seat and sent up a cloud of grey powder. "It's really in good condition."

Alberto waved the air with his handkerchief.

I, too, thought Milali would like the vintage piece, but I'd visited their flat and couldn't imagine where she would find room for it. I didn't say anything and moved toward a camel-backed sofa that had caught my eye.

In spite of its dark threadbare covering, the sofa had an elegant shape and I envisioned it newly covered and sitting against our living room wall. Alberto looked skeptical but pulled out his tape measure.

"Yes, it would fit," he said. "I just can't picture it."

"But you like the way the bookcase turned out, don't you? Remember when you wanted everything grey and black like in your office?"

He nodded.

"Then trust me on this. I promise not to recover it unless you first approve of the fabric. I'll bring you swatches from the fabric store if you don't have time to shop with me. OK?"

Alberto nodded again and turned to Ramón.

"The things we do for our wives," he said.

Ramón looked at me and winked.

Then I saw a pair of comfortable-looking armchairs. They needed work, too, and my creative juices bubbled with possibilities. I found a long, very Spanish-looking table with turned legs and a wrought iron support, and a wooden bench with a carved back that would serve as seating along one side. The table may once have stood in a reception hall. I now imagined it in our dining area.

Alberto followed me with his tape measure and didn't object again until we came to the straight chairs.

"*¡Por Dios, Diana!* We can't take those chairs."

"Why not?" They had tooled leather seats and backs held in place by sturdy brass studs, perfect with the table.

"Don't you see the insignia?"

I looked more closely at the tooled design: two overlapping wheels and a large *F*. I shrugged.

"*Ferrocarril*," Alberto said. "Railroads."

I knew the word for railroads. I just didn't recognize their embossed escutcheon.

I looked at the chairs again—solid, straight. The dark wood matched the table.

"Look," I said, "If anyone ever asks—which I seriously doubt—we'll just say you inherited the chairs from your great grandfather. The *F* stands for Fernando Fernandez."

"And he invented the wheel?" Ramón said.

I could always count on Ramón, though we had nearly missed his friendship.

Several months earlier, Alberto had voiced a concern. He often talked about office projects with me. I liked that but I was surprised when he came to the kitchen where I was experimenting with a meat loaf, leaned against the sink and said, "I don't know what to do about one of the men at the office."

"In what sense?"

"I like him and he's very good at what he does."

"That doesn't sound like a problem."

"I think we could be friends but…"

"But what?"

"He isn't an engineer. I don't know what you'd call it in the States. He has a two-year technical degree."

Alberto's degree, *Ingeniero de Caminos, Canales y Puertos*, had required six years of intense studies. I appreciated that he was proud of it, but I didn't like what he was doing now.

"I don't understand," I said. "You like and respect this man, and you think he would be a good friend?

"Yes, but … well, I don't know if he would fit in. You know what I mean."

Unfortunately, I did. All of our male friends had the same degree. It ranked as one of the highest in the country and guaranteed not only a comfortable income but also a certain social prestige. As far as friends were concerned, we were all in the same boat, so to speak. What bothered me was the way Alberto seemed to be weighing whether or not he could invite a person without that degree on board.

"What would you do?" he said.

"I never had to think about it," I said. "I don't think I could *plan* my friends."

I had never known anyone so premeditated as my husband. I didn't want to look at him. Alberto changed the subject.

"Let me mix the meatloaf," he said.

A few days later he invited Ramón home for a drink. By the time we went foraging in the Ministry's cellars, we were close friends.

⁂

I would happily have spent more time among the relics, but I sensed urgency in our mission, which, while not illegal, was clearly unusual. To have it known that Alberto Benítez, *Ingeniero de Caminos, Canales y Puertos* and a frequent contributor to the *Public Works Review*, had scavenged his home furnishings from the underground storeroom of the Ministry of Public Works accompanied by his cobweb-trailing colleague and his dust-covered American wife would have been, well, awkward. And now we had to figure out how to take possession.

Fortunately, Ramón knew a man with a truck. To be more precise, Ramón had a cousin who knew a man with a truck. A truck! Lucky for us. I had seen what looked like complete bedroom suites delivered on a motorcycle—bed frames sticking out of the sidecar, or giant armoires hauled in a two-wheeled cart by a kid on a bicycle. Unlike the shifting Americans, Spaniards tended to stay in one place. Based on my observation, this tendency may have had less to do with love of place and more to do with a lack of moving vans.

Milali gave me the name of an upholsterer. Alberto and I settled amicably on the fabrics, and I spent hours in our storage room bringing a tired table and some weary chairs to life. Our baby, healthy and easy-to-care-for, laughed often. Aurora and I settled into a comfortable routine. I was making a home, and those were the happiest days of my married life.

# Chapter 15

We had moved to a neighborhood north of *Bernabeu* Stadium where the *Real Madrid* kicked its way through soccer season on Sundays from September to June. There, at the end of the bus line, a group of private homes from the early twentieth century—the kind the Spaniards called *chalets*—stood sedately behind stucco walls as noisy newcomers moved in. This northern-most edge of Madrid had begun life as a genteel summer colony. The remaining undeveloped acres and the unpaved streets gave the false impression of being in the country. The *Puerta del Sol*, the very heart of Madrid, throbbed with commotion less than ten miles away while in our new neighborhood, some ancient Spanish law protected the grazing routes for sheep and twice a day they passed the front door of our building.

They were a dusty lot, the shepherd, the sheep and the nondescript canine that trailed them. I hurried to the balcony whenever I heard their approach. The sheep bleated. The bell some wore round the neck clanged like a rock in a tin can—maybe it was. The noisy bunch acted like they owned the neighborhood which, in a way, they did. They had been traveling the road long before we arrived. If the sheep stopped to nibble the flowers by our gate, the shepherd whistled a command and the dog nipped the flock forward again. Periodically a sheep would raise her head and look around as though she had temporarily forgotten where she was. A moment later she lowered it and resumed her travels. I loved watching them, but eventually the sheep disappeared. I don't know if the shepherd found another line of work, or if the sheep found an alternative route to pastures. Sometimes I imagine the whole gang taking the metro. The shepherd holds one of the special thirty-day tickets that allows unlimited subway trips. The sheep line up to pass through the turnstile and the little dog brings up the rear. Even as I watched it, our landscape was changing and we were part of the change.

I was excited about life in one of the new buildings. At the same time, I felt sorry for my neighbors as bossy building cranes muscled through the narrow streets that were better suited for horse and buggy travel. I imagined the aging homes shuddered. They looked vulnerable as a trio of six-story condos shouldered their way onto the scene, part of a 1960's building boom.

The old buildings had the look of things made by hand, wooden shutters and carved doors, iron hinges and painted tiles. Often the date the house was built was worked into a wrought iron grill above the door. A statue of the owner's patron saint sometimes stood in a niche beside the gate. Frequently the house had a name. A hand-painted tile set into the stucco wall or attached to the gate might identify it as *Villa Teresita* or *Los Almendros,* and we knew at once that Little Theresa had lived there, or that almond trees grew in the garden. For reasons known only to the builders, the new condos were named for two groups of indigenous Venezuelans, *Tiuna* and *Arichuna.* A third condo, ours, had no name. We were a number. In September 1967, as we settled into our new home, the expansion of Madrid encroached around us. I would have stopped it if I could.

⁂

I stood with Alberto on our balcony in the warmth of a lazy October sun. Aurora had cleared the lunch dishes and Ana lay deep in siesta land.

"Is this what you wanted?" Alberto waved a cigarette toward the bench.

"Yes," I said. "Exactly."

The bench had been my idea, but Alberto had made it in our basement storage room. The storage room now housed his long-dreamed-of workshop. To date, he had created a glass topped kitchen table, a rack to hold placemats, a shelf for the entrance hall and a brassbound coffee table. All I needed to do was admire a piece of furniture in a shop window and my husband sprang into action. "I can make that," he would say. It helped that his father still had a small industrial warehouse where Alberto could use a welding torch. Alberto had turned into a torch wielding do-it-yourself *aficionado* and a capable craftsman.

We looked over the railing as the sound of hoof-falls and bells grew louder. This time the hooves belonged to a donkey drawing a wagon, and the bells, instead of rock-in-a-can cacophony, gave out a bouncy jingle rather like sleigh bells. A man wearing baggy pants and a smock ambled beside the wagon until halting in front of our building where he scanned the rows of balconies, threw back his head and shouted *Chatarrero!* Junkman! He waited a few minutes, but no one had anything to dispose of that afternoon, and he nudged his animal on again.

"Look, Diana," Alberto said. "It's 1967 and the donkey carts finally have rubber tires.

Until recently, the carts ran on iron-bound wheels.

"They eat up the edges of the road," Alberto had complained. An engineer noticed things like that. But something else had caught my eye. Attached to the rear of the junkman's cart with a length of cord, a little bent and out of date, was a license plate that read *Diplomatic Corps.*

*"La raza mejora,"* my husband said, still fixed on the tires and using one of his favorite expressions. The race is improving.

"Oh for Pete's sake," I grumbled. "The next thing you know we'll have paved streets!"

# Chapter 16

July 1969. I didn't know if was the heat, the seemingly endless drive, or *Tia* Anita's non-stop chatter that made me feel unwell. My head throbbed, and instead of appreciating *Tia* Anita's generous invitation to a few days at the beach, I resented it. Aunt Ana, everyone called her *Tia* Anita, was my father-in-law's sister, my husband's favorite aunt, and our little Ana's godmother.

Anita, a retired teacher, glowed when we asked her and her husband Juan, a medical researcher, to act as our daughter's godparents. They had no children of their own. We didn't have the heart to contradict Anita's assumption that we had named our daughter in her honor. That had been a matter of practical semantics—*Ana* sounded the same in English as it did in Spanish. The American grandparents wouldn't find the pronunciation difficult. Alberto said he liked names that began with *A*. I liked *Ana* because it seemed old and universal. So, for various reasons, everyone approved.

Anita phoned early in July to invite little Ana, Aurora and me to Alicante where she had two vacation apartments. One she kept for herself; the other she rented out. Alicante had served as a vibrant trading port for the Greeks and Romans in 1000 BC. By 1969, owing to an ideal climate and vast kilometers of fine sand the *Costa Blanca,* the White Coast, was fast becoming a version of Miami Beach. Foreign tourists had discovered *Sunny Spain,* and high-rise hotels were gradually replacing the humble fishermen's homes. Normally, Juan went with her, but this time her husband had business that kept him in Madrid. The only thing Anita asked in return for her hospitality was transportation. Would I drive?

Anita belonged to a generation of women who didn't drive. In all her sixty-plus years I doubt the thought of getting behind the wheel of a car ever entered her head. And she certainly would not have taken the train to Alicante alone. Anita was not spoiled or fearful. She simply reflected the cultural and generational attitudes of her day. She didn't drive and she didn't travel alone. I, on the other hand, enjoyed a certain status in the Benítez family because I did both. Neither Ana nor Aurora had ever seen the ocean, so I looked forward to their reactions when I took them to the beach for the first time.

⁂

Ana, two years and three months old, giggled with excitement as she climbed into the car the morning we began our trip. Aurora followed with her suitcase, the toddler's bag and a picnic basket. I stowed my own case in the front trunk under what, in my previous life, had always been called the hood and which housed the motor. In our *Seat 600,* a two-door, four-speed, stick shift with a top speed of 59 MPH, the motor was in the rear. I hoped *Tia* Anita would travel light but when we picked her up at her apartment a few minutes later, she looked prepared for a much longer expedition. In addition to a suitcase, she had several bulging shopping bags and a gallon-sized jug of olive oil.

A branch of the Benítez family produced olive oil in Córdoba. As a result, Anita was always well supplied and was so convinced of the product's superiority that she took her own olive oil wherever she went. Even when she accompanied Juan to an international medical conference, she had no compunction about pulling a flask from her purse to dress her salad. They might be in a café in Paris or a hotel in Prague; it didn't matter to her. The day of our trip, she sat with the jug braced between her feet and I hoped she had a firm grip as I pointed the car toward the *N-IV.*

The roads on the Iberian Peninsula followed the ancient paths marked centuries earlier by the feet of donkeys and pilgrims and Romans and were still marked with Roman numerals. The national highways were two shoulder-less lanes peppered with potholes, and, I found it fascinating that when the road met a river, we traveled over intact Romans bridges. In theory the shade from trees planted at the edge of the road kept the asphalt from melting completely, but the sun softened the blacktop and it took on the contours of the land like a carpet, bumps and all.

Aurora murmured stories to Ana in the back seat, her soft voice barely audible above the whirr of the motor, which sounded like an electric cake mixer. When Ana tired of the stories, they played rounds of *Veo, Veo,* a version of *I Spy.*

*Tia* Anita perched like a parrot on my right shoulder—at least it seemed so in that cramped space—chattering non-stop in a high-pitched voice that was clearly *Andaluz*. In spite of her many years in Madrid, Anita, like her brother Manuel, never lost the southern accent. It seemed as if every time Ana fell asleep and Aurora's eyes began to close, *Tia* Anita would turn in her seat and screech "*Como van las niñas?*" How are the girls doing? Their eyes would snap open, any chance for a nap shattered.

For the first few miles, *Tia* Anita fussed about her husband, irritated that Juan had not taken her to Alicante himself. I didn't find it odd that he had a business meeting of some kind. It wasn't until twenty-five years later that we discovered the real nature of his *business.* The respected doctor had been living a double life with his mistress and their daughter. By the time the shocking news came to light, the daughter had graduated from medical school. If Anita knew, she kept the secret.

⁂

I drove most of the day—over four hundred kilometers—stopping only long enough for a lunch of *tortilla* and ham sandwiches under the trees, or for a bathroom break.

Decent rest stops were rare but Ana, unabashedly, thought peeing behind a bush was fun. We washed our hands with bottled water, splashed a few drops on our temples, then squished back in the car. I couldn't tell which was better, being roasted with the windows closed or seared with them open. With a constant shifting of gears, I restrained our little vehicle as we descended the long hill toward the *Rio Tajo,* then urged the reluctant *Seat* up again to the brown plateaus. Alberto liked to name things—he called the office computer *Carlota* and named his rifle *Matilda,* but to date our car had not been christened so I decided to call it *Rocinante* in honor of *Don Quijote's* sway-backed nag and to commemorate our crossing the area of Spain called *La Mancha.*

Cervantes wrote *Don Quijote* in 1605. I doubt the landscape had changed since then: stretches of nearly treeless plains, crossed by flocks of sheep tended by shepherds on foot, and fields planted in grapes and wheat. Occasionally on a rise, the windmills *Don Quijote* mistook for giants came into view: white cylinders with black roofs, their canvas arms twisting slowly in the wind. In the village of *Mota del Cuervo* a few windmills stood close to the road and the entire village smelled like *queso manchego*—sheep's cheese, a favorite of mine.

Unlike the American superhighways my husband admired, which sidestepped towns and cities, Spanish roads passed directly through the middle of the *pueblos.* Traffic laid its noise and pollution on the very doorsteps of the villagers. Rural women dressed in traditional black sat on rickety wooden chairs, knitting by their front doors a mere few meters from a string of moving cars. And it seemed to me that when they had a chance to escape it, they didn't.

Alberto often took us to the country on a Sunday. There, entire families sauntered at the edge of the road with apparently no thought of danger: young mothers in espadrilles with babies in their arms; fathers in work pants but wearing a glistening white Sunday shirt, sleeves rolled to the elbows; kerchief-covered *abuelas;* weathered old men in black berets, hunched over their walking sticks; teen-aged boys, cocky in their first pair of jeans (jeans being a recent import). I never understood why they chose to walk in a haze of car fumes beside the buzz of traffic when just next to them lay the wheat-smelling fields and the sounds of birds. But maybe the fields belonged to the workweek.

We lumbered on under the blaze of July sky from village to village, each with its own unique product: *Arranjuez*—strawberries and asparagus. *Valdepeñas*—wine. *Albacete*—knives. *Roda*—*Juanitos* (little Johnnies), a kind of candy. *Novelda*—grapes. The landscape changed as we left behind the flat plains and straight roads of *La Mancha.* Once we crossed the province of *Albacete*, the terrain became irregular, and instead of grain fields and swaths of sunflowers, we saw the jagged sierra in the distance dotted with castles and increasing stands of Roman pines. These lands once separated the Moors from the Christians, and later divided the kingdoms of Castille and Aragon.

As we neared *Alicante,* the vineyards increased and now included not only grapes for wine but also grapes trained on poles and wires intended as table grapes. We saw the first palm trees and the vast olive orchards and almonds farms. The road curved into hills. The sun was lower in the sky, the air cooler. At last, on a hill called *Monte Benacantil*, the castle of *Santa Barbara* came into view and behind the hill, the blue line of the sea.

"Look! There's the water," I said as we descended to the coast. I was looking toward the horizon and the endless field of blue. Silence from the back seat. After a moment Ana spoke.

"Who's having a birthday?" she said.

*"Cumpleaños?"* I repeated to make sure I understood. Sometimes my daughter spoke English, other times Spanish.

"*Sí, sí,*" she said. "Look at all the candles!"

In addition to the beach and the climate, *Alicante* was famous for the *explanade*, a stretch of public walk along the waterfront, bordered by towering date palm trees. The day Ana saw them, the clusters of fruit were wrapped in a white gauze-like fabric that prevented a rain of dates on the strolling pedestrians. From our vantage point, with a little imagination, they resembled colossal birthday candles.

I loved Ana's observations. A week earlier she had told me she now understood the difference between a spoon and a fork.

"What is it?" I said.

"Forks have fingers."

⁂

We found Anita's apartment, one of the first to be built, in a nondescript concrete cube of four floors, the maximum allowed in a building with no elevator. Sticky and tired, we dragged our luggage to Anita's third-floor apartment. The only one with energy was the child, who busied herself opening and closing doors and cupboards. Once she had finished her inspection, she did it all over again.

"Tomorrow," I said when she asked to go to the ocean. "Right now you can help me make our bed." The cupboard held clean linens. "And then we can go for a walk before supper."

I had to escape the sound of *Tia* Anita's voice. I could hear her in the kitchen pelting Aurora with questions. Did she have enough soap powder? Did she know how to use a washing machine? Had she brought enough bread for the evening meal? Were there enough eggs? Could she make gazpacho for the next day? Would she remember to turn off the gas stove? Would she make a grocery list for Anita's inspection? Was the melon she brought from Madrid ripe? I swallowed two aspirins with a handful of water from the bathroom sink, took my daughter's hand and bolted for the door.

"*Volveremos en una hora,*" I said as we sailed past the kitchen. Surely in an hour *Tia* Anita would have finished her interrogation and my Ana should have burned off some energy.

The aspirin took effect within minutes. We found a children's playground behind the building, and I felt rejuvenated enough to push a swing for Ana and to hold her waist while she crawled along the monkey bars. When she tired of that, we walked the short distance to the water's edge.

"Yes, yes," I said. "Tomorrow. I won't forget."

My head was clear when we started home but the smells of our supper—or someone else's, it didn't matter—filled the stairwell, and by the time we reached the second floor, I felt sick.

Normally, I would have relished a supper of fried eggs on white rice with a splash of tomato sauce. But I shook my head when Aurora asked if I wanted one egg or two. I didn't want any. I blamed my aversion on *Tia* Anita's olive oil. By all accounts the orchards in Anita's corner of *Andalucia* produced the finest oil in the country. It was graded according to acidity and labeled according to region, rather like wine. In spite of its reputation, I had never liked it. The light yellow oil I used in Madrid had a delicate flavor. But Anita's pride was a translucent pale green with a heavy, almost smoky flavor. I didn't care for the taste and now I couldn't stand the smell as it sputtered in a skillet waiting for Aurora to slip in an egg. The odor hung in the air long after the eggs had been fried and hours after the dishes had been washed.

In the morning I thought something in Alicante's water made the coffee bitter. All I wanted for breakfast was a chunk of stale bread. *Tia* Anita fussed that I wasn't eating enough. I didn't want to complain about the smell of her oil. No one else seemed bothered. My daughter had put on her bathing suit as soon as she got out of bed. After breakfast Aurora and I took her to the beach while Anita went to the rental office. By one p.m. we were all back together again. Ana was exhausted from chasing waves, and the bridge of Aurora's nose was sunburned.

Ana could barely keep her eyes open during lunch. I didn't need to coax her to bed for a nap. And I knew that *Tia* Anita, too, would go to her room after lunch. She followed the old Spanish refrain *la comida reposada y la cena paseada,* a nap after lunch and a walk after supper. She looked astonished when I said I was going out. *Alone? Where? Everything would be closed for siesta. Was I angry? Had she upset me? And why wasn't I eating?*

I assured her I wasn't upset, and blamed my restlessness on an American upbringing; I just couldn't get used to *siestas.* I tried to explain that the automatic shutdown after lunch felt unnatural to me. But I couldn't explain the loss of appetite even to myself. I never told her what I did next.

I walked along the beach occupied now only by tourists baking in the sun—northern Europeans determined to return home with a tan. I knew the locals were still at lunch, or sleeping it off. I slipped off my sandals, rolled up my slacks and stepped ankle-deep into the Mediterranean. For a moment I wished that I didn't live in a country where wearing shorts was akin to a crime against public morality. I was tempted to lie down in the furrow of a gentle wave and allow the restorative water to roll over me. Instead, I walked on absentminded until I saw the sign *Restaurante La Playa*, and the wave that washed over me was hunger and a craving for red meat.

Silly, I suppose, to order meat in a seaside restaurant that featured fish. The waiter looked surprised when I asked for *solomilo,* a tender fillet of beef, and a *copita de tinto.* I probably should have ordered the house specialty *sangria,* too, but I had an appetite for unadulterated red wine. The waiter poured a glass, left the bottle on my table and returned a moment later with a saucer of green olives, another of tissue-thin potato chips and a small hard roll. By the time he brought the fillet and salad, everything but the wine had disappeared. Over an hour later, renewed in body and spirit, I sauntered back to the apartment.

I found Ana sitting beside Aurora at the kitchen table, playing with bits of colored embroidery floss. On quiet afternoons Aurora worked on her *ajuar,* a collection of towels and linens she embroidered and put away until the day she married. My little girl was always content in Aurora's company, lining up threads according to color or folding scraps of material. Aurora was not yet twenty years old, but she had a gentle and firm manner with my daughter, maternal beyond her years.

⁂

Anita treated me differently from that day forward. I tried to compensate for what she thought was my—actually, I don't know what she thought. I had always liked her in spite of her voice and I was truly sorry about the olive oil aroma. I knew she would never understand my need that particular afternoon for peace and quiet and red meat, so I kept quiet about that and tried to ignore the tension. I was glad we had not planned for more than four days in Alicante.

Alberto phoned the day before we returned to Madrid.

"How are things in my harem?" he said. He liked to call us that.

"We're all fine," I said. "Anita resolved her issues with the rental office. I think Ana will be a good swimmer in no time. Aurora is sunburned. I had a two-day headache but I'm fine now. And you?"

"I had the most amazing evening with Blanca and Jorge," he said. "They invited me for dinner."

"What did you have?" I knew Blanca liked to cook.

"It wasn't what we ate. It's what we saw!"

I remembered our friends had television. We did not.

"The moon!" Alberto said before I could ask. "Absolutely amazing! We watched the landing on the moon."

On July 21, 1969 the United States landed the first astronaut on the moon where Neil Armstrong walked on the lunar surface called the Sea of Tranquility. While Armstrong took what he called *one small step for man and a giant leap for mankind,* I had shambled on the shore of the Mediterranean unaware that I was pregnant again.

# Chapter 17

I thought we already had the perfect child. Ana had been easy in every way from the day she was born. She slept and ate on schedule, had a sociable nature and laughed easily. When Julina told me the second baby was always easier, I couldn't imagine how.

Alberto and I, without any particular time frame, had always thought to have another child. We were not surprised when I learned I was pregnant. Our families were happy with the news. If anyone teased Alberto about wanting a boy this time, he said he didn't have a preference, "Just so long as the child is healthy." I had not married a stereotypical Latin male. In fact, I didn't even know any.

We knew without thinking twice that if we had a boy we would call him Luis in honor of the many beloved Luises in the family. A girl's name took a little longer.

I favored Eva, but Alberto said there had been some family sadness surrounding a girl named Eva so that was out.

"I still like the sound of *A,*" he said for the umpteenth time. So we ran down a list.

*Amalia*—we knew one and she was nuts. *Arancha*—too regional. *Asunción*—never! *Agustina*—looked painful to me, like anguish. *Almudena*—too popular. The *Virgin de Almudena* was the patron saint of Madrid and there were already countless numbers of girls called *Almudena.* We stopped at *Alicia.* It rolled off the tongue in Spanish and was translatable to English. Once we had chosen a name and I continued to enjoy perfect health, the only thing I wondered about was the actual birth date.

I worried I might have the baby on March 15, Ana's birthday. I'm sure that's happened before—siblings born on the same day though years apart. I felt sorry for children obliged to share everything from a room (that would be our case) and toys and maybe even the birthday cake itself. But when Ana celebrated her third birthday I was still pregnant. Then, because of the way Lent fell that year, I fretted that the baby might be born on Good Friday.

Catholic Spain observes *Semana Santa,* Holy Week, from Holy Thursday to the culmination on Easter Sunday. Of all those days, the Good Friday rituals are the most solemn. I didn't want to have a baby on such a somber day but at the rate things were going a Good Friday birth seemed likely. The doctor had given me an estimated due date that had come and gone—twice.

The first time I believed I was going into labor, I phoned the doctor, made an appointment to meet him at the hospital and dragged Alberto from his slumber at the ungodly hour of 9 a.m. For him it was still night.

"I think today's the day," I said. But it wasn't.

After a few minutes of scrutiny in the examining room at *La Virgen del Mar*—I loved the name of the little clinic, Virgin of the Sea—the doctor diagnosed false labor and sent me home with instructions to return the following Monday. If the baby had not arrived by then, he would induce labor. His tone carried a hint of reprimand, and I longed for the charming Dr. Varela who had delivered Ana. But Dr. Varela had never billed us for his services and I didn't want him to think we expected another favor. Instead, I went to a doctor from Alberto's medical plan, a man devoid of charm, with an equally graceless midwife. Nevertheless, I followed his instructions on the appointed day.

I crossed our lobby and felt the eyes of Pedro, the *portero,* assessing the situation. Alberto carried my pale blue overnight case as he had the previous week. He shrugged a *Buenos Dias* in Pedro's direction. I pulled back my shoulders and nodded. I felt silly. I could practically hear the *portero's* thoughts. *Does la Americana know what she's doing?* Apparently I didn't. I was home again in less than two hours.

"*Todavia no,*" the doctor had said. Not yet.

The baby waited a few more days then came howling into the world shortly before noon on Palm Sunday. The details of Ana's birth had escaped me due to an unanticipated dose of anesthesia, but when the new baby arrived I was completely conscious and drug free. The delivery could not have been easier. I speak for myself, of course, I don't know what the doctor and his assistant thought. A few gulps of oxygen and some curt instructions from the grumpy midwife were all I needed. The baby girl, however, protested loudly. The doctor could find no reason and pronounced her healthy. I couldn't imagine the protests would continue for weeks. A nearly constant wail shook the walls of our flat. Alicia cried before and after meals, before and after a bath, before and after a diaper change. A nap? What was a nap? Her specialty was the 2 a.m. howl. I lost weight. Julina could not have had this in mind when she said the second baby was easier.

Before I left *La Virgin del Mar,* Aurora brought Ana to see me and meet the baby. We lived a fifteen-minute walk from the clinic. We had prepared Ana. She had been excited when we told her the baby might be the size of her new doll and perplexed when we said we didn't know yet if the baby would be a boy or a girl. Regardless, the infant would need lots of meals and if she were very careful, Ana could hold the baby on her lap. We looked forward to her reaction. Aurora was holding Ana's hand as they came into the room but as soon as she saw me, Ana lunged toward my bed.

"*Ay, Mamá*!" She said. "Something bad happened in the street!"

I looked at Aurora who smiled and shook her head.

"*Sí?*" I said. "What happened?"

"I stepped in dog *caca*! Now my shoe smells bad!"

She had sailed right past the baby's crib and never noticed her new sister. That wasn't the reaction we expected.

I wondered if Ana would be jealous. I needn't have worried, even though Alicia required much of my time. With Aurora as a second mother and a father who took her out for treats, the big sister had no reason to feel neglected. Ana happily ate ice cream at the corner café while her father sipped brandy, and she eagerly accompanied him to the pharmacy for one of his periodic vitamin injections (he tended toward hypochondria) and where the lady pharmacist filled her pockets with *caramelos.* I protested. I didn't approve of taking Ana out in the evening and I didn't approve of all the sugar. He did it anyway. And why couldn't he use the pharmacy across the street instead driving to the one in his old neighborhood?

⁂

On the other side of the world, Richard Nixon inhabited the White House. Over 100,000 people demonstrated in Washington against the Viet Nam War. The National Guard fired on student protesters at Kent State University, killing four. I didn't miss the United States. My parents had spent several weeks with us shortly after Ana's birth, and I had taken Ana to visit the States when she was a year and a half old. I would take Alicia, too, when she was a bit older. But I didn't want to live in the US. I liked my Spanish life.

⁂

On a late spring afternoon Alberto and I sat at our dining room table enjoying a post-lunch coffee with our friend Ramón. He lived with his wife, Milali, on the other side of Madrid, but since the office where he worked with Alberto was only a few blocks from our flat, he often came for lunch. I didn't mind if Alberto phoned even at the last minute to ask if another person at the lunch table would be convenient. Aurora and I could always find a way to stretch the soup or add more rice to a *paella*, and there were always eggs for an omelet. Ramón was easy company. He had a soft baritone speaking voice and a particular tenderness with Ana and Alicia that I found endearing.

Aurora had cleared the table of everything except the tiny coffee cups and two brandy snifters. I rested my arms on the table toying with breadcrumbs, pushing them into little piles under the edge of my saucer. An angle of afternoon sun crossed the embroidered tablecloth. The curtains swayed in a gentle draft from the open balcony door. It was my favorite time of day, *la sobremesa.* The word translates as *the period after a meal.* But more than a specific hour, the *sobremesa* to me meant conversation.

When I first came to Spain, I found the Spanish lunch excessive both in quantity and length. As a working girl in the States my hour-long lunch at noon had consisted of a tuna sandwich and black coffee. Now I lived among people who ate three courses accompanied by wine in the middle of the afternoon. They didn't even think about lunch before 2 or 3 p.m. and could often be found still talking at the table at 4 or 5. It didn't take long for me to embrace the custom.

We talked that afternoon about the current highway project at the Ministry, and recounted the antics—or "*antiques*" as Alberto called them in one of his memorable mispronunciations—of our children. We relaxed and laughed easily in those languid moments as though we had all the time in the world. Gradually, the subject of vacations arose, a topic to which most of our friends gave a great deal of thought.

So far, I had convinced Alberto that staying in Madrid for the month of August was preferable to joining the mass exodus of *Madrileños* heading to some crowded beach. My idea of a vacation was a long weekend in the mountains with friends. At the moment, I couldn't imagine traveling with a baby and a three-year old to unknown territory for four weeks. Aurora, too, would go to her parents' village for the month. No, I'd rather stay home and enjoy the pool at our building, which would be nearly deserted. But Ramón was raving about Galicia, his favorite holiday spot.

I knew that remote northwest corner of Spain only from what Alberto had told me. I had visited the south with its spreading olive orchards and whitewashed pueblos and Moorish influenced architecture. What Ramón described differed greatly. The Moors had never reached Galicia. The foreign influence there came from the Celts who inhabited the region in the fifth and sixth centuries. Guitars and flamenco dances typified southern Spain but the Gallegos of the northwest played *gaitas,* a kind of a bagpipe, and danced the *jota,* which looked rather like an Irish jig. Instead of a sprawling landscape under a blazing sun, the green hills of Galicia were often wrapped in fog. *Meigas,* the witches frequently depicted as beautiful seductresses, figured in Galician folklore. The houses—even the granaries built on stilts to prevent an infestation of rodents—were made of stone.

"The Romans called the area *Finisterre,* Land's End," Alberto said. "I think you'd like it. It never gets hot."

By now Ramón had launched into the glories of Galician gastronomy. In spite of being a poor province in many respects, Galicia produced an abundance of seafood: lobsters, langostinos, shrimp, mussels, clams, octopus, cockles and others I'd never heard of. And the famous Gooseneck barnacles called *percebes,* which are unsightly sea creatures that attach themselves in clusters to the wave-smacked rocks and in coves along the coast. They have nothing to do with the barnacles found on ships. Fishermen, working in pairs attached by a line like mountain climbers, risk life and limb to harvest them by hand. Alberto had introduced me to barnacles in an old tavern in the heart of Madrid.

A platter of barnacles is not a pretty sight. What I saw looked like a clump of giant weathered thumbs. The shell-like tips made me think of fingernails. Appearance to the contrary, there is a long tradition of eating barnacles in this part of the world where they are an expensive delicacy. But I didn't know how to approach the unattractive creatures.

"This way," Alberto said, peeling back the brown leathery skin. "Then bite."

The slightly chewy pinkish flesh smelled and tasted like sea water. I liked it.

"To be absolutely authentic," Alberto said, taking a sip of white wine, "we should be drinking cider."

Cider was another typical Galician product, but unlike the *percebes,* I never developed a taste for it.

⁂

Ramón could have worked for Galicia's Board of Tourism. He described the city of Santiago de Campostela with its cathedral and the Cies Islands where he and Milali took their little boy on a ferry with a picnic lunch to spend a day on the beach. When I asked where they planned to stay, Ramón said they always rented a fisherman's cottage. It didn't come equipped and they had to supply their own bedding and towels and cooking pots, though he didn't seem to mind. The humble cottage didn't have a washing machine or a dryer either, but he said it was easy to find a village woman to do the laundry. He managed to make it sound quaint and reminded us that another couple we knew well was also planning to vacation nearby. We could have a grand time together. He had it all figured out. I couldn't deny that some of this, especially the climate, appealed to me.

Alberto swirled the caramel-colored liquid in his brandy glass, a gesture I knew well.

"Yes, but I don't know if a damp stone cottage is the best place to take a three-year old and a baby in diapers," he said.

He pretended to shiver. My husband's aversion to cold bordered on the phobic. I enjoyed chilly weather. But Alberto had made a good point.

Ramón thought we were being overly cautious. He and Milali had taken their son when he was just months old. He claimed the sea air was beneficial for everyone.

Alberto took a sip of brandy, reflected a moment, and then turned to me.

"Look, the only thing I want to do on my vacation is sleep till noon. So why don't you go up for a couple of days and see for yourself? You could fly to Vigo, rent a car and explore. If you find a place you think is suitable, just book it. All I want is a dark room and a warm bed."

It was a perfectly logical idea. But…

*"¿Sola?"* I said. "You want me to go alone? To a place with witches called Land's End?"

I may have exaggerated a bit. I looked at Ramón for support. He pointed out that Alberto could easily take a long weekend from the office, but my husband didn't find that convenient. *"Mi esposa Americana es totalmente capaz de organizarlo todo,"* he said. *Well, three cheers for the American wife and her organizational capabilities. What about a bit of reassurance and some company?* But I'd be darned before I would say that. My husband wasn't the reassuring type. He would point the way and pay without protest, but he never held my hand.

I went alone.

⁂

Alberto's secretary booked a car for me and reserved a room at the *parador*—the word means stopping place. King Alfonso XIII inaugurated the first *parador* in 1928 in the Gredos Mountains north of Madrid, part of his plan to develop tourism by providing reliable lodgings. The enterprise had the added advantage of preserving many historically important buildings—monasteries and convents, castles and palaces—by transforming them into comfortable accommodations while protecting their architecture. I looked forward to a stay at the *Parador del Conde de Gondomar*, a medieval fortress originally constructed to protect the coast from pirates.

*

Two weeks after our lunch with Ramón, I boarded the smallest plane I had ever seen and flew north. I wasn't sure I would understand the Galician vernacular though Alberto had said most of the people spoke Castilian. Franco had made sure of that. Following the Civil War, he had stripped three areas of Spain of their language. He prohibited Gallego, Catalan and Basque from being taught in school and required all official dealings to be transacted in Castilian Spanish. Alberto thought that made sense.

"One of the reasons the United States is so great is that everyone speaks the same language," he said. "Here in this country roughly the size of Texas we have four dialects. More if you throw in the province of Valencia and the Balearic Islands."

I didn't think to question that generations educated in schools under the Franco regime might not understand their own parents who still spoke in hushed tones in their age-old tongue.

As the plane neared Vigo, I recalled Ramón's forewarning about the angle of descent and the proximity of the landing strip to a mountain. I was still a nervous flier and unenthusiastic about heights in general, and it was a discomforting image. I concentrated on my small guidebook that compared the land below to Ireland. I read about a Galicia that had been a pilgrim destination since the ninth century when legend said a star directed shepherds to the burial place of St. James the Apostle.

*Santiago de Compostela*, St. James of the Field of Stars, became the patron of Spain. During the Reconquest, when the country fought to expel the Moors and Jews, his name rang out as the rallying cry. For hundreds of years, devout pilgrims had walked *El Camino,* The Way to Santiago, and worshiped at the eleventh century cathedral. Forty-three years later, I would walk the *camino* with my daughters. Like those early travelers, we, too, would wear a scallop shell to mark us as pilgrims, but in 1970, I could not have imagined such a thing.

I picked up the car at the airport, spread a map on the passenger seat and headed toward the *parador* on the bay of Bayona twenty kilometers south. Alone in the chilly dampness, I drove through wisps of fog along the narrow road that edged the Atlantic.

Bayona's main street faced the bay. I could have walked the length of its gentle curve in ten minutes. A dozen small boats bobbled on the water. I would see later that the remaining streets were a series of narrow lanes with low-slung stone buildings some of which housed a shop at street level and a dwelling on the second floor. At the end of the main street, an arrow pointed to a hillside battlement and a square crenellated tower. Alberto had taken me to several *paradores*. I loved the antique appointments and the architecture, but I wasn't prepared for the grandiose entrance to the *Parador del Conde de Gondomar.*

I parked the car beside a stone balustrade and entered the hotel lobby through a reconstructed tower. Huge banners suspended from lances hung on the walls. A wide stone staircase led to a second-floor gallery. A suit of antique armor stood on the landing. I could imagine a blare of trumpets heralding a royal arrival.

My room, furnished with heavy reproduction sixteenth century furniture, smelled pleasantly of *La Toja* soap. The bellhop set my suitcase on a stand at the foot of a canopied bed. Walking to the window, he pulled aside the thick linen draperies and opened a shuttered window that overlooked the bay. The only thing missing from the scene below was the *Pinta* on the horizon. The *Pinta,* one of Columbus' ships, had brought the first word of the new world to Europe—and it had moored here in Bayona. I knew that from the guidebook. I didn't stay long at the window. I was hungry and I had business to attend to. The dining room was still serving lunch and the view through the tall glass doors was equally spectacular, but I chose a sandwich at the bar instead of a heavy lunch and then went about my mission.

I drove back the way I had come, wondering what a rental agency looked like in this fishing village. Maybe I would begin my inquiries at the post office, if I could find one. I parked with no problem in front of a restaurant that had a *closed-for-the-season* sign on the door. It, along with the variety of small shops that lined the street, looked as though it might have opened the same day Columbus' ship sailed into the bay. In the midst of the stubby structures, rose a brand new four-story building. I could smell fresh paint as soon as I opened the car door. A billboard strung from the second story balcony of the new building advertised summer rentals. I stepped inside the little office and asked for more information.

The middle-aged woman behind the desk spoke with a strong sing-song accent, but at least I could understand her. Yes, she had rentals available for the summer, right upstairs. The second floor apartment had just been furnished with wicker chairs and glass-topped tables. It had two bedrooms, a bathroom with a full-sized tub, a living room with a round dining table, and a galley kitchen with a refrigerator that looked ample enough for a couple of bottles of milk and a chicken but not much more. The view from the balcony stretched across the water to what I guessed were the Cies Islands. Even better, the sheets and towels and cooking pots were included. What clinched the deal was a woman named Asun who could come three mornings a week to wash diapers and assorted laundry and to cook or clean. I remembered Alberto's words … *if you find something you like, just book it.* I dismissed the idea of a picturesque cottage and gave the woman a deposit. I knew Alberto would approve.

With my business concluded in less than an hour, I turned to exploration. A light rain began to fall as I returned to the car and headed south. I wanted to see what lay beyond the *parador*. The only thing I knew for sure was that, if I followed the road long enough, I would end up in Portugal.

The drizzle had a soothing effect—for a while. I lowered the window, stuck my hand out to feel the wet air and inhaled a blend of seaweed and mossy rocks and wood smoke from the cottages. The sea gulls cried in spite of the gentle *shush-shush* of windshield wipers. I thought I could hear the sea—not the sound of waves crashing the shore or their retreating whisper, but a kind of vibration and low moan. Or maybe it was the sound of the witches plotting mischief.

As the afternoon darkened, I found myself driving along a ledge several meters above the surf. The altitude made me nervous, and I felt clammy in a way that had nothing to do with sea air. I wondered who had built this road and how. Alberto could have told me, but my husband was elsewhere. I had an image of workmen falling from the cliff and dashed to bits during the road construction. My guidebook (maybe I should stop reading) had called it *La Costa de Morte*, The Coast of Death. No, that stretch of road was farther north and the deaths were due to shipwrecks not dizzy Americans who missed a turn and plunged through the guardrails.

I knew my fear of being sucked over the edge was irrational, but I couldn't loosen my sweaty grip on the steering wheel. There was little traffic, so I drove in the left lane: a head-on collision seemed less likely and less terrifying than a plunge to the sea. Once, a pair of oxen pulling an overloaded wagon came toward me and I was forced to spend a few dizzy moments back in my right lane. But the wagon passed and I was alone again. I began to think I had made a mistake by driving this far and I looked for a place to turn around. The drizzle and solitude that I had enjoyed minutes earlier now made me uneasy.

The fog crossed the road in front of me and bumped into the rock face. It recoiled for a moment then slowly raised itself up and over the cliff, making its way inland. It reminded me of a woman in a long skirt who lifts it to climb the stairs, releasing it once she reaches the top. Then, to my right, above the layer of fog a black cross appeared to float in the air. The guidebook hadn't said anything about floating crosses. I slowed the car and a moment later, when the fog parted, I saw that the cross was attached to a church spire. I could not resist the impulse to turn toward it. I didn't even care that it was growing dark. I had been in Spain long enough to know that for me the side road was always the most interesting one. I pulled off to the right and descended a jagged wagon track toward the water's edge.

The solitary church stood on a bare stretch of land. Everything about the place was gray—the stones of the church, the rocks on the shore, the gulls, the sea and the sky. The only bits of color came from the reflectors on the wooden bed of a dilapidated truck that sagged by the church wall.

I parked the car beside the truck and stepped out onto flat stone slabs that I took to be flagstones until I noticed the incised names and dates, and came to the unsettling realization that I was standing on gravestones. The stones spread to the water's edge where they fell victim to the uncompromising tide that crept slowly over them even as I stood there.

I had not arrived on a Sunday or a Holy Day, the normal occasions for Mass, but the iron bound wooden door of the church was open and I heard voices. I pulled a scarf from my pocket, covered my head and went inside. The grayness outside seeped into the church as well, softened now by the light of flickering candles. An assortment of votives burned and sputtered in front of the statues along the side aisles—tokens of supplication or thanksgiving. And on the main altar tall tapers in heavy gilded holders flanked a carved wooden crucifix. It was a typical Spanish crucifix.

Flecks of red paint dotted the crown of thorns, and the wound in the side of Christ seemed to drip with blood.

I stood in the rear of the church, wondering what kind of a service I had stumbled upon and not wanting to intrude or be noticed. The group inside consisted mostly of men, aside from four or five women wearing heavy black shawls over their heads. I strained to recognize the words as the men, fifteen or so, sang in a dialect I didn't know. It wasn't until the priest raised his hands in blessing that I recalled the rising tide and the time of day. The men were preparing for a night's fishing and, in what must have been an ancient invocation, they asked for a safe boat and a good catch. I left before the final *amen.* I didn't want my presence to interrupt their prayer. I was an outsider, but for a short time I had been part of a haunting and primal beauty. It wrapped itself around me like the fog. I felt it still when I fell asleep that night. It floats on the edge of my memory to this day.

I would describe the vacation apartment to Alberto, but I could never describe how I felt in that stone church.

⁂

"*Perfecto*," Alberto said when I told him about the slightly revised plan for vacation housing. I think he was relieved. "I just hope the bedroom is dark and quiet so I can sleep till noon for a month." He'd already made that clear. *And what you and your daughters do is your business—just don't bother me.* He didn't actually say that, but that's what I heard.

On the last day of July, we loaded the car. Even without the linens and the kitchen equipment, the car bulged. Ana sat in front—three-years old, wide eyed and excited. I sat in back with Alicia. The basket I used to carry the baby fit well enough but I had to sit with my knees nearly under my chin. I hoped the car's motion would lull Alicia to sleep. But the only thing the rocking car did was make Ana carsick on a mountain road shortly after an abundant lunch of *croquetas* and ham and a strawberry ice cream.

Nine hours and 600 kilometers later we reached Bayona. Alberto was worn out, but he liked the apartment. I, after a day cramped in the backseat, had lost the feeling in my legs. Only Ana was full of life and curiosity. She entertained herself on a stool at the kitchen counter—the kind with a pass-through window to the dining area—opening and closing the screen, pretending to be on television. I opened the balcony door to let in the cool air and called to Ana.

"Look," I said. "Can you see the islands way out in the water?"

"Can we go there?" she said.

Alberto had come to stand beside us. "Of course," he said. "We'll go in a boat with Ramón and Milali and their little boy."

⁂

As it turned out we were four couples from Madrid—only two of us had children— who met periodically during the following weeks. One of the men had been born nearby, but it was Ramón who acted as chief tour leader. He organized a trip to the islands for an afternoon on the beach. We went on an open-sided ferry, putt-putting across the bay with not much more horsepower than a child's toy. The children and I were thrilled. Another day we drove to *Gijón* and drank cider from glasses so thin they flexed if you squeezed them. The cider didn't interest me, but I bought six glasses to use as water tumblers at home. In *Padrón* we lunched on baby clams in wine sauce and ate the tiny grilled peppers for which the town is famous. And we visited the magnificent cathedral in *Santiago.* Everything around me was green and delicious and felt slightly wild. If only the background noise had been something other than Alicia's protests.

I tried to calm the fussy baby. I fed her, I walked the floor, I jiggled her in her stroller, and I took her to bed with me. She cried anyway. On the beach, she wailed at the waves. If I set her in a little seat with a sweet sunbonnet on her head and poured warm sand over her bare feet, she howled. And then there was my husband.

Alberto lived up to his words; he slept until noon. I can't say I wasn't forewarned. I had just temporarily forgotten his other words. That he'd never push a baby buggy.

I would do that myself. I hadn't imagined when he first said it that I would feel so lonely.

⁂

Sitting at a waterfront café a week or so after our arrival in Galicia, Milali peered over the top of her sunglasses. "You look awful!" she said.

I didn't need a reminder. I had circles under my eyes and dry skin. Milali was tanned and smiling. She looked relaxed like someone on vacation. I jumped at sudden noises. Eight hours of uninterrupted sleep was a distant memory. My slacks bagged. After Alicia's birth, I had returned almost immediately to my pre-baby weight of 115 pounds. Since then I had lost six. Three simple things might have made life easier: disposable diapers, frozen foods and sandwiches, but the first two didn't exist and my husband wouldn't eat the latter. Of the many things Alberto liked about the United States, sandwiches were not among them. "Uncivilized," he called them.

⁕

I shopped at the farmers' market nearly every morning. I loved the markets in Madrid, but Madrid was familiar territory. Here I didn't recognize many of the strange looking fish, and I couldn't pronounce the vegetable names in Gallego. Having two small children with me didn't help. Asun came three mornings a week and kept the balcony aflutter with lines of drying diapers. I was grateful for her help, but I felt I needed three Asuns to keep me afloat.

"Look, Diana," Milali said. "Leave the girls with me for a few hours. I'll manage. You and Alberto can go out with Ramón. He wants to show you the fish auction."

At that moment, she could not have given me a more precious gift.

⁕

We stood on the wharf watching the fishermen unload their catch. They piled the fish on stone slabs inside a building that was more corrugated metal roof than anything else. An auctioneer in rubber boots surveyed the lots and when everything seemed to be in order, he opened the bidding. In the States, an auctioneer begins at a certain point and increases the bid in segments until the potential buyers fall silent, then he shouts *Sold to the highest bidder!* But here, the auctioneer began high and decreased bit by bit until a rough voice called out, *"mio."* Mine!

Outside, three or four fishermen—apparently independents with a very small catch and no need for an auctioneer—had laid their fish on tarps on the ground, waiting for someone to make an offer, sometimes singing out a line about the freshness or the size of their fish. We walked along the wharf with no intention to buy. We had come strictly as spectators—until we saw the three lobsters. I'm sure we all had the same thought—chilled with garlicky mayonnaise. That's how we'd eaten them in a restaurant in Madrid. But what would we do if we bought them? Ramón said he knew how to cook them but he didn't have a refrigerator to store them overnight or a pot large enough to hold them. I had both, although no idea of what to actually do with the wiggly creatures that appeared very much alive and didn't look friendly. But Asun was coming the following day. She would know. The next thing I knew we had changed from casual spectators to slightly intimidated owners of several kilos of crustaceans, and I had invited our friends to lunch the next day. I remembered the mesh shopping bag that for some reason I had stuck in the trunk of the car. None of us wanted to handle the lobsters that now looked downright hostile, and the old fisherman gave us an amused look when we asked him to put them in the bag for us. I stuck the bag back in the trunk. When we returned to the apartment later and removed the bag of lobsters, they no longer moved. Dead, I thought. Alberto stuffed them into our pint-sized fridge, bag and all. In the morning I would ask Asun what else I could bring from the market to make a festive lunch.

Alicia woke me with her crying. I didn't know what time it was. It was still dark and I was still very tired. I changed her diaper automatically and made my way to the kitchen to heat one of the bottles I had prepared earlier. I cradled the baby in one arm, opened the fridge with my free hand, then screamed and nearly dropped the poor child. I won't say they were cavorting exactly, but something in the chill interior of the refrigerator had revived the lobsters. They had escaped the mesh constraints of my shopping bag. Their antennae waved in time to music only they could hear as they fixed their reproachful eyes on mine. I slammed the door and woke Alberto. He could fuss all he wanted, but there was no way in hell I was going to stick my arm in that refrigerator.

⁂

Asun boiled the lobsters to perfection, cracked some of the difficult bits and made a bowl of *alioli*. The lunch with our friends was delicious. Alberto, always a good storyteller, gave his own version of the midnight lobster attack. He embellished and exaggerated with a perfectly straight face and had the rest of us laughing until, apropos of nothing, his demeanor changed.

"Women!" he said in a voice laced with unexpected venom. "Who the hell understands them?"

Milali looked at me in surprise. I shrugged.

"More wine anyone?" I said in an attempt to brush off the comment. I couldn't think of anything else to say.

But Ramón turned toward Alberto and, in a tone mixed with kindness and reproach, he said, "You don't have to understand them to love them." Without respoding, Alberto left the table to look for cigarettes. The rest of us moved conversation in another direction.

I could have asked Alberto for an explanation, but I didn't want to engage. *Don't make a scene. Don't make matters worse. He'll forget he said it or say he was just kidding and that I didn't have a sense of humor.* In spite of dear friends, affectionate in-laws and a country and language that I had grown to love, I realized I was living my marriage through clenched teeth. We never took another family vacation.

*

The girls and I visited my parents periodically, but Alberto didn't come with us. From time to time my husband and I went away for a long weekend with friends, and sometimes I joined him on a business trip. By then the girls were old enough to leave with Aurora. One July, I took the girls and Aurora to *El Escorial* for a couple of weeks. The town, the site of Philip II's monastery, was an hour north of Madrid and much cooler. Alberto said he would come on the weekends, but he didn't. Later, when he took his vacations in the month of August, we stayed at home. He slept till noon, and I sat by the pool with Ana and Alicia. Everyone was happier.

# Chapter 18

Our neighborhood was changing. The dust settled once the road was paved, the street name changed from *Cuesta del Zarzal (*Bramble Bush Hill) to *Menéndez Pidál* in honor of the writer who had lived for years at the foot of the hill, and the lobby of our building sounded like the United Nations. A rambunctious family of Argentinians occupied the sixth floor and a Spanish journalist lived with his German wife across the hall. A French couple and their toddler son inhabited the second floor. Whenever he saw us, little Nicolas called out a greeting in Spanish with a heavy French accent that made me smile. Everywhere I turned, I heard an accent. Even my Ana's English had a Spanish accent.

I don't know what the Japanese lady spoke, aside from Japanese. I never met her, but from my bedroom window I could see the other wing of the building where she hung her fish to dry. She folded the tails of what looked like sole over a line strung across the balcony and attached them with a clothespin. The fish flapped in the sun for a couple of days and then disappeared. The Japanese lady, too, disappeared shortly and was replaced for a brief time by an Iranian woman with a baby. We smiled and nodded to our neighbors in the lobby, but we didn't become friends with any of them until the Americans arrived.

*

We met by the pool. I sat on a folding canvas stool working the crossword puzzle in the International Herald Tribune. I didn't read the Tribune on a regular basis, but I bought it occasionally from the kiosk by the market and kept it until I finished the puzzle. Ana was feeding sand to her doll. Alicia, in a rare moment of silence, was sleeping in a bouncy seat. I looked up when I heard the gate open. In walked my new blond neighbors and *poof* my life changed. In an instant, my daughters found an American playmate, and I made a friend for life. But, of course, we didn't know that at the time.

"Heather, look," said the new arrival, pointing to Ana, "Maybe that little girl will play with you." She turned toward me and raised her eyebrows. "*¿Habla Ingles?*" I noted the relief on her face when I said yes. She put out her hand and said, "Hi, I'm Diane."

"Well, that's coincidence for you," I said. "I'm Diane, too."

The new Diane spread a towel on the sand beside me and began to add to the data I had already gleaned from my bedroom window. I didn't normally spy on my neighbors, but a few days earlier I had yielded to temptation. The bedroom window that had allowed me to observe the Japanese lady with her fish also afforded a view of my neighbor's dining room, and I already knew a few things about her. She smoked and wore contact lenses. Her husband came home for lunch every day, and she read on the balcony after putting her little girl down for an afternoon nap. Heather was a year younger than Ana, but the girls played well together while Diane chatted easily.

Diane and Ed Lyons came originally from Connecticut. Ed worked as Chief Financial Officer for an international tire company. Diane had taught primary school until they began their nomadic life three years earlier with a stint in Brazil. Their daughter had been born in the States between overseas assignments. I calculated that Diane and Ed were roughly five or six years younger than I was, which made them fifteen years younger than Alberto. One of the first things Diane told me was that she and Ed were taking Spanish lessons.

"I keep mixing Castilian Spanish with Brazilian Portuguese," she said. "We just hired a *muchacha,* and I know she doesn't understand a word I say. She just looks blank every time I open my mouth."

"I remember those days," I said. "You get good at charades."

That's how our friendship began. Diane was the first American I met in Spain—aside from a few customers while working at the boutique. I had been married nearly six years and in that time, I was so busy being Spanish I hadn't felt the need for Americans. However, Diane and I soon fell into a comfortable routine, and I found myself going to the market twice a week with a native New Englander. You can't get more American than that! Diane always came with a list. She was the most organized shopper I had ever known and had meals planned days in advance. I bought what looked good, but I never knew for certain what we were going to have for dinner until I laid eyes on it. While I was dawdling over the freshest vegetables or scrutinizing the clarity of a fish's eye, Diane had already filled her shopping bag and was ready for the second feature of the morning—coffee and pastry.

We would sit at the counter by the market door with a *café con leche* and a *bollo* and exchange information. On a particular morning I was explaining the difference between *suizo,* a sweet breakfast roll, and *Suiza,* Switzerland.

"You've got to be careful with the vowels," I said. "And just to confuse you a bit more we have *sucio,* dirty, *Suecia,* Sweden, *Sueca,* a Swedish girl and *zuecos,* clogs."

Diane looked puzzled for a minute.

"What does *tirar* mean, exactly?" she said.

"Well, it can mean toss or throw or throw away."

"And what about *retirar?*"

"That means to remove or take away."

She groaned.

"What's the matter?"

"Instead of telling the *muchacha* to remove the dinner plates, I've been telling her to throw them away!"

⁂

While I added to her Spanish vocabulary, Diane brought me up to date on American pop culture. During those morning coffees I felt I had been away from the States for a very long time. I didn't want to return, but I was losing track of the changes. I had never heard of a television program called *All in the Family* until Diane told me and then I was surprised.

"You mean the characters really use racist, vulgar language on TV?"

"Yep. That Archie Bunker is a bigot and makes no bones about it."

I hadn't read *The Godfather* or *The Exorcist* either and Diane promised to lend them to me. Her openness and genuine interest in Spain and her willingness to go anywhere and eat anything made her easy company. We introduced our husbands and were soon a compatible foursome going out for dinner or taking the children to the country for a long Saturday lunch. I sensed Diane and Ed's appreciation for Alberto, which didn't surprise me. My husband was an interesting man and a great source of Spanish information, and, of course, he spoke English. But sometimes I wished he would keep his opinions to himself.

For most of his life, Alberto had had his clothes custom-made. This was true in Spain for most men of his generation. Until recently, ready-to wear clothes were a novelty. My husband had very conservative taste and definite ideas as to what was acceptable. He wore beautiful jackets and trousers to the office. On weekends in summer he wore linen slacks, polo shirts—always with a sweater draped over his shoulders—and espadrilles. That's what he wore the day we planned to take Diane and Ed to *El Meson* for lunch.

Diane and Ed stood waiting beside the *portero's* desk in the lobby. I leaned to give Diane a hug and when I turned I saw that Alberto had stopped behind me with an odd look on his face, his eyes fixed on our neighbor's knees. Both Diane and Ed were wearing sandals and Bermuda shorts. He took a deep breath.

"*Amigos,*" he said, "we don't wear shorts in this country."

That was true. I had never seen a Spaniard in shorts. I didn't own any myself. Women wore sleeveless dresses in summer or cotton slacks but never shorts. On the other hand, I thought nobody but my husband would make a scene. I nudged him.

"Oh, Alberto, don't be so fussy. We're just going to the country." But he went on.

"Seriously," Alberto said, "no self-respecting Spaniard would wear those silly pants."

Diane looked embarrassed. Ed just headed toward the door.

"We're not Spaniards," he said. "Let's go."

That should have been the end of the discussion but Alberto was like a dog with a bone. When we arrived at the restaurant, he asked for a table indoors.

"Let's sit on the patio," I said. "It's too nice to sit inside."

"True," he said, "but we'll be less visible indoors." And he looked pointedly at Ed's legs. I felt uneasy but Diane and Ed laughed, though I thought Diane was a bit reserved.

"Well, anything to keep *Don* Alberto happy," I said, and I linked arms with Diane and Ed. I didn't like this mean streak in my husband. Good-humored teasing was one thing. This was something else, and I was noticing it more and more, even with Ana and Alicia.

A few days earlier, Alberto had been playing with Alicia. He set her on top of the refrigerator, which the two-year old thought was fun for a moment. But then he left her there alone in the kitchen. I came out of the bedroom when I heard her cry. Later he would try to say it was all a joke. He was the only one who thought so. On another occasion, he didn't even apologize when his carelessness caused Ana's parakeet—a bird he insisted on buying—to escape. He had said he could train the bird to fly in the flat—outside the cage. But he never bothered to close the balcony door and the bird flew away. Ana was heartbroken. I was angry. If Diane and Ed saw this side of Alberto, they kept quiet about it.

Occasionally, we spent a long weekend together at the beach or in the mountains and on one of these outings, Diane asked rather timidly about Alberto's experiences during the Civil War. I supposed she was hesitant because I had already warned her that Alberto wasn't interested in talking about flamenco dancing or bullfights that foreigners usually wanted to discuss. She might have thought the war would be a painful subject, but he didn't seem to mind her question. I already knew the story. He had told me before we were married, but I had never heard him describe his escape to anyone else. I leaned back in my chair—we were sitting on a hotel patio with a bottle of wine—and watched for my friends' reaction.

"I was twelve," he said. "And Madrid was hell. We all ate very poorly. I couldn't leave the house because of the fighting. I had no friends, no physical exercise and spent my days reading novels. One day in October of '37 my father called me into his office—he worked from home— and laid out his plan."

I had been in my father-in-law's office and could imagine him seated at the carved desk surrounded by three walls of books and a window that faced the *Jardin Botanico*. But I couldn't imagine what the botanical garden looked like in a war-ravaged city.

"My father said he had been in contact with the International Red Cross. No one knew when the siege of Madrid would end. I had already missed an entire year of school and he said I couldn't continue like that. He had finally been able to secure my transfer to join my sister at our uncle's house in Huelva. My father explained that on the night of November 10th, a taxi with my sister's school friend, Maria Antonia, and two of her aunts who were also leaving Madrid would come for me and take us to Valencia and a boat bound for Marseilles, France. From there we would take a train, also operated by the Red Cross, pass through Hendaye and cross the border into Spain at Irún. That is where Maria Antonia and her aunts had to leave me and take another route to family in France. My father said he realized I was only twelve years old, but that he had to ask me to continue the journey alone. He gave me tickets and enough money to last until I arrived in Sevilla where my uncle waited to meet the train and take me to Huelva."

Alberto paused, added a splash of wine to his glass and asked if anyone had a pencil. Diane found a ballpoint in her purse, and Alberto pulled a paper napkin from the basket on the table. I think even blindfolded my husband could draw the map of Spain including all its rivers and mountains and provincial borders. Now, on the napkin he outlined Portugal, Spain, North Africa and France, and then marked with dots his convoluted trajectory.

Huelva, his final destination, sits on the gulf of Cadiz roughly 380 miles southwest of Madrid. But in order to avoid the fighting, Alberto's escape took him south*east* to Valencia, northeast to Marseilles, nearly due west to Hendaye and Irún and finally south to Sevilla and west again to Huelva skirting Madrid on its western side. A 380-mile trip turned into an odyssey of nearly 2,000. When he connected the dots, they formed a spiral on the napkin.

"Wow!" Ed said.

Alberto smiled. "I'm not sure that was the worst of it," he said. "Because then my dear father asked me a favor. He said that he wanted me to make a great effort to complete both the first and second year of *Bachillerato* in one. That would be like your finishing freshman and sophomore year of high school simultaneously. In that way, I could make up the year I had lost and begin my third year the following summer. 'All for the good of my future,' he said."

"So, on that November night, I waited in the doorway with my parents. Everyone was crying, but I was relieved to see a large red cross painted on the side of the taxi. That always alleviated our fears. Inside, just as my father said, three ladies sat in the back seat, which allowed me the privilege of sitting in front, something I always enjoyed. The kindly driver and I chatted all through the night. Because of the bad roads in those days, the trip was tedious and I thought it a good idea to make conversation so he wouldn't fall asleep."

Alberto was able to smile at the thought of the bumpy roads.

"We arrived the following day and found the Inmérité II, a small boat from a French fleet rented by the Red Cross to transport Spanish refugees to France. We docked in Marseilles the following night. On the tracks just next to the port, a sealed Red Cross train was waiting. By sealed, I mean no other passengers could board and the window curtains were closed. We traveled through the night and all the following day. Just before reaching the border with Spain, the train stopped. That's where the ladies left me, and a woman from the Red Cross took me to a large building."

Alberto pointed to one of the dots on the napkin map.

"It was late and dark but I could see we were in a town. We walked up a wide flight of steps and entered a building through double doors though only one side was open. I followed the woman to a row of cots where people were sleeping. She handed me the blanket that was folded on an empty cot and said she would come for me in the morning to make sure I boarded the train to Sevilla. I took off my shoes and tried to make myself comfortable, but the cot was too short and my legs dangled over the end. I slept off and on. I dreamed, and at one point I looked up and saw the stars shining over my head. But how could I see stars? I was inside. Nevertheless, I saw bright specks shimmering in the darkness. That was when I thought I had died and must be on my way to heaven."

Alberto stopped and laughed again.

"In the morning I saw what had produced the stars. But I wouldn't realize for a long time that I had spent the night under the Baccarat crystal chandelier in the casino at Biarritz. Then the insane trip really began."

With his eyes slightly closed, the map of Spain unfolded in his memory, and Alberto ticked off the cities and towns of his journey.

"From Irún the train went to San Sebastian, Zumárraga, Vitoria, Burgos, Venta de Baños, Valladolid, Salamanca, Alba de Tormes, Béjar, Plasencia, Cáceres, Mérida, Zafra, Cumbres Mayores, and finally, thank God, Sevilla."

He smoothed a wrinkle from the napkin and continued.

"I tried to form some kind of strategy along the way. Naturally, I was traveling third class. I had to carry only my overcoat and a small suitcase so I was quite mobile. I would walk along the corridor of the third-class car observing the people as they got on. If I detected a fat lady with a basket and preferably a muscular husband, I tried to get in their compartment. I reasoned that if a fat lady was carrying a basket, the probability of its containing food was quite high. And also if the husband was muscular, he might be useful in an emergency. I tried to look for compartments where there might also be other boys of my age to talk to. The trains were extremely crowded. I could not always find these ideal conditions. But sometimes fortune took pity on me."

*Fortune took pity on me!* My husband was showing off his English.

"I would ask very politely," he continued. "If I might take a seat next to the fat lady with the basket. When she said I could, I would open the conversation with a phrase that always caused a sensation. *Pardon me, Señores,* I would say. *I am going to try to sleep a little. I have come alone all the way from Madrid and I am a bit tired.* The passengers would look at one another in surprise and then begin to question me.

*But how could your parents allow you to travel alone?*

*Have you run away from home?*

*How did you bypass the blockade?*

And, finally, the question that was music to my ears, *Have you eaten recently?*

Automatically, the fat lady would hand me a phenomenal slice of egg and potato omelet on crusty bread and something to drink, usually sparkling water mixed with red wine."

"Weren't you scared?" Diane was staring.

Alberto just shrugged and lit a cigarette. "As I ate, I told them my adventures."

As I said, Alberto had always been a good storyteller. I watched him sometimes with Ana as he built the suspense in some old folk tale until she wiggled on her chair. *And then what happened, Papá? What happened next?* But before he would continue with the action, he described every detail of a beggar's rags or the rich man's jewels. His stories had a distinct style and, now, the way he recounted his war experiences made me think of *Lazarillo de Tormes,* a sixteenth-century picaresque novel.

I had read portions of the novel in a university course I took before Alicia's birth. The novel, like Alberto's story, is a survival tale. Young *Lazarillo*, a rogue, lives by his wits and recounts his misadventures in a series of satirical episodes.

In spite of his difficulties, *Lazarillo* tells his story with wit and energy, at one moment self-deprecating, in the next confident of his own cleverness. Alberto sounded that way to me—both victim and hero in his own story. And in a strange way, detached.

"Once, after I had eaten," he said. "I asked the muscular husband if he could show me to the toilet. He led me down the corridor and in a loud voice, appropriate to his size, shouted, *Out of the way, please. Out of the way! This young man needs to answer a call of nature.*"

"So, more or less that is how I solved my physiological problems until I arrived in Sevilla three days later. My uncle was waiting at the train station. I expected him to hug me but he only took my hand and said *My son, we are faced with unleashed barbarism.* I will never forget those words. But in spite of them, after the sordidness, the fear and the scarcity of food in the Red Zone of Madrid, my uncle's house in Huelva seemed like Paradise on earth to me."

Alberto didn't say, but I knew from Julina, that he arrived malnourished, filthy and covered with lice. And no sooner had he somewhat recovered, his uncle began what Alberto would later call *a forced march* to make up his lost studies. He was enrolled in a private school and allowed to read only textbooks. The mystery novels Alberto so loved were forbidden. Somehow he managed to cram two school terms into one and when the time came for final examinations, he received a Certificate of Honor for the first year and a Certificate of Excellence for the second. And I knew, too, that when he completed his third year of *Bacillerato,* the next term, he also received a Certificate of Excellence.

"How long did you stay with your uncle?" Diane asked.

Alberto took a sip of wine and tapped the end of a cigarette before lighting it. "A bit over two years," he said. "Even as the war came to an end, the circumstances in Madrid were still very difficult. My parents thought it would be best if I spent another summer in Huelva where I could be out of doors in a healthful environment and eat well. My sister and uncle made sure I had friends of my own age. My best friend, Tony, and I spent hours in an abandoned fisherman's hut on the beach or making explosives with the gunpowder we found in a workshop belonging to Tony's father."

I remembered Alberto's telling me that Tony taught him to ride a bicycle and that one of their explosive experiments rocked the neighborhood, whereupon Tony's father locked the workshop.

"You might think it strange," Alberto said, "but I remember that summer, in the middle of the Civil War, as one of the happiest times of my life."

Julina had told me she felt that way, too. "I was happy to be out of my father's house," she'd said.

"So," Alberto continued, "I returned to Madrid and that fall I entered the most progressive school in Madrid. I realize that most of the world has an unfavorable opinion of Dictator Franco. But I can tell you, at that time, he had a tremendous interest to make of my school a kind of paragon of education. We had the best laboratories, the finest sports complex, beautiful classrooms. As I said, Franco wanted to showcase a new education for the New Spain. For the final two years of my *Bachillerato*, I was part of a system that inculcated a belief that we were the best of the best—liberal, progressive, modern and elite. We were the brightest and the cutest."

Alberto laughed. He had actually used the word cutest.

"I'm not saying that I think this system is right," he said. "I'm just saying that's the way it was."

# Chapter 19

I had no intention of joining the American Women's Club of Madrid, but when Diane said she was interested in knowing more about it and wanted to visit the clubhouse on *Plaza de la República de Ecuador*, I offered to take her.

"Do you know where it is?" she said

"More or less. I think it is near my favorite market, *Chamartín*, but I've never noticed a clubhouse."

The clubhouse turned out not to be a house at all. The space, designed for commercial purposes, sat between a yarn shop and a cubbyhole-sized establishment that sold light bulbs and electrical supplies. With its blue door and a lace curtain at the window, it could have passed for a beauty salon were it not for a discreet polished brass plaque that read *American Women's Club.*

"Oh, it's cute!" Diane said as she pushed open the door.

Inside, a large-boned sixtyish woman sat behind a wooden desk. In reality, the bosomy blonde may have been as neat as a pin, but in my memory her bleached hair flies in all directions and the buttons on her white nylon blouse threaten to pop at any moment. Around her, the air smelled like Lily of the Valley and something else—toast, I think.

"Come in, come in," she said. Her strong British accent surprised me. I hadn't known about the international makeup of the club.

"I'm Tess la Touche." She offered her hand.

The wooden sign on her desk read *Tess la Touche, Clubhouse Manager,* but the sound of her name made me think *Exotic Dancer.*

Diane went straight to the point. What exactly did the AWC offer? Diane wanted to know more about Spanish history and culture but hadn't been in Spain long enough to be fluent in the language.

"I quite understand," Tess la Touche said. "My husband, Pat, and I came to Madrid twenty-five years ago, and I still haven't sorted it out."

Tess la Touche had come to Spain during the most restrictive period of the Franco regime. I wondered why. She told us later that she was an actress— maybe that accounted for her name—and sometimes made commercials, but that didn't explain why she had moved to Spain when Franco held such a tight reign.

As Mrs. la Touche rummaged through her folders for a list of pertinent information, she asked if I, too, were a recent arrival. "Not exactly," I said.

"Oh? How long have you been in Madrid?

"Six years."

She looked confused. "But I've never seen you here," she said.

"No, this is my first time."

Her expression changed from puzzled to reproachful, as if my absence had been an affront to the organization. There were, she said, over three hundred women who looked to the AWC as a source of companionship and inspiration, and a place where they could stay in touch with their cultural roots, so to speak. I wanted to say I'd had no time to contact my roots because I'd been fully engaged in putting down new ones.

Tess la Touche handed Diane a list of Spanish teachers and showed us a telephone directory of all the club members. We could have our own directory if we joined. She smiled as she gave each of us a copy of the AWC monthly newsletter and said, with what I thought was a trace of challenge, "You'll find some of our activities listed here."

The list included arts and crafts classes, bridge games, the monthly luncheon, a Tuesday evening slide show on art history, the trip of the month, an Easter party with spouses, and, although it was April, an announcement for the annual Christmas bazaar to benefit Spanish charities.

"Wow!" Diane said. "This looks really interesting."

I nodded.

"Let me show you the downstairs," Tess la Touche said.

Aside from the desk, the ground floor was furnished with sofas and coffee tables. As she led us toward the stairwell, I noticed the counter and a kitchenette barely large enough for the two girls in pink uniforms, and some kind of cooking surface. That explained the smell of toast I had noticed earlier.

Downstairs, Tess la Touche pointed to the book-filled, floor-to-ceiling shelves. "We have a growing library," she said. "Every time a member returns to the States we inherit more books. And this is where the various committees meet as well as the Toastmistress International group."

Ever since Diane and I had entered, there had been a steady stream of traffic: women exchanging notes or sharing a pot of tea prepared by one of the girls in the kitchenette or, now, a foursome seated at a card table playing Mah Jong. In a short time, Tess la Touche had introduced us to a club member from Germany, another from Argentina, (both married to Americans) and the current president, a former nurse from Nebraska, who had worked for a time in Lebanon until she married a Swiss journalist and moved to Spain. These were not the blue-haired, sherry-sipping women I had imagined.

On our way back to the ground floor we stopped to read the notices on a corkboard at the foot of the stairs.

*Maid wanted, live-in, near Parque del Retiro – Portable sewing machine for sale (needs transformer) – Interested in yoga? Call Becky Flynn. – Tuesday evening, 7 p.m., Helen Lemley de Liencres speaks about the Convento de las Descalcas Reales (Convent of the Royal Barefoot Nuns) 50 pesetas, pay at the door.*

I'd seen all I needed to see. I paid my dues on the spot, enrolled in a pewter-embossing class and asked for information about the Toastmistress organization. Diane signed up for bridge classes.

"Would you like a bite of lunch?" Tess la Touche said. The girls in pink could prepare a simple snack and beverage. "Toasted cheese sandwiches and a glass of red wine?"

"Fine with me," Diane said.

"Fine with me, too," I said and watched as Tess la Touche went to the counter and called out our order.

"Marta," she said, "dos señoras quieren dos grilled queso sandwiches, por favor. And also dos glasses of red vino. Thank you muy mucho."

*Poor Marta,* I thought. But Marta must have been used to Tess la Touche's *Spanglish* because she answered, "Sí, lady."

Before Diane and I took a seat on the sofa, we watched the girl in pink clamp sliced bread and cheese in a metal mold that simultaneously removed the crusts and sealed the edges. She held it by a long handle turning it back and forth over a gas flame until the bread turned brown. A few minutes later she set a battered aluminum tray on the coffee table in front of us. It held two crisp pockets of molten cheese and two stubby glasses of red wine. The cheese burned our tongue. It didn't matter; we were having a grand time. When Diane turned to me and said, "This is the worst wine I have ever tasted," we burst out laughing.

Meanwhile, Tess la Touche had returned to her desk where she answered the frequently ringing phone, dispensing information on everything from where to find a butcher who spoke English (there were none, but she knew one who spoke French) and should you give your maid the month of August for vacation? (Of course!) When she wasn't answering the phone, Tess chatted with the club members who came and went according to the activities of the day. She called everyone by name. Clearly, Tess la Touche knew everything worth knowing in Madrid. I wasn't surprised when I read James Michener's acknowledgements in his book *Iberia* that he credited Mrs. Tess la Touche of the American Women's Club of Madrid as his source for "daily gossip."

*

I couldn't have imagined how the American Women's Club would influence my life. A year later, I was chairman of the annual Bazaar, and the following year I was the club's vice president and a regular member of Toastmistress International. But I'm getting ahead of my story.

One morning, after finishing my shopping at the *Chamartín* market, I stopped at the club for a cup of coffee. I had just taken a seat on the sofa when another member, Peggy, the club president, sat down beside me. We had attended the same book discussion a week earlier, and now she was telling me about the mystery she had just finished.

"I have the name of it here somewhere," she said as she pulled a wad of Kleenex from her raincoat pocket.

"You keep notes on Kleenex?"

"Well, sometimes I write on my coat lining but I think I used Kleenex this time."

Even on the calmest day, Peggy managed to look wind-blown—her hair in perpetual turbulence. It was clear she applied her lipstick without benefit of a mirror. Her stockings invariably had runs and her sensible black suede flats were scuffed in back. The red knit suit, a favorite, judging from the number of times she wore it, was so fanny-sprung that it looked sizes larger than her fragile frame required. But after five minutes in her intelligent, droll company, one forgot what she wore and looked instead into her lively blue eyes.

"I know I'm a disaster," she giggled. "You can imagine how this affects my exceedingly neat and organized Swiss spouse." She continued to rummage.

"When Bernard is home," Peggy said, "he expects proper nutritious meals scheduled with the precision of the proverbial Swiss watch. I try to oblige. But when he leaves town, life is much more relaxed. The kids and I hit the peanut butter trail and just snack when we feel hungry. Last week he went to cover a story in North Africa for a few days." I had met Bernard once, a journalist from Zurich, now based in Madrid.

"I was behind in my reading," Peggy said. "So, on Thursday night I went to bed early with a box of crackers, a jar of peanut butter—one of the six I brought back from the States—a history of Spain—I'm still trying to figure out the Carlist Wars—and my notebook. It was chilly in the flat; I'd put on a flannel nightgown and Bernard's old cardigan. I was feeling quite cozy propped up on pillows, sprinkled with cracker crumbs, and a jar of *Skippy* on the nightstand when I heard the front door open.

"'I got away early,' Bernard calls out. And the next thing I know he's standing at the foot of the bed. I licked the peanut butter off my teeth and shoved the cracker box under the sheet, but not before Bernard had assessed the situation. He didn't speak but I could read his expression. I think he would have preferred to find me in bed with another man rather than in my sorry condition."

Making fun of herself was part of Peggy's charm.

"I don't like to indulge in stereotypes," she said. "But I married a man who embodies everything Swiss—punctual, thorough, neat and moderate. Sometimes he drives me nuts! But you married a Spaniard," she said. "Your husband must be, I don't know, livelier."

"Never a dull moment," I said and changed the subject. I could have told her about the episode with Alberto the previous night but, unlike Peggy's lighthearted anecdote, there was no humor in what had happened in my house, only a growing disquiet.

⁂

Alberto and I never went to bed at the same time. By 11 p.m. I was ready to call it a day but my husband stayed up late pacing the floor, alternating a glass of brandy or a cigarette in one hand and holding a book in the other. Lately, the book was the one he had written about the capture of underground water. He planned a second.

That previous evening, I had sat working on a piece of embroidery until I couldn't keep my eyes open.

"I'll check on the girls," I said. "Then I'm going to bed."

"*Buenas noches*," he said without looking up.

I fell asleep immediately and when I woke again, I didn't know why. The alarm clock on the bedside table said 2:30 a.m. Alberto wasn't in bed and something in the air made me cough. Without bothering to turn on the light, I opened the bedroom door to find Alberto slapping at the armchair. Puffs of smoke rose around him and the room smelled like burning horsehair, or whatever that old chair had as stuffing.

"I dropped my cigarette," he said.

I looked at the chair; I didn't believe him.

"You fell asleep," I said.

He didn't answer. Opening the balcony door, he dragged the chair outside.

If Alberto had simply dropped a cigarette, he would have picked it up immediately leaving only a scorched mark, but the hole burned in the chair cushion was the size of a soup bowl. His brandy glass lay on the floor. And our daughters were asleep in the next room.

⁂

Peggy had found the humor in her domestic misadventure. I could not find any in mine.

# Chapter 20

I wished I had seen Alberto drunk, at least in a way I could recognize. I might have known what to expect. But my husband never staggered or slurred his speech, which were the only behaviors I associated with drunkenness. And he never lost his self-control. He remained deliberate and articulate no matter what he drank. As a result, I didn't see danger in the brandy. The signs along the way that suggested caution appeared only in the rearview mirror.

Shortly after we were married my father-in-law told me that he thought Alberto drank too much. I disagreed. I saw no indication. Besides, how much was too much for teetotalers? However, one evening when we still lived in the furnished apartment, before Ana was born, Alberto raised the question himself.

We'd spread the plans for our new flat on the coffee table and, as we waited for the after dinner coffee to filter, Alberto opened the sideboard and reached for the bottle of *Osborne 103*. I was used to that, but surprised by what he said next.

"Do you think I drink too much?"

*One question too many*, a friend would comment to me later. That, too, was hindsight.

"No," I said. "You're never intoxicated, but I think I'd rather see you go out on a Friday night with some guys from the office and get kinda silly instead of sipping away on a daily basis."

"Well, you'll never see *that!*" he said.

I never did. The insidious poison festered beneath the surface and worked its mischief out of sight.

# Chapter 21

Urged by a desert breeze, the Palo Verde tree scattered its petals across my parents' patio like yellow confetti. Alicia sat on the floor stroking Snipper, a neighbor's dog who shortly after meeting my daughters had installed himself as part-time resident and self-appointed defender of little girls. This surprised us because Snipper's real home was three miles away. Nevertheless, he cut across the desert to have breakfast with us every morning and didn't return to his own home until supper. Once, when I pretended to chase Alicia, Snipper had growled at me, but I didn't take it personally.

I lay on a chaise absorbing the atmosphere. Ana and my father sat at a wooden picnic table engrossed in a craft project. Earlier in the week they had molded a snail with white plaster.

"Sure," my father said now. "It's *your* snail. You can paint stripes on it if you want. Just don't get paint on your dress."

"Will it be dry by the time we go home, Granpa?"

"By the time you go home? Yes, I believe so," he said, but his tone had changed.

I didn't want to think about it, either.

*

Two years earlier, my parents had retired to Arizona.

"No more Pennsylvania winters for us," my mother said. "No more boots and no more shovels."

They bought three acres of desert near a town called Carefree and built a house. Here, on a three-week visit to the States, the girls and I were seeing the Wild West for the first time—the endless variety of cacti (some with Spanish-sounding names), roads that sent up a cloud of dust every time a vehicle passed, and a glimpse now and then of an elusive roadrunner. Doves cooed in the morning and coyotes yip-yapped at night—a bark I first mistook for dogs. My father's warning about rattlesnakes only added to the excitement of this place, in every way so different from Madrid.

The sky that day seemed bluer than normal and the air smelled of plants I couldn't define except for a hint of orange blossom. I felt at ease, released into a world inhabited only by my parents and my daughters. And the dog. Alicia's chronic cough had disappeared and Ana had stopped apologizing for actions that didn't require an apology. *I'm sorry! I'm sorry!* She would say when she couldn't remember a word in English or if she dropped a pencil, or some other trivial matter. And her face would go red. But not that day. That day God was in his heaven, as the poet wrote, and all was right with the world—until the mailman came.

"I'm going for the mail," my mother called from the arcadia door. "Anyone want to come with me?"

"I do, Nana. I do," Ana looked up from her half-painted snail.

"Not before you clean your brush," my father said.

"I want," Alicia said. As soon as she rose and took a few steps, the dog did, too.

"You girls go," my father said. "I need a break from snail painting, and some iced tea. But don't forget to close the gate."

I just waved and called out from my chaise, "*Cuidado con los rattlesnakes!*"

For city girls aged four and seven, the trek for mail spelled adventure. It meant walking half way around the circular driveway, then down to the gate at the edge of the property—the kind of swinging gate cowboys leaned against in the movies. My father had fenced his tract to keep out the roaming, open-range cattle. From the gate, you walked several yards, turned left at the ocotillo and followed a rough track cut by the tires of a pick-up truck to an unpaved two-lane road where the mailbox stood in the afternoon shade of a 200-year-old saguaro. An S-shaped sidewinder might slither across the road. Invariably, a family of quail scurried out of your way. For sure, you didn't see another human.

"You got a letter, mama!" Ana waved an airmail envelope and ran across the patio.

"Really?"

I hadn't expected any mail, but I recognized Diane's handwriting and wondered what she had to say that couldn't wait till we returned in another week. I read the first three lines and stood up.

"Go play with your sister," I said to Ana and walked toward the house. I didn't want the girls to see me cry.

I'd always known that Diane and Ed would eventually leave Spain. That was the nature of ex-pat life. But knowing didn't mean I was prepared. I thought we'd have another year together. Instead, I had to be grateful for two weeks, the time between our return to Madrid and Diane's departure. I leaned against the kitchen sink weeping.

"I know you're disappointed," my mother said as she handed me a Kleenex.

My parents had met Diane and Ed when they visited.

"You have other nice friends and you'll stay in touch."

"Yes, but it won't be the same."

Diane and I had never exchanged what Alberto called *los secretos de la alcoba.* I kept my marital misgivings to myself. What could she have done with the information anyway? But we had shared so many other things, both big and small, and I didn't want to imagine life without the friend who had become so much a part of it.

I remembered the day Diane's only child, Heather, and my Alicia went to pre-school for the first time. Diane choked back sobs as she took their pictures by our front door and kept repeating, "They look so little. They look so little." And then, "Oh, no! Here's the school van."

I tried to reassure her.

"They'll be fine. It's a lovely, little school."

I had already gone through the *first day of school* drama with Ana three years earlier. I knew how it felt to send one's child into the world for the first time. But little Heather wouldn't be an only child much longer. Her brother was born in the spring. We named him Ian. I say *we* because Diane and Ed asked Alberto and me to be their son's godparents.

Ed and I were both practicing Catholics; Alberto didn't practice anything and Diane attended non-denominational services under the direction of an American pastor. Religions other than Roman Catholic were tolerated in Spain but few had their own premises. As a result, Diane went to church in a hotel room rented for that purpose and where, under the Franco regime, the congregation could not exceed twenty-five.

Ed had become friends with a Jesuit priest, a charming man in charge of an American university program in Madrid. The priest agreed to baptize the baby. So did Diane's pastor. On a sunny April morning we stood in a neighborhood chapel as two clerics took turns praying over the baby in what Ed later called Spain's first ecumenical baptism. We held lighted candles and vowed to set a good example for the child. Then, continuing in the ecumenical spirit, we all returned to the Lyons' flat for lunch: the Americans, the Spaniard, the Jesuit, the pastor and the pastor's wife.

⁂

I remembered our first Thanksgiving dinner together and how we laughed the next day when Diane said "I wonder what Pedro the *portero* thought when he saw *la señora de Benítez* all decked out in her long evening skirt toting a turkey across the lobby."

"After that second martini," I said, "I didn't much care what he thought."

Our dinner had been a combined effort. Diane and Ed had a roomy flat but a smallish oven, too small for the holiday turkey. Alberto and I had the reverse.

"I'll make the side dishes if you can bake the turkey," Diane had said.

That was fine with me. Aurora, under my supervision and with Diane's recipe for stuffing, roasted the bird.

The turkey had entered the final baking stage when Alberto and I went to the Lyon's Den (our name for Diane and Ed's flat) for a pre-dinner drink. An hour later Aurora called to say the turkey had reached the proper temperature. I excused myself from the cocktail-sipping guests, among them an American priest and a Spanish antiques dealer and went to retrieve the main course.

*"Fiesta Americana,"* was all I said when I passed Pedro the *portero* and tried to look dignified while keeping the turkey centered on the platter.

But there would be no more Thanksgivings like that. No more *Fiestas Americanas.* I dabbed my eyes.

Mother opened the fridge. "Iced tea?"

I wadded the Kleenex and threw it in the container under the sink.

"I don't even want to go back!"

Mother turned toward me.

"What did you say?"

"Nothing. Never mind."

I didn't mean to say that. And if I said it, I couldn't mean it. The feeling of homelessness had lasted only a moment.

A week later the girls and I returned to Madrid.

⁂

We had been home less than a week when Alberto's parents came for the customary Thursday evening tea. Aurora always had Thursdays off so I set the table and put out a tray of *Don* Manuel's favorite cookies. My mother-in-law, increasingly vague and forgetful, played with Ana and Alicia and their dolls. Alberto would stay late at the office until his parents were ready to leave, and come home in time to say goodbye. That was one way to avoid the inevitable father-son argument.

*Don* Manuel thanked me for *"un té esquisito."* Exquisite is how he described a table set with napkins folded in triangles and cookies arranged in a pattern. He was easy to please in that respect. I smiled and patted his hand, but his next words puzzled me. Mari-Carmen, he said, had prepared a nice tea for them when I was in the States. Mari-Carmen? Who on earth was Mari-Carmen?

For a split second I thought maybe Alberto had asked his sister to send her *muchacha* over for the afternoon. But that seemed very unlikely, and besides, her name was Pilar. Or maybe he had taken his parents to a café, but that seemed just as improbable, and I had never heard of one called Mari-Carmen.

*Don* Manuel must have read the confusion on my face because he seemed flustered for a moment. He said he assumed the woman Alberto had introduced to them was a friend of mine. After all, she had come to my house to serve their tea. I couldn't imagine what he was talking about. He went on to say she owned the pharmacy near Alberto's old apartment and all of a sudden I remembered.

Alberto had told me about the pharmacist years ago. He laughed when he said he thought she was dispensing more than medicines in her back room. The *portero* in his building had made remarks to that effect. These doormen know everything. Alberto went to her pharmacy occasionally when he wanted a shot of the vitamins he thought prevented the flu. (You pay 50 pesetas and the pharmacist gives the injection.) He made no secret of that. I thought nothing of it at the time. I never imagined he was visiting the back room for any other reason. Ana had told me that when her Papá took her out for an ice cream, they sometimes stopped to say hello to the lady at the pharmacy. It didn't occur to me that my husband was being unfaithful when he took our daughter out for ice cream.

Now I felt the shock and anger rise like a sudden fever. The pharmacist had a name and was on such friendly terms with my husband (and our daughter!) that he invited her to our house to make tea for his parents. I must have mumbled something to my father-in-law, but I can't remember what.

What was Alberto doing? What kind of woman takes a liberty like this in another woman's home? What had my husband said when he invited her?

I looked at the drawers under the bar where I kept the table linen. The idea of that woman touching MY napkins, MY silver tray, MY teapot and, even though Ana wasn't there that day, MY daughter—I wanted to throw up. I wanted to take the girls to the bathroom and wash their hands. Instead, I stayed at the table listening to *Don* Manuel tell me for the hundredth time that the anis liqueur he used to sweeten his tea was produced in Rute, the village where he was born. I was glad he had old stories to tell. I couldn't think of a thing to say.

Alberto came home in time to chat briefly with his father. I couldn't look at him. For once they avoided an argument. I took the teacups to the kitchen, not knowing what I would say to him later. But after my in-laws left and the girls were in their room, I asked him why he had never mentioned that another woman had been playing hostess while I was away.

"I didn't think you would mind," he said.

"Well, I do."

"OK, I won't do it again."

There was no hint of regret or contrition in his voice and no explanation. He reacted as though I had asked him not to leave his socks in the middle of the living room. Did I want to scream at him? Yes! And I think he would have liked that. In the peculiar way he had of turning the tables, he could then accuse me of hysterics.

*Where can I take this fire? The rage burning behind my breastbone leaves me breathless. I try to spit it out. I want to burn him, but the flames fizzle. My anger doesn't reach him. Cold in the face of it, Alberto doesn't flinch.*

# Chapter 22

We made most of our decisions at the dining room table—usually between two and five p.m. Under the eyes of an American flamingo—the framed Audubon print that hung on a wall I'd painted the color of cooked shrimp—we discussed everything from career moves to household minutia. The drawn-out Spanish lunch hour allowed for lengthy conversation. With businesses closed for three or four hours, the children in school or napping and a home devoid of television, we had nothing else to do but talk.

"I think I'll buy a gun," my husband said *a propos* of nothing.

"Whatever for?" We didn't hunt and we didn't need a gun for self-protection.

"Target practice," he said. "We could take it on picnics in the country."

It seemed a good idea. Marksmanship was an activity we could pursue together. Alberto and I enjoyed being out of doors. We just didn't like to do much while we were out there. We tended toward sedentary picnics and gentle walks through castle ruins. After an *al fresco* lunch of *tortilla de patata*, grilled chops and a bottle of wine, the only exertion that appealed to us was a stroll through the nearest village in search of a café and a strong espresso. Firing a gun, however, didn't sound strenuous.

To be fair, Alberto played tennis, but he failed in his attempts to recruit me as a partner. I have never felt inclined to serve, strike, heave, hurl, toss, throw, pitch, pass or bat a ball of any kind. I'm a nonviolent soul; I don't want to hit anything. And a speeding sphere swirling in my direction scares me. The only thing I want to do when faced with an on-coming ball is duck. I have no competitive spirit, and I don't like to sweat.

This general aversion towards sports, however, does not include swimming—a tranquil motion, at least in my case, that does not require a team or a partner—an activity that does not leave you hot and sticky. You can slip into a pool, swim several laps and emerge feeling cool and refreshed. Or just roll over and float. But my husband and I no longer went to the pool together because Alberto couldn't swim. He did try. He tossed his well-developed sense of dignity to the wind, equipped himself with goggles and inflated armbands, and flailed around the shallow end of the pool with our four-year old daughter and a toddler from the fifth floor. He was much better at tennis. Given our athletic proclivities, the gun seemed a good idea. I would later change my mind about the wisdom of Alberto's owning a firearm—though no one ever came to harm—but the Saturday he bought a Remington, I had no cause for misgivings.

The sporting goods store on *Serrano* had been outfitting serious hunting and fishing enthusiasts for generations. Inside, aside from the racks of rifles and shotguns and fishing rods, the walls displayed an assortment of antlers and shelves of trophies. Interspersed among them hung several photographs of Franco. The photographs didn't surprise me; the *Generalíssimo's* penchant for outdoor life was well documented.

Franco often posed for the press (which he controlled) while fishing in his native Galicia or hunting big game in the Spanish Pyrenees. Pictures I'd seen in the glossy magazines I read at the beauty shop frequently showed him after a shooting party. Attired in a green hunting jacket with a leather recoil patch at the shoulder and a felt hat with a feather, he smiled with his fellow hunters, members of his cabinet and the aristocracy, amid knee-high piles of quail and partridges. From the size of the mounds I think the fowl had been easy prey. In other photos, Franco wore a military uniform and posed beneath a banner that read *Treinta Años de Paz!* Thirty Years of Peace. (Tell that to the quail.) You couldn't go anywhere in Spain without seeing Franco's face. Throughout the country in hotel lobbies and city halls, his image stared from the walls. If you toured a museum, a sign under his portrait at the entrance said Franco had added the new wing. If you attended Mass at a cathedral, the label below his picture in the vestibule declared he had refurbished the cloister. Beneath his photograph on a castle wall, the words chiseled into the stone proclaimed the *Generalíssimo* had rebuilt the drawbridge. Franco's features were carved into the limestone at the entrance to mountain tunnels, and on the side of bridges, his bronze profile gazed into the future. Currency and postage stamps, too, bore his likeness. The images, however, were misleading.

Dressed in military uniform and positioned so that his figure or profile filled the picture plane, Franco looked imposing. In reality his stature—he stood barely five feet three inches—was fodder for jokes. When he addressed the nation on radio or television his thin voice cracked like that of a nervous twelve-year old boy, and he punctuated his speech with a mechanical rise and fall of his right arm that made him look like a toy soldier.

The paradox in Franco's regime was the ease with which we bought the gun. We needed a permit, but compared to the ordeal of my driver's license, the gun permit proved unusually straightforward. I don't remember if Alberto's position in the ministry smoothed the process; it may have. Whatever the reason, it didn't take long to complete his purchase of a .22 rifle, and the following weekend we left Madrid with an overnight bag in the trunk, a picnic basket on the floor and Matilda lying across the back seat of the car. Alberto had christened his firearm Matilda. I don't know why he liked to name things, but I thought his choice was fitting, and we headed toward the province of *Guadalajara* singing an Australian bush song, *Waltzing Matilda, waltzing Matilda. I'll go a'waltzing Matilda with you.* My husband knew the most surprising things.

⁂

"You should come to *Solana* for the weekend," Maria Rosa said between bites of chicken with grapes, my sister-in-law Julina's specialty. Julina had invited us to lunch with her childhood friend, an unmarried multilingual woman who worked at a radio station in Germany. She returned to Spain for a few weeks every summer.

"*Solana?*" Alberto said. "I've never heard of the place."

"Oh, it's not a town," Maria Rosa said. "It's the name of a house in the middle of nowhere that we inherited years ago. It means *Sunny Place,*" she said, looking at me.

"My grandparents grew wheat. The farmhouse isn't exactly up-to-date but it has four bedrooms and indoor plumbing. I'd love to have you all visit."

"I'm sorry, we have other commitments," Julina said. "Perhaps next year?"

"Of course," Maria Rosa said. She turned to Alberto. "But that doesn't mean you and Diana can't come, and if you come this weekend, you can meet my brother."

I'd already heard about José-Mari, a bachelor in his fifties and a doctor with the ski patrol in the Pyrenees.

"A car on the road is such a rare event that we spend hours trying to imagine who it might have been," Maria Rosa had said.

And now the mention of a ski patrol doctor who was bound to be dashing—I was dying to go.

Alberto looked at me and raised his eyebrows.

"It sounds great," I said.

"Don't expect anything fancy," Maria Rosa said. "The house has some quirks. For example, when the only phone we have rings in the hall the lights go out." She laughed.

"I'm not complaining. It took ages to get a phone line installed in the first place, and I'm just glad to have it."

The conveniences we took for granted in the city frequently failed to reach the rural areas. Aurora had grown up in a village house with no running water. In 1968, her mother still walked to the public fountain in the village square and carried water home in buckets.

*

Shortly before noon, we parked on a gravel driveway in front of *Solana*, the only building for miles around. The flat-faced two-story rectangle, sat on a rise behind a bright-green wrought iron fence. A pair of scrub pines grew by the gate and several pots of geraniums—some more robust than others—sat by the double front door. The shutters of the upstairs windows were closed against the June sun. The front of the house overlooked a blanket of ankle-deep green shoots that spread to the horizon. In July, when the wheat turned blond and reached waist high, the nearby villagers would harvest it by hand. Maria Rosa had told us they leased the fields, which meant they could maintain the house even though they visited only twice a year.

We sat for a moment wondering if there were a bell or if we should try to open the gate ourselves, but as soon as Alberto opened the car door Maria Rosa sprang from the house.

*"Bienvenidos a Solana!* Welcome!" She said, her red espadrilles scattering the gravel.

Beside Maria Rosa, a compact man with tanned cheeks and a mass of white hair swept back from his face waved in our direction and bent to unlatch the gate. One could recognize them at once as brother and sister. José-Mari's mustache, too, was pure white but the color of his hair didn't age him. It gave him a sparkle. I imagined him on skis, bareheaded, the wind whipping through his hair as he swooped down a snowy slope to rescue some poor stranded soul. How had he remained a bachelor?

Maria-Rosa made the introductions and showed us to a large second floor bedroom. We stowed our bag and reunited in the kitchen where José-Mari was opening a bottle of wine and his sister was setting the table. Together, supplemented with the contents of my picnic basket, we concocted a lunch—a platter that held sliced tomatoes, olives, hard-boiled eggs, sardines in olive oil, white asparagus, *Serrano* ham, and links of chorizo. Half a round of *Manchego* cheese and two loaves of village bread rested in a straw basket. It wasn't until the second bottle of wine was nearly empty and the coffee grounds had cooled that Maria Rosa suggested we leave the dishes and go for a walk.

Unlike the cultivated fields in front of the house, the rough land behind it seemed a life and death struggle between some gnarled trees I couldn't identify and the outcroppings of jagged granite. We walked with no particular purpose—the best kind of walk—crossing the road at one point to follow the track beside a fallow field. Alberto, an ambling encyclopedia of engineering data, marched ahead. He stopped periodically to discourse on aquifers and wells, two subjects dear to his heart. While my husband scanned the ground for clues to subterranean water sources, I watched the sky where a hawk glided on the updrafts. Against the cloudless backdrop, a church spire rose in the distance. Did it still toll the *Angelus?* Did the villagers pause at noon for an *Ave Maria*? I stopped when Maria Rosa stooped to pull a few leaves from an inconspicuous plant and crush them between her palms.

"Smell!" she said, waving a warm hand in front of my face. "*Es el olor de una tierra seca.* This is the smell of a dry land."

I inhaled the peppery aroma and wondered what healing properties lay in the crushed leaves. In this landscape that looked the way it must have looked centuries earlier, I imagined a local healer finding cures in its plants. At the end of the month, Maria Rosa would return to Germany, but I knew from something in her voice that this *tierra seca* would call her back as long as she had breath. Her roots ran deep. Often, at times like this, I felt my own shallow shoots stretch for a tighter grasp. I thought of the quote by Cesare Pavese, "*We do not remember days. We remember moments.*"

⁂

Jose-Mari took the lead on our return to the house—a particularly rocky trail. When he paused for us to catch up, he pointed to the abandoned granite quarry, a gouge in the earth, the size of a small chapel.

"There's been no activity here for years," he said.

No activity? And yet, just as the crushed leaves in the field a few minutes earlier, the abandoned quarry evoked life—not my life, but one that spoke to me in spite of all our differences. I stood motionless in the quarry and felt the blast of dynamite and the earth's responding shudder. I tasted grit on my lips. I heard the workers' shouts and the clank of chains as donkeys strained to move the rock. I wondered what had caused the activity to cease, but before I could ask, Alberto pointed to the stone wall several yards away.

"This would make an ideal shooting gallery," he said.

Jose-Mari nodded. "We can use empty bottles for targets."

⁂

The following morning, we amassed the *cascos*—ours plus every other empty bottle we could scavenge from the trash barrel. We made our way to the quarry shooting gallery with two bulging shopping bags. As though someone had known we were coming, a knee-high block of stone rested on a level stretch of ground, a perfect rifle support when we sat behind it. Jose-Mari placed the bottles at intervals along the far wall. Our targets glistened in the sunlight. The greens had once held wine, the amber Alberto's brandy. The clear bottles labeled *Solares* still dripped with mineral water.

"Ladies first," Jose-Mari said.

Alberto motioned to Maria Rosa but she shook her head.

"Then it's up to you, *Cazadora,*" my husband said, calling me *Huntress* as he sometimes did after the Greek goddess, *Diana the Huntress.*

I sighted along Matilda's barrel and took aim at the defenseless dregs of a full-bodied red. I held my breath the way Alberto had instructed and slowly squeezed the trigger. A crack echoed off the stones. I tried again, and again. Finally, the crack was accompanied by the satisfying sound of shattered glass and a burst of green shards. My father would have been proud.

⁂

We returned to Madrid invigorated by country air and stimulating hosts, and grateful that, thanks to Aurora, we had enjoyed a weekend of shooting without the children. Aurora had given up her Sunday afternoon off so Alberto and I could get away, but I wouldn't expect her to do that again, especially now that she had a serious boyfriend.

"We'll just leave the gun at home when we take the girls for picnics," I said.

Alberto nodded.

⁂

Two weeks later we had planned a Sunday in the country with our new British friends, Jan, whom I met at the AWC, and her husband John.

Ana and Alicia were dressed and ready, the packed picnic basket stood by the door, but I couldn't get Alberto out of bed. We had discussed many times before that if we didn't leave before noon, the roads would get so congested that it took hours just to go a few miles.

"We are not the *only* people in Madrid who think Sunday in the country is a good idea," I said.

When our friends arrived, he still wasn't up.

"You go ahead," he said. "I'll catch up with you later at the usual place."

I'd heard those words before. By now I knew I couldn't change his mind. I apologized every which way as the girls and I crawled in the back seat of John's car. They must have wondered about such an unusual arrangement.

"No problem, love," John said with a smile.

We drove to a familiar spot near the *Escorial.* Jan had brought what she called her bag of tricks—a kind of duffle filled with scarves and feather boas and hats and gloves, leftovers from her days as a teacher and perhaps playthings in readiness for her own child due in a few months. Ana and Alicia played dress-up. John arranged a circle of stones for a fire. We waited for over an hour but when hunger finally overtook us, we grilled the chorizos and ate lunch. It was after 3:00 p.m. when Alberto showed up.

He sauntered down the path—not the least self-conscious or apologetic—balancing the damn rifle in the crook of his elbow. He didn't point the gun, and I believed it wasn't loaded, but when Ana shouted "Papá" and started to run toward him, I grabbed her shoulder.

"Slow down!" I said, stepping in front of her. The rush of anger I felt toward Alberto made my hands shake. *We had agreed not to bring the gun where there were children.* I could smell the gin when he reached to pat Ana on the head.

"Why did you bring it? We weren't going to shoot today, remember?"

"Oh, but I knew John would enjoy playing with Matilda," he said. "Right, John?"

John had been scraping charred bits off the grill. "Maybe later, Alberto," he said.

"We saved some lunch for you," Jan said. "Let me fix you a plate." But our lighthearted picnic had changed to one charged with tension, and I knew everyone except Alberto and four-year old Alicia felt it. John suggested they leave the shooting for another day, but Alberto insisted on setting out paper plates for targets. I took the girls to the far side of our parked cars to play. Of course, the men didn't fire in our direction, but I shuddered every time I heard a shot.

I could have caused a scene. It would only have magnified the situation. Alberto had a knack for twisting my words and, worse yet, involving my daughters.

*Don't shoot today, Alberto, the girls are here.*

*Ana, isn't Mamá silly? She thinks I'm going to shoot you. You know I would never do that, don't you?*

I kept quiet.

# Chapter 23

Diane had left Madrid. I used to smile when I looked from my bedroom window and saw Diane reading or watering the plants on her balcony. All that remained now were a few empty flower pots. In Julina I had found a loving sister-in-law, and I enjoyed a special closeness with my Spanish friend, Paloma, but they were part of Alberto's family or a group of his old friends. Everyone I knew had a previous connection with my husband—until Diane. I discovered Diane on my own. With or without Alberto, Diane would always be my friend. I met other women at the club—lovely and interesting—but due to the nomadic nature of ex-pat life, our relationships were superficial and temporary.

And then I met Jan.

Tess la Touche introduced us at the American Women's Club in late summer. I remember well because Diane left Spain a few days earlier. I couldn't have imagined that as I said goodbye to one dear friend, I was making another.

"Oh, lovely to meet you," Jan said with an accent that came from somewhere in Britain, though at the time I didn't know it was London.

Tess, who had a talent for finding out absolutely everything about absolutely everybody, may have supplied the additional information, or it could have been Jan herself, because the ebullient 5'2" woman in her mid-twenties did not fit the pattern of English Reserve. She was one of the most out-going people I had ever met—the kind who could befriend a signpost, even if the signpost spoke another language.

The day I met her, Jan was newly arrived from Iran where she had taught school for an international oil company and where she met John, a fellow countryman, who worked in the oil industry. They had been married less than a year when he transferred to Madrid. The new Mr. and Mrs. Devey, now expecting their first child, packed up their wedding gifts, several Iranian carpets and Jan's collection of copper pots, and moved to an apartment on *Avenida del Generalísimo,* not far from where I lived. John, like so many ex-pat husbands, traveled often. And Jan, like so many ex-pat wives, looked to the Club as an outlet for her energy and a source of companionship with fellow English speakers. Our friendship blossomed over eggplants.

We probably volunteered, though the details of how Jan and I formed a two-woman committee to provide centerpieces for the AWC September luncheon remain hazy. I don't remember who decided to incorporate purple eggplants—aubergines, Jan called them—into the centerpieces.

"They look rather dusty," Jan said looking into her shopping bag. We were standing on the steps of the *Chamartin* market.

"We can fix that at my house," I said, which explains why, when Aurora returned from the playground with Alicia just before lunch, she found us at the kitchen sink polishing the produce with a kitchen towel and olive oil.

"Your *muchacha* must think we're totally bonkers," Jan said.

"Not Aurora," I said. "She's been with us nearly seven years. We haven't scared her off yet." I laughed at Jan's expression, *totally bonkers.* She had already added *wellies, nappies* and *cuppa* to my vocabulary.

Later, after our husbands had met and we often played bridge or had dinner together, Alberto would quote from his inexhaustible source of memorable phrases.

"In the words of George Bernard Shaw," he said. "Britain and America are two nations divided by a common language."

⁂

The success of our eggplant centerpieces—we nestled them in baskets with bright yellow straw flowers—propelled Jan and me into another project. Before we had time to consider carefully, we were chairladies of the Christmas Decoration booth at the annual bazaar. I had the perfect partner.

In addition to her enthusiasm, Jan had a lot of stuff to work with. Byproducts from her teaching days included paints and papers and lots of patterns for—I don't know—*things*. Handicrafts she called them. Over several weeks we transformed our homes into cottage industries, creating candles and *creches* and anything Christmasy. Most of our projects involved a *whoosh* of gold from a can of spray paint. Our favorite was the Madonna and Child; we made dozens of them.

Prior to painting, the fabric-draped Styrofoam forms looked rustic—to put it kindly. But three coats of gold worked a kind of Christmas miracle. We had finished the front of the figures, allowed them to dry on my balcony and were applying the final touches when Alberto opened the balcony door.

"You're home early," I said.

He waved the air with his hand and wrinkled his nose at the paint fumes.

"What are you ladies doing?" he said.

"Spraying the Madonnas' backsides," Jan said.

"Interesting," Alberto said, and closed the door.

Jan and I giggled.

"I don't think that came out right," she said.

"It was perfect!"

Later we would boast that the Devey/Benitez Christmas Decorations booth had been a complete sell-out.

⁂

Alberto had always encouraged me, whether it meant taking a job or enrolling in a university course. When I expressed an interest in the Prado Museum he bought me three volumes of art history. He paid, he just didn't participate in the way I would have liked. The evening of the Ritz Hotel cocktail party was no exception.

I was proud of the cocktail party I had organized at the Ritz Hotel for the AWC members and their spouses. I had worked with the banquet manager to select the room, the hors d'oeuvres and a classical guitarist. The idea of cocktails at the prestigious Ritz Hotel was well received. Becky, the club president was impressed, and the club members were excited. We didn't do *this* everyday.

The evening of the event I had already dressed in a black jersey top and a floor-length grey skirt when Alberto came into the bedroom and said he didn't feel like going.

"What? Alberto, this is an evening meant especially for couples. And I'm kinda the hostess. I don't want to stand at the entrance and greet people by myself."

Or worse—shrink behind a potted palm while ninety couples mingle in animated conversation. I felt like a teenager without a prom date.

"But Jan and John will be there," I said, thinking he might have suddenly developed a case of shyness. "And you know Becky and her husband."

"No, you go ahead. I'm not in the mood." Alberto wouldn't change his mind.

I crossed our lobby certain that Pedro the *portero* wondered where *la señora* was going all dressed-up and alone at night.

⁂

The room at the Ritz was softly lit and the guitarist was strumming chords when I arrived. The bartenders stood ready for action. I was talking with the waiters dressed in short white jackets who would later circulate among the guests with large oval trays of assorted finger foods when I saw Jan and John. How like them to be the first to arrive to show support and to offer help if needed.

"Lovely room!" Jan said as she kissed me on both cheeks.

"Where's the *marido?*" John said, looking over my shoulder.

"Oh, Alberto has the flu."

"No!" they said in unison. I wondered if they remembered the day of the picnic when Alberto arrived late with the gun.

*He has the flu.* That seemed the most credible explanation, but I cringed every time someone expressed regret that my husband couldn't be with me. I felt abandoned—dismissed. And yet, a few months later Alberto helped me with another club project in a way I could not have imagined.

⁂

I felt flattered when the new club president asked me to chair the bazaar, a fundraiser for Spanish charities. The bazaar had outgrown the club's basement, its location in years past, and had moved to the neighborhood school hall. Now, given the increasing success of the event, that venue seemed likely to be too small as well.

"You need the *Palacio de Congresos,*" Alberto said one evening after he heard me discussing the situation on the phone with Jan.

"I don't think we're *that* ambitious," I said. The *Palacio de Congresos* was a recently inaugurated state-of-the-art conference facility with façade decorations by the Catalan artist Miró. I didn't think a group of American women wanting to sell arts and crafts and homemade cookies had a chance of securing the *Palacio* no matter how laudable their intentions. And I felt certain we couldn't afford it.

"*Mira, Diana,* you already have no for an answer," Alberto said, using one of his favorite phrases. "If you contact the director of the *Palacio* and state your case, you might get a yes." I couldn't argue with his logic.

Alberto helped me craft a letter. I don't know what broke the ice, addressing the letter to *Estimado Directór,* or the gentle reminder that he had once been a classmate of my husband's. At any rate, esteemed director suggested we meet. I went to the appointment wearing a navy suit, the diamond brooch my in-laws had given me, pumps with a matching bag and leather gloves. Along with encouragement, Alberto had also given me the impression that the director's position was just a notch below the Pope's. When I reached the gentleman's office, I didn't know if I should say *Buenas Tardes* or genuflect.

Also wearing a navy suit, the director bowed his patrician head over my hand (a gentleman never actually kissed a lady's hand), pulled a chair for me in front of his desk and asked how he could be of service. I was aware, not for the first time, of the courtliness of Spanish men, at least the ones I met, well-educated with lovely manners. It was not only the bow; it was the way they looked at women. Maybe that was it—they looked, and I always sensed a flirt behind their formal exterior. The gentleman in front of me leaned forward waiting for me to speak as though he had nothing else in the world to do.

I extolled the fund-raising goals of the AWC and wondered if he had a space appropriate for such an activity. He did. And would it be available for the dates we planned? It would. And, here I paused looking for just the right word, could we arrive at a reasonable rental fee?

"*Claro, señora,*" he said. "*No se preocupe.*" Of course, madam. Don't worry. It would be an honor to provide the space free of charge. Free of charge! I'd just won the lottery!

⁂

"Well?" my husband said when I met him after work that evening at the little restaurant next to his office.

"You were right," I said. "We got the *Palacio.* Gratis!"

Alberto pulled a pack of Kents from his jacket pocket, flipped open the top and tapped up a few cigarettes. I took one. He reached into his other pocket, removed his lighter and lit my cigarette, then lit his own. He moved slowly and deliberately as though deciding how to respond. Then with just the suggestion of a smile he said, "Of course." But I knew he was more pleased than his brief acknowledgement indicated.

"Now I just have to figure out how I am going to stock this illustrious hall, and with what."

"Sorry," he said. "I can't help you there."

"I know," I said. "I need committees."

⁂

What a paradox! I had joined a club that I thought held no interest for me and here I was forming committees after vowing never to even serve on one. I loved it.

Now groups of ladies around Madrid prepared for the annual AWC bazaar. They made table decorations, poured candles, knit baby clothes, planned a bake sale, stitched aprons, and requested from relatives in the States any article that could be sold with a *Made in USA* label, including paper napkins. Jan assumed the responsibility for advertising the bazaar. I don't know how she managed it with a baby at home and another on the way, though her parents came from London to help.

The night before the bazaar I sat at the dinner table talking with Alberto, telling him how I had spent the afternoon setting up the exhibition hall. The phone rang a couple of times with a last minute question or two, but I felt confident that everything was calm and organized. I just prayed for customers. I should have prayed to the patron saint of migraines instead. I rubbed my neck wishing off the warning signs, but I felt worse by the minute. I couldn't afford to be ill. I took two *Optalidón* and crawled into bed.

Migraine sufferers will understand; I thought I was going to die. But I couldn't stop vomiting long enough to die. The knives in my head grazed my eyeballs. A fire burned across my shoulders; at the same time, I was freezing. I spent most of the night on the bathroom floor.

The bazaar doors opened at ten the next morning. I was still in bed. The phone rang in the bedroom. I couldn't talk. I managed a few words to Jan, but I told Aurora to tell anyone else who called that I was ill. I would try to go later. Finally, at four o'clock Alberto, who didn't work on Saturdays, drove me to the *Palacio.* I looked a wreck and felt worse—embarrassed that I hadn't been there from the beginning.

There were a few people milling about. I knew Jan wouldn't be there in the afternoon. Her parents had returned to London and she had a babysitter only for the mornings. The tables and booths were nearly bare. I didn't know what to think. Had everyone packed up and gone home early? Then several ladies gathered around me and one of them, the club treasurer, said we had made over $6,000. No bazaar had ever come close to that.

I introduced Alberto to the ladies, who told him how sorry they were I had missed the event after putting so much work into it. He looked proud and nodded. Becky, the club president, said she thought obtaining the *Palacio* had contributed to our success.

"Well," I said, "we had a little help with that." I tapped my husband on the arm.

"You're lucky, Diane, to have such a good helper," Becky said. "Sometimes I wish I had a Spanish husband."

*Be careful what you wish for, Becky.*

# Chapter 24

21 de Noviembre 1974. *VIVO EN LA HISTORIA*

The entire front page of the newspaper showed a photograph of Franco dressed in military uniform lying in an open casket. The banner in heavy caps read *Living on in History*.

The death of 82-year-old Francisco Franco Bahamonde surprised no one. He had suffered from Parkinson's disease for years and had not been seen in public since October, when he appeared particularly frail. On several occasions Prince Juan Carlos, designated as heir-apparent by Franco in 1969, acted as head of state due to Franco's declining health. For nearly 40 years, *El Generalísimo* had controlled the country, but now Spain went from a dictator on Wednesday to a King on Friday in a process Franco himself had orchestrated. He had always declared himself a monarchist and promised to restore the monarchy when the time came—that is, after his death. In the meantime, Franco had overseen the education of the young Prince, believing he had created a figure to follow in his own authoritarian footsteps. He could not have foreseen how the now *King* Juan Carlos would gradually and peacefully transition the country to a liberal constitutional monarchy far different from the war years of Alberto's childhood and the years of political reprisals that followed. Even in the years of my marriage under Franco's repressive regime, a mother could not travel with her children unless she had permission from her husband.

⁂

Alberto stood in front of the television, barefooted and half dressed. He had pulled on his trousers but apparently gave up after that. Instead of a shirt he wore his pajama top. It was shortly before 9 a.m. Carlos Arias Navarro, the prime minister, had just communicated the news of Franco's death. He eulogized *El Generalísimo's* lifelong dedication to the country and then, fighting tears and trying to control his voice, he pulled a sheet of paper from his breast pocket.

"I will now read Franco's last testament to the country," he said.

We learned later that Franco had written it after his first heart attack. In it he begged forgiveness from anyone he may have harmed. His only enemies, he wrote, were the enemies of Spain, and he cautioned the country to be wary of them. He loved his country and his God, he wrote, and was proud to have lived and died a Catholic.

Alberto's hands shook as he raised a coffee cup to his lips. I felt no particular emotion, only a curiosity as to what would happen next. Uncharacteristically, Alberto seemed affected. The black and white image on our 19-inch TV changed to one of the Spanish flag undulating to the sound of a funeral dirge.

"Come on, girls," I said.

"Where are you going?" Alberto said.

"To meet the school bus."

"Today of all days there won't be school."

"Well, if the bus comes, I'm putting them on it, and if it doesn't come … well, then no school."

The bus arrived at the usual time, I put the girls on it and headed to the market. Some of the stalls were closed, some had condolences taped to the wall and some went about business as usual, though somewhat subdued. When I came home again an hour later, Pedro the *portero* told me the school bus had returned the girls and he had just taken them upstairs. By then I'd had time to digest the news, and I knew what I wanted to do.

Aurora was the *business-as-usual* sort. She was peeling potatoes for a *tortilla* when I came in. Ana, on the contrary, ran toward me flushed and out of breath.

"Papá's crying!" she said. "Papá says our leader is *dead!*"

I entered the living room to find Alberto with a handkerchief in one hand and a beer in the other. I knew my husband appreciated Franco's commitment to improving the country's infrastructure, but his emotional reaction to the news of the *Generalísimo's* death surprised me. Since when had he become such a devoted Francoist? And why was he telling a child that her leader was dead? Surely there was another way to explain the news that day. I suggested he go to the office. I felt certain some of his colleagues would be there, if not to work, at least to commiserate. I just wanted him and his drama out of the house. Before he left, I told Alberto what I wanted to do.

I wasn't afraid of another civil war breaking out, although now surely the anti-Franco voices would sound loud and clear. There wasn't an opposing army waiting to take over. But there were factions capable of causing disruption. Two years earlier, Prime Minister Carrero Blanco had been assassinated by the explosion of a bomb placed in a tunnel under the street where he passed every morning on his way to Mass. *Euskadi Ta Askatasuna,* the Basque separatist group commonly referred to as ETA, was to blame. Recently, a jewelry store in my neighborhood had been robbed. Once again, the separatists were blamed. Robberies were a means to collect funds for their activities, it was said, and bank robberies were increasing. I thought leaving the capital for a couple of days might be a good idea. I didn't want to get caught in a crossfire or some kind of protest.

"I'd like to take the girls to Gredos," I said. "There is sure to be snow in the mountains. They would like that. We can stay in the *parador.* Just for a couple of days. In case there is any trouble here."

Alberto didn't object.

After lunch I asked Aurora to pack the leftover *tortilla* and some fruit—in case the girls got hungry on the road—bundled the bare essentials in the car and drove north for nearly three hours. The *parador,* surrounded by pine forests, had once been a hunting lodge for Alfonso XIII. Since 1928 the building had served as a hotel.

⁂

At the base of the mountains, enough snow had fallen that the girls flopped on their backs, waved their arms and made snow angels. When they tired of that, they collected pine cones and stored them in the trunk of the car. By the time the dining room opened for dinner, we were starving. Aside from a table of six occupied by what appeared to be hunters or hikers, we were the only diners. The waiters made a fuss over my daughters. Once Ana and Alicia had finished their dessert of *helado de chocolate*, the server suggested he bring my coffee to the lounge where we could sit in front of the fireplace. I could not have felt any farther from the death of Franco if I had been on the moon.

We slept with the window ajar. A crisp mountain air filled the room, overlaid with the scent of the hotel's bath gel. Alberto always insisted on a hermetically sealed sleeping chamber. I had not had such a peaceful night in months. Though I knew some of the history of the *Parador de Gredos*, I could never have dreamed of its future—that exactly three years later, in 1978, in this very place, King Juan Carlos and his ministers would meet to finalize the Spanish constitution.

⁂

There were no major disturbances in Madrid. We drove home a day later. The political transition suffered its trials, but for the most part, the restored monarchy brought a continuation of peace and stability for the country. Unfortunately, the peace and stability did not extend to my home.

# Chapter 25

Ana had wedged herself between the bride and groom at the head table, wailing as though her seven-year-old life was falling apart. She had no right to be there disrupting Aurora's wedding banquet, but Aurora thought that allowing Ana to sit with her would have a calming effect. It hadn't. I was angry and embarrassed. Furthermore, if anyone's life was falling apart, it was mine but, unlike my daughter, I couldn't let it show.

⁂

Aurora had known Paco, a kind, responsible young man, for over four years. We knew they planned to marry. In that sense I was happy for her when she set a wedding date. She deserved a full life of her own. She would make a wonderful mother, but the thought of my home without her calm, efficient presence brought back the feelings I had when Diane left. Ana was inconsolable. She liked Paco, too, and didn't object to the marriage, but she couldn't understand why Aurora had to leave.

"*Pero tú vives con nosotros!*" she said. You live with *us*.

Ana didn't feel any better when we explained that Aurora would still come to us for a few hours every day.

"I'll come every day to take you to the school bus," Aurora told her. "And before I leave in the afternoon, I'll make *croquetas* for your after school snack."

For me that was the saving grace. I didn't want another live-in *muchacha*. No one could ever take Aurora's place.

When it came to the simple wedding Aurora preferred, her mother had other ideas. Aurora's parents lived in a village of seven families in a house devoid of central heating, a refrigerator, a cook stove and indoor plumbing. The wheat they grew provided a modest income. For food they depended on a kitchen garden plus the rabbits and chickens and pigs that Aurora's mother tended. For transportation, they used a donkey. By any standards, they lived in humble circumstances, but when Aurora expressed concern at her mother's growing guest list and the expense that implied, *Señora* Sanchez put her foot down. For over twenty-five years she had saved for the *boda* of her only daughter and no one was going to take that pleasure from her.

The morning of the wedding the photographer came to our house. He posed the bride in her long white gown in front of the bookcase and took several shots of Aurora and Alberto together. Alberto, elegant in a dark navy suit, looked especially proud when Aurora took his arm. She had asked him to walk her down the aisle. Her father didn't mind inviting one hundred of his nearest friends and far-flung relatives to a four-course banquet after the wedding Mass, but he felt shy about walking down the aisle. Ana alternated between excitement and despair as Aurora turned this way and that adjusting her veil. Quiet as usual, Alicia just watched. If the photographer's eyes followed me when I went to the bedroom for my earrings, I didn't notice.

The newlyweds took a week-long honeymoon trip to the Canary Islands. Ana eventually calmed down, though she counted the days until Aurora's return. She wasn't the only one; the house felt empty.

The following Sunday we went to *Paseo del Prado* for the usual family lunch. On the way home Alberto said he wanted to work on a new project.

"I'll drop you off at home and then go to the office for a couple of hours. OK?"

"That's fine," I said. Maybe the girls and I would take a little siesta.

Our building was quiet as a tomb on Sundays. Pedro the *portero* had the afternoon off and was probably napping himself. I unlocked the door to our flat, sent the girls to change their clothes and went to my bedroom to do the same.

My first reaction was anger. The room was a mess. The drawers in the bedside tables were overturned on the bed. My slant top desk was open and ransacked.

"Girls!" I shouted. "Come here this minute."

But even as I shouted my hands grew cold and fear replaced the anger.

The expression on their faces told me the girls were innocent, and when I looked more closely at the contents of the drawers spilled on the bed, I realized we had been robbed. My jewelry was gone. I didn't have a great deal, but the diamond brooch Alberto's parents had given me, plus an 18k gold charm bracelet, some earrings and a ring were missing. Immediately I thought of the sterling silver place settings I had collected before I was married, and the sterling trays we received as wedding gifts. I was shaking when I opened the cupboard, but nothing there had been touched. I phoned Alberto who arrived a few minutes later with the police.

There was no sign of forced entry. Whoever did this must have had a key. The policeman looked at our door, formidable in appearance but, he explained, with a lock so simple it could be opened with a strip of flexible plastic. No key necessary. Alberto and the police spoke to the few neighbors who were home on a Sunday. No one had seen or heard anything except for the seven-year-old girl next door, who said she saw a man in a yellow plaid jacket on the stairs. We dismissed that immediately. Men didn't wear yellow plaid jackets. The policemen were sympathetic but said I would never see the jewelry again. They knew how the robbers operated. They would have fenced their ill-gotten goods before nightfall. As for my silver, no need to worry about that. Thieves found the trays too bulky and no one seemed interested in sterling silver place settings these days.

"You're lucky you didn't have ham," the shorter of the two policemen said.

"Ham?" I said, thinking of the slices in the fridge. *Would the robbers have stopped to make a sandwich before absconding with my brooch?*

"Some people have an entire *Serrano* ham hanging in their pantry," the taller man said. "I'd need a whole month's salary to pay for one. Your *ladrones* would have thought they'd won the *Loteria de Navidad.*"

I knew the kind of ham he meant—the air-dried delicacy from the mountains that cost a fortune. But that wasn't the kind of ham I bought to add to the girls' grilled cheese.

The policeman closed his note pad. "So if there's nothing else—"

"They took the TV," Alberto said.

Until then I hadn't even noticed the new television set was missing—probably because I hadn't grown used to it yet and wasn't accustomed to seeing it on a little bench the size of a footstool beside the dining table where it looked absolutely ridiculous. Alberto and I had fought over it.

"We don't need a second TV," I argued.

"Well, I can't see the one in the bookcase from my seat at the dining table and I want to watch the news while I eat."

He came home on Friday carrying a box. On Saturday he watched the lunch-time news and the evening broadcast on a screen not three feet from his soup never dreaming that by Sunday afternoon the TV would be gone.

This kind of crime was common, the policemen told us, and unfortunately the criminals usually got away. They hadn't counted on Alberto Manuel Benitez, who grew up reading Agatha Christie and Conan Doyle. He wasn't about to let this go.

I had a creepy feeling every time I looked at my bedside table, imagining strange hands rifling through my belongings, but I resigned myself to the loss. My husband, however, paced the floor every evening looking for clues to the puzzle until the night, long after midnight, when he burst into the bedroom where I was sleeping and snapped on the light.

"I know who did it!" he shouted. "And I know how!" He bounced from one foot to the other.

I sat up and leaned against the headboard.

"And your evidence, Sherlock..."

"Never mind evidence, this is what happened."

The robber had entered our building through the basement garage whose door was often left open. He took the service elevator from the garage directly to our floor, bypassing the lobby. He slipped his bit of plastic in our door lock and walked straight to the bedroom where he knew I kept my jewelry. He knew because he had seen me come out of the room adjusting my earrings the day of Aurora's wedding. The robber was the wedding photographer!

"You're right," I said. "And he was wearing a yellow plaid jacket! How could I have forgotten that?"

Alberto wasted no time in communicating his findings to the authorities, who hauled in the photographer—apparently a known entity in police circles—plus a few other likely suspects. With her mother's approval, I took our little neighbor to the police station to identify the culprit. I felt certain we had our man. Unfortunately, the photographer had changed his wardrobe and appeared in a black leather jacket. Without the yellow plaid item crucial to our cause, the little girl couldn't make a positive identification. Alberto had solved the case; we just couldn't prove it.

I don't remember how or when we received the photographs, but I clearly recall the day the bill came. I handed Alberto the envelope when he came home that evening.

"A *bill?*" Alberto yelled. "He thinks we're going to *pay* him?"

He opened the bar. "Bring me some ice, will you?" he said. "And a sheet of stationery."

A few minutes later Alberto showed me his reply. In essence it read, *It'll be a cold day in Hell…!*

The photographer went silent.

The morning after the robbery, I had gone to Aurora's room where I had stashed the empty TV box. Aurora wouldn't live with us again, but when she returned from her honeymoon and began to come for a few hours daily, I didn't want her to think I was using her room for trash. I planned to keep her room as she left it. That meant taking the box to the basement bin. I opened the door. The box was gone. Not satisfied with just the TV, the robber had packed it in its original container. In addition to the feelings of violation, loss and fear, I added indignation. And the notion that some petty criminal had invaded a room that still smelled faintly of Aurora's floral cologne gave me the creeps all over again.

When I opened the other door—the carved one that led to the landing—the wooden panels felt solid, but now I knew they held a dangerous flaw.

# Chapter 26

I never expected to hear voices from out of nowhere. I didn't believe in ghosts. And in spite of my religious upbringing, I didn't think God or the Saints were trying to communicate. In that regard I had suffered an early disappointment when, as an eight-year-old, I had prayed fervently to the Virgin Mary to grant me a two-wheeled bike. She hadn't answered and she didn't deliver the bike either. But that's another story. The point is, I wasn't the type to hear voices when no one was there. But I did.

I was sitting on the edge of the pool in the deserted back garden, feeling confident in my new black bikini. Two babies later and I still had a slightly boyish figure free of stretch marks. I had an hour before lunch to work on my tan. Alberto was at the office, Ana and Alicia were at school, and Aurora, who still came to us for a few hours every day, was preparing a roast with a green pepper and red vermouth sauce—an infallible recipe we had developed together that owed much of its success to a new pressure cooker.

I swirled my legs and watched twin whirlpools form in the warm June water. I hadn't been thinking of anything in particular—perhaps whether or not Alberto would bring someone home for lunch, nothing more. I was alone when I heard the voice, a woman's voice that said *This isn't right.* Instinctively I looked over my shoulder. There was no one there, but immediately I knew the meaning of the words.

⁂

From the back of my brain, the countless images of Alberto that I had never been able to erase flashed one after the other like a movie reel gone mad: Alberto being rude to our friends with never an apology; throwing his new sweater across the room because I had bought beige, a color he said only queers wore; screaming at his father on the phone and slamming down the receiver; making sexually ambiguous remarks to the young girl who sometimes babysat when Aurora was away; insisting, when I once coughed at the dinner table, that I was choking and slapping me so hard on the back that he knocked the glass from my hand; embarrassing Ana in front of strangers because of what she ate or didn't eat; yelling at her for what he considered a breach of etiquette no matter who was present (I watched her face turn red in shame); telling her she looked like a prostitute the day she played with Heather and painted her fingernails; grilling her over homework assignments until I thought she would become ill while Alicia cowered beside me on the sofa; asking our daughters if they would like a little brother then saying it was my fault they did not have one; telling Jan at the bridge table she should talk to me about having another child as Jan squirmed, ill at ease, at a loss for words. When I intervened or made light of a situation, he became more aggressive. Though he never struck us physically, I constantly played emotional dodge ball.

And I watched him drink. I remembered that when he'd asked, I'd told him I didn't think he drank excessively. But one day, when we were spending a weekend in *Cáceres* with Ramón and Milali, I counted his drinks.

The weekend had started out well enough. It was my first visit to that city, and I loved the layers of history that Alberto and Ramón uncovered for me.

In 35 BCE the Romans founded a settlement 190 miles west of Madrid calling it *Norba Caesarina.* The Visigoths arrived around 400 AD. The Moors invaded in 711 and Alfonso IX expelled them in 1229. By the time we arrived, the name had changed from *Norba Caesarina* to *Quazris* to *Cáceres,* and the city had been home at one time or another to Romans, Moors, Jews and Christians. In the stone wall that surrounded the old city center, Alberto pointed out the vestiges of those previous civilizations.

"Look," he said. "The base of the wall is clearly Roman. You can tell by the shape of the granite blocks, but the building material of the upper part is different."

"From the *Almohades*, perhaps," Ramón said, citing another civilization I would have to research.

It was early evening when we walked the cobblestoned streets and crossed the *plaza mayor* looking for a café to while away an hour or so till dinner. Cobblestones and *plazas* are not unique to *Cáceres,* nor are walls that shelter Gothic and Renaissance architecture. These same features—in varying degrees—form the foundation of countless towns across the Iberian Peninsula. What distinguished *Cáceres* was the noise.

Every tower and turret and belfry and spire held a stork's nest—sometimes as many as four—and the racket of their clacking beaks nearly drowned the church bell tolling the hours. *Tak-a-tak-a-tak-a-tak-a-tak* they declared, arching their long necks backward as though about to execute a reverse somersault. The sound, like a stick scraped along a picket fence, ricocheted around the plaza.

Alberto called the birds Master Builders.

"I don't know how they do it," he said. "Their nests of twigs appear vulnerable, as though they might fall at any minute. And yet they resist wind and storm. Amazing!"

"I know," Ramón said. "Once I saw a nest on top of a weather vane. *Increible!"*

Warmth from the noontime sun lingered on the plaza. We sipped our drinks and ate almonds at a sidewalk table and watched the storks. Sometimes a pair stood side by side clacking away in stork talk—at other times a lone bird stood on one spindly leg as though undecided about his flight path.

"Do you know the story about the two storks?" Alberto said.

We shook our heads. Alberto took a sip of his gin.

"Well…," he said. "Two storks met just as the sun was going down. One asked the other if he had had a busy day. 'Indeed!' was the reply. 'I delivered one baby boy and two sets of twins. How 'bout you?' The first stork adjusted his wings and shook his head. 'Naw. All I managed was to scare the crap out of a couple of secretaries.'"

We all laughed but the joke left a bad taste and when Alberto ordered another drink, although no one else wanted one, tension inched into the evening.

For a reason I can't remember, the conversation at dinner turned to men's pajamas. My husband had remarked about the unnecessary pocket on his pajama top. Why a pocket? It must have been a female who had designed the pajamas in the first place—some woman who expected men to pay for everything to such a degree that she created a place to carry money even to bed. He ranted for several minutes against scheming women. The idea seemed ludicrous from the beginning, but he wouldn't let it go. I grew increasingly uncomfortable, afraid Ramón and Milali would think he was talking about me. I wasn't a spendthrift. Twice I had taken a job wanting to pay for the trips I took with the girls to the States. He had dismissed my efforts. What had prompted this tirade? Then Milali, who never said anything the least bit contrary, patted my hand across the table. *"Desde luego Diana, has ganado tu rincon en el cielo,"* You have truly earned your corner in heaven, she said. I felt doubly embarrassed. Not only did she find Alberto's comments ridiculous, she felt sorry for me.

Later, after we had said good night to our friends and returned to our hotel room, I reminded Alberto of his question when we were newlyweds: Did he drink too much?

"Do you realize," I said, "that you have had eleven drinks today?" I counted off the beers in the morning, the gins before lunch, the lunchtime wine, the brandies after lunch, the mid-afternoon *copita*, the pre-dinner martinis, and the wine with dinner and the brandies till bedtime.

Alberto stood perfectly still for a moment. He seemed shocked; for once at a loss for words. Was this the man I had married—this paunchy middle-aged figure with greasy-looking receding hair and rumpled slacks? He turned abruptly, reached for the newspaper on the desk and kicked off his shoes.

"Don't ever do that again," he screamed. "I'm not a child!"

Only moments earlier I had watched our friends walk toward their room holding hands, speaking softly.

⁂

We never took another trip together. Over time our evenings of bridge with the Spanish group grew less frequent. When I invited Julina and Luis for *merienda*, they often had something else on their schedule. Paloma included my girls at her daughter's birthday parties, but she no longer hosted her Mardi Gras evenings.

⁂

*This isn't right*, the peculiar voice said that day at the pool. In addition to stating the obvious, I wished the voice had offered some advice, but it didn't speak again until Christmas.

# Chapter 27

I think the purchase of the tree was symptomatic. Under normal conditions I would never have bought an artificial Christmas tree. I didn't like artificial, and the aluminum abomination standing in front of the bookcase looked more like a July Fourth firework than a fir befitting the Yuletide. The fun had gone out of the annual haggling with the gypsy tree sellers at the market, and I didn't smile any more at the thought of pushing a pine through the open back windows of the car to get it home. The look of resignation on Pedro the *portero's* face when I asked him to drag the tree across the lobby no longer amused me. And finally, I didn't want to find dried needles stuck in the parquet months after Aurora and I had hauled the skeleton to the garbage bin in the basement. None of that, however, would have mattered if all else had been well—if I'd been married to just about anybody other than Alberto Benitez, whose behavior was growing increasingly unpredictable.

⁂

For years my sister-in-law and I had alternated Christmas Eve dinner. Alberto's parents, now in their 80s, no longer went out in the evening, but Julina and I continued to prepare and enjoy our holiday tradition.

We both put up Christmas trees. In Julina's house, we had the added attraction of an elaborate Nativity tableau that Luis assembled with his collection of antique figures. The children liked to count the tiny shepherds in the scene and to locate the Three Kings with camels, and the baby Jesus on a bed of straw. His own children, Isabel, now 18, and César, 14, had outgrown the wonder of it, but they fell into the spirit when Ana and Alicia visited. Alicia, at five, was especially engaged. But eight-year-old Ana had begun to ask questions.

The Saturday before Christmas I stood at the kitchen counter mixing chocolate into Ana's milk—part of an ongoing battle to get her to drink it.

"Mamá," she said.

"Ummm?"

"Is there really a Santa Claus?"

"Well, of course," I said, hoping I sounded credible.

"I *knew* it! You'd never spend money on all those things!"

I turned away so she couldn't see my smile, but I didn't know how much longer I could maintain the magic. At that moment Alberto came into the kitchen.

"Finish your milk and get your coat," he said. "I need your help with an errand."

"What kind of errand?" Ana said between gulps of milk.

"It's a secret."

"Are we going to see the lady at the pharmacy?"

*Ah, yes. The "nice" lady pharmacist who served tea in my house. Ugh!*

"No, not today." Alberto didn't look at me. "Now hurry up."

They left the house shortly before noon looking like co-conspirators and wouldn't say where they were going. At two p.m., just when I was beginning to think they weren't coming home for lunch, I heard the front door open. I looked up from the sofa where I had been reading *The Cat in the Hat* with Alicia. Alberto looked blasé as he crossed the room with an oddly-shaped package under his arm. Ana was all giggles.

"*Es un violín,*" she said. *"Hemos comprado un violín!"*

Indeed, the package was shaped like a violin, but it was wrapped in brown butcher's paper and had a smell I recognized.

*"Feliz Navidad,"* Alberto said, and laid the ham on the coffee table—leg bone, hoof and all.

"A whole ham! Alberto, what on earth am I going to do with it?"

"I don't know. You said you liked ham. Now you've got one."

"I do. I mean, thank you. It's just … well … a bit much."

"Mamá, you don't like it?" Ana patted my arm.

*You can't tell a child her father's grandiose gift bordered on thoughtlessness. I didn't imagine we would be robbed a second time, but I wondered if he remembered the policemen's story about ham thiefs?*

"*Sí, mucho,*" I said. That was true.

Although I loved barnacles and baby eels the first moment, I tasted them, I had needed time to develop an appreciation for *jamón Serrano.* In butcher shops, cafes and country restaurants, the hams hung from the rafters. In the *Puerta del Sol* in a shop call *El Museo del Jamón*, the Ham Museum, at least a hundred hams hung like stalactites from the ceiling. By now I relished the dry salty taste and served it as an appetizer with a drink or sautéed with vegetables. I had become an enthusiastic convert, but I never bought more than a hundred grams at a time—the ham was extremely expensive; an entire one was out of the question. Besides, I didn't have a rafter from which to hang it. I did the only thing I could with Alberto's gift. I pulled a pillow case over it and hung it from the faucet on the balcony. And that's where it dangled on Christmas Eve.

*

The year of the artificial tree was my turn to host Christmas Eve dinner. In spite of my feelings about the stupid tree and my life in general at that moment, I looked forward to spending the evening with Julina and Luis and the children. I planned a menu of crab meat and shrimp cocktail piled in special glass cups nestled in ice, ham loaf (from my mother's recipe), creamed new potatoes with peas and for dessert, pear halves stuffed with pureed raspberries and flamed with vodka.

Ana helped with the preparations by folding napkins, Alicia filled nut bowls and Alberto sliced ham for *hors d'oeuvres*. We couldn't all fit at the dining table so I put up the card table where I hoped César would keep Ana and Alicia entertained. Isabél would sit with the grownups. Ana and Alicia were especially excited and tried to outrun each other when they heard the doorbell. *¡Los tios! ¡Los tios!* they squealed.

I opened the door and was greeted with more squeals and kisses and smiles and hugs and a box of chocolates and a bunch of red carnations from the dearest people I knew. Alberto had already poured himself a Scotch and offered to do the same for Julina and Luis, knowing full well they didn't drink alcohol. Instead, they all accepted a *Fanta de naranja*, nibbled the nuts and strips of *Serrano* the girls passed around and laughed when I showed them the ham hanging on the balcony. I went to the kitchen periodically to be sure the ham loaf didn't burn. When I finally announced that dinner was ready, Alberto had just refreshed his drink and was in the midst of showing César a numerical puzzle. Ten minutes later I said if we didn't go to the table soon, the food would be unfit to eat. César, with a flourish, pulled out the chairs for his little cousins while the rest of us took our places at the big table. Halfway through the shrimp cocktail Alberto began to tease Isabél, now blossomed into a lovely teenager.

Our niece had her first boyfriend, a nice boy we had met and liked. A few weeks earlier we had all been to the country home of mutual friends, the boyfriend too. Now Alberto was telling her that he had observed them doing things they should not have been doing. Isabél blushed.

"Please, Uncle," she said. She looked at her parents. "We didn't do anything."

I believed her. But Alberto insisted that he had seen them in the courtyard petting and French kissing. His expressions made me cringe.

"Alberto, for heaven's sake leave the girl alone," I said. I had been there too. The only thing the *novios* had done was hold hands under the lunch table. But he would not stop his perverse insinuations. Julina and Luis tried to change the subject. That seemed to encourage him. They fell silent. Only the little girls at the card table laughed at something their cousin said. I was thankful when the time came to change the plates and I could go to the kitchen for a few moments. When I returned, Julina and Luis sat rigid and grim-faced. Isabél was wiping away tears. My nails dug into the dessert tray and I felt a prickle on the back of my neck. *Not on Christmas Eve!* The voice hissed. *Not in my house! Not with these dear people! I won't have it!*

I wondered for a moment if I had blurted the words myself. No, the others seemed not to have heard.

I served a flaming dessert of pears stuffed with raspberry puree. Everyone raved over the show, but no one wanted to linger for coffee. The long-faced people who said good-night were not the same jolly group who had come for dinner.

I put the girls in their pajamas and tucked them in bed. Would Santa come in the night? I assured them he would—I had stashed their gifts in the back of my closet planning to put them under the tree once they were asleep. Of course, Santa would come, and on January 6th the Three Kings would leave a gift for them at Julina's house where we would go to eat *roscón de Reyes,* each of us hoping to find the good luck charm hidden in the traditional holiday cake.

When I went to clear the remains of dinner, Alberto was sipping brandy in the brown armchair—the one he had nearly incinerated. I wanted to slap the glass from his hand. I wanted to slap *him* for his callous behavior.

"Why did you persist on speaking to Isabel that way?" I said. "All you did was upset her. You *know* none of that was true."

"Well then, she shouldn't have been upset," he said, and picked up the newspaper.

"Alberto!" I felt the rage again. "You can't treat—"

*"Wait,"* This time I recognized the voice. *"You'll never reach him. Just wait."*

I clamped my mouth shut and carried the tray of empty glasses to the kitchen, unaware of what Luis had said when he left us that evening. I wouldn't know for years that as the elevator door closed, he'd turned to Isabel and put his arms around her. "We'll never set foot in that house again, *hija.*"

Maybe if I had known that, I wouldn't have waited.

# Chapter 28

We watched the arrival of the New Year on television. A crowd of merrymakers gathered in *Puerta del Sol* looking with anticipation at the clock tower on the building that once housed Franco's infamous Ministry of Security, the jail where political prisoners suffered atrocities or death. It was a young crowd with no memory of the Civil War, able to look at the building without trembling. We couldn't see the details on TV, but I felt certain most of the revelers held parcels of grapes. I, too, had placed a plate of grapes on the coffee table by the sofa where I sat with Ana.

The custom of eating grapes to welcome the New Year began in the late 1800s, though I don't know why. According to tradition, if you ate one white grape each time the clock struck at midnight you would enjoy good fortune in the New Year. It sounded easy, but by grape eight or nine I always found my mouth full of the fruit of the vine and unable to swallow. I couldn't chew fast enough for the Good Luck Fairy or whoever was in charge of things. And neither could Ana.

The girls had wanted to stay up till midnight, which was fine with me, though Alicia had fallen asleep in an armchair. Alberto sat at the dining table working on his second book. He looked up when the clock began to strike.

*"Feliz Año, niñas,"* he said, raising his glass and coming across the room to kiss us on the head. "Let's hope it's better than the last one." He held Ana's gaze a moment too long.

"I think it's bedtime now," I said as I scooped up Alicia. "Come along Ana," and I led the way to the bedroom.

"But no school tomorrow, right Mamá?"

"Not until after Three Kings Day," I said, knowing that if I'd said she never had to return at all, she would feel relieved. Ana had struggled with school for over a year and now I thought the fault was mine.

I had practically insisted Ana skip second grade. She had attended *Santa Margarita,* a bi-lingual school, since she was two and a half years old, where she flew through pre-school, kindergarten and first grade. When it came time for second grade, I spoke with the teacher regarding the curriculum, which sounded very repetitive. Ana already spoke two languages and I didn't think I could bear another year of the *pollito*-chicken, *gallina*-hen song. As a result, she went directly to third grade and just as I was congratulating myself on our shared brilliance (I had skipped second grade myself), Ana slowed down. By the time she entered fourth grade her struggles had increased in spite of the extra work during vacations and Alberto's help with math. Julina said she had had the same situation with César.

"It's a matter of age," she said.

The children were simply too young. She recommended Ana either repeat the year or be moved back to be with her contemporaries. It pained me to admit this might be a good idea, and better now than later. Alberto had a fit when I suggested it. He blamed the teachers at *Santa Margarita* and sent an insulting letter to the directress requesting an appointment. That's how I ended up in the principal's office.

"Your husband isn't with you?" the directress said, motioning me to a chair and looking over my shoulder toward the door. The hand she extended felt warm against my icy fingers.

"No."

The directress arched an eyebrow. I clenched my fists in my lap.

"My husband has a business meeting this afternoon," I lied.

"Surprising," she said. "His letter expressed such strong dissatisfaction. I expected to see him."

*My husband likes to throw stones in the air but is rarely around when they fall. This isn't the first time he's sent me to pick up the pieces.*

I waited.

"Tell me about your husband," she said.

*Señorita, I don't know where to start!*

"Well," I said. "He's a civil engineer. What else would you like to know?"

"Does he get along well with your daughters?"

"He gets impatient sometimes. I suppose all fathers do." I attempted a smile.

"Hmm," the directress said, opening a manila folder that lay on the desk in front of her. She pulled out two sheets of construction paper and pushed them toward me. I thought I recognized Ana's handiwork, but I didn't see what two drawings had to do with anything.

"Yes?" I said.

"I find this work very disturbing."

*Disturbing? What on earth was she talking about?*

"Disturbing?"

"We are trained to interpret children's art," the directress said.

I focused on the sheets more closely. One sheet was marked *Papá,* the other *Mamá.* The pastel-colored, lightly-penciled mother figure wore a long strand of small beads, each one perfectly round. I wondered how long Ana had worked on those beads. How careful and patient she had been! The other drawing was different. In real life Alberto and I were almost the same height, but the father on the page appeared much taller and larger than the mother. Wide strokes from a black felt pen outlined the figure and Ana had painted the father in dark clothes. He wore a black hat. She had even underscored the word *Papá* with a slash of black pen.

The directress tapped the father. "This image is sinister."

I felt at once cold and light-headed and frightened. *Sinister!* Beyond rude and thoughtless, beyond erratic and impatient, beyond brandy and gin, beyond difficult there was sinister? And a woman I barely knew had to tell me?

What about Alicia? Dear Lord, what was *she* drawing that I didn't know about? Her bright depiction of the

Arizona desert had won a ten-dollar prize at the AWC, and she had made me a drawing she titled *Alicia in the Rain with Freckles* that I found charming. Was there more? True, she always clung to me or to Aurora whenever anyone else was around. A friend of ours called her The Little Philosopher.

"Quiet but wide-eyed," he said. "Always thinking."

"She's just shy," I'd replied.

⁂

I remember nothing else from the meeting at school; I'd gone deaf after the word *sinister.* If the directress made a recommendation, I didn't hear it. As I left her office, the only thing I knew for certain was that I dared not tell my husband about the assessment of Ana's drawings. Aside from that, I didn't know what I was going to do.

*Stall,* I heard the voice say. *Stall until you think of something.*

# Chapter 29

I had bought the paperback and slipped it into my purse before my mother could notice. I'd left her in the produce section squeezing avocados while I looked at the magazine rack in a Carefree, Arizona supermarket. The girls and I had only one day left of our visit with my parents.

"I need something to read on the plane back," I'd said, intending to buy a couple of magazines. Instead I reached for a shiny paperback with the promising title—as nearly as I can recall—*Seven Steps to a Happy Marriage.*

The chapter headings implied solutions for everything from sexual incompatibility and conflicts in child rearing to antisocial behavior—three issues very familiar to me. The nature of the book came as a surprise. The self-help industry that was growing in the States didn't even exist in Spain. Spaniards didn't air their problems publicly. I guessed they found the help they needed among family or with their priest. I couldn't do either. I bought the book.

After a decade in Madrid, I had no confidant—not when it came to my marriage. I could hardly complain to my husband's own family about him. What kind of position would that put them in? And what would they think of me? I felt close enough to Jan and my Spanish friend Paloma to tell them how I felt, but these friendships also included husbands. We were all mutual friends. I couldn't force them to choose a side, which I believed would have been inevitable. I imagined going out to dinner where one of them looked across the table at Alberto or at me and started making judgments or began to treat us differently because of something I had divulged. I shared some of my worries with Diane but that wasn't until the day before she and Ed left Spain. I took her for a farewell lunch. Her impending departure and the bottle of *Señoria de Sarriá* facilitated a franker than usual conversation. Diane was shocked. That surely would have affected our friendship had she stayed in Madrid. As for seeking solace from the clergy, I had a good idea of where that would lead, after my conversation with a local priest regarding birth control.

My marriage was crumbling, and I saw no way to shore it up. Communications with Alberto—if indeed there had ever been any beyond the superficial—had broken down. If I found a way to repair the situation, I was ashamed to admit I no longer even wanted to communicate with a man I couldn't trust with my feelings or with anyone or anything I cared about. But I had to find a solution somehow. Without any financial resources, leaving was out of the question. And the law was not on my side. In Spain a married woman could not open a bank account, buy a car, work, apply for a passport, or take her children out of the country without her husband's consent. If there had been books written about conjugal discord, they would not have been written from a woman's point of view and they would never have been displayed in a Madrid bookstore. Franco's censorship and rigid Catholicism would have prevented it.

I didn't wait to read the book on the plane. That night when everyone else was asleep, I took the book from my purse. My parents would have worried had they seen it and there was no point in that; they could do nothing anyway. I read the book without stopping and when I reached the end, I took a pencil from Alicia's coloring box and began to underline in red.

Although it was only a paperback, I felt uncomfortable marking the pages. In my Catholic school days, *Thou shalt not deface a book* was the eleventh commandment, and writing in red was just plain rude. Before we were married, Alberto had written letters to me and often underlined portions in red.

"Where I come from that's considered impolite," I said.

"I want to make a point," he said.

"I think I can get the point without the red underline."

He did it anyway. Now, I was doing the same thing because I planned to give him the book and I was determined to get his attention. The book's authors, an MD and a PhD psychologist, had a language and a vocabulary for things that I was too intimidated, embarrassed or ignorant to say for myself, but I could express my feelings with a red underscore.

One evening two or three days after our return to Madrid, I took the little book from the bottom of my lingerie drawer where I had tucked it. Alberto and I had finished dinner, the girls were asleep, and Aurora had gone for the day—back to her new husband. I hadn't rehearsed what I was going to say; I concentrated on staying calm.

"I found this in the States," I said, handing him the book. "I underlined some sections for you. I don't think I am the only person in the world to feel the way I do. Anyway, read it when you have time."

He looked surprised. "Of course," he said. I went to bed.

The book lay on the bar the next morning. I was positive Alberto had read it. But I left for the market before he was out of bed and by the time I came back, he had gone to the office. I didn't touch the book. When he came home for lunch and went to pour himself a pre-lunch cocktail, he saw it.

"By the way," he said, "I read your book last night."

"And?"

"Well of course, it is a typically biased work. Very one-sided, very American. And all you have pointed out are some absurd details plus your own exaggerated emphasis on body hygiene."

I shuddered inside. My husband came to bed mumbling obscenities— brandy on his breath, cigarette smoke in his hair and a body that smelled of stale sweat. I was supposed to find that alluring?

Maybe he had skipped some pages—the ones that dealt with tenderness, respect, tolerance.

"You couldn't have read all of it."

"I read enough," he said.

Before the idea had fully formed in my head, Alberto seemed to read my mind.

"By the way, I can't afford to send all three of you to the States again next summer," he said. "You can go alone if you want. Or you can take one of the girls. You just can't take both."

He had a little smile on his face. As though it were a complete after-thought he said, "As a friend of mine said, 'You never have to worry about Diana leaving you. She doesn't have any money.'"

He picked up a pad of paper and continued to work on the notes for his new book as though we had been talking about the weather. I said nothing, but I heard a rustling at the base of my skull.

"*You just watch me!*" the voice said.

# Chapter 30

I stood in the silent, empty waiting room of the psychiatrist's office, too nervous to sit down. The beige sofa and a pair of chairs looked comfortable, but I preferred to stand and look out the window. I had already checked for signs of a hidden camera. I wondered if Dr. Calderon observed his patients from a concealed device in the light switch. Did psychiatrists evaluate the movements of their next appointment before opening the door to the inner sanctum? *Well, so what!* I had nothing to hide, but I never imagined that a spontaneous remark to my sister-in-law a week earlier would lead to this.

⁂

Julina had worked at the American library for over twenty years. I stopped sometimes after my errands for a brief chat. As she walked me to the door one morning, we were still laughing about my failure to appreciate the writer Gabriel Garcia Marquez.

"I think magic realism isn't for me," I said and gave her a good-by hug.

"I know," she said. "You always want your feet on the ground." She kissed my cheek.

I turned to leave and for some reason Conchita popped into my head, a mutual friend I hadn't seen for some time.

"How's Conchita?" I said.

"Getting better."

"Better from what?"

"Her husband's an alcoholic," Julina said. "She's had a difficult time."

"Oh, I didn't know."

"Yes, but Conchita told me that ever since they started seeing a psychiatrist, things have improved. Light at the end of the tunnel, as you Americans say."

"A psychiatrist?"

"Conchita says he's wonderful."

We said goodbye a few moments later. By the time I pulled into our garage I knew what I was going to do. Diane had left town with the abbreviated version of my unhappy marriage, but I needed to tell someone the whole story. I was going to find that psychiatrist.

I waited a few days before visiting Julina again. This time with the pretext of giving her a recipe she had asked for.

"By the way, do you know the name of Conchita's psychiatrist?" I said.

Julina looked surprised, and then laughed.

"Diana, don't tell me *you* need a psychiatrist?"

"Of course not," I said. "It's for someone else."

Instead of the truth, I told her my prepared story—a friend from the American Women's Club needed some help. I wasn't sure why. When she asked if I knew of a therapist, I told her I would ask my sister-in-law.

"I believe his name is Antonio Calderon," Julina said. "But I don't know his address."

"Never mind," I said. "My friend can find that out for herself."

"But does your friend speak Spanish?"

"I think she can manage," I said.

⁂

I didn't know how I was going to broach the subject with Alberto, but that came about quite naturally after a disagreement about Alicia's bedding. Alberto insisted her constant cough occurred because she kicked off her blanket at night. I maintained she kicked it off because she was too warm. Alberto would go into the girls' room after they were asleep and tuck Alicia's blanket so tight the poor child could barely move. That was all it took for me to explode one evening.

"Alberto, I can't go on like this. I need to talk to someone and one of the women at the Club gave me the name of a psychiatrist. (I would never tell him the information came from his sister.) He's Spanish. I don't know what he charges." I was about to continue but before I could go on, Alberto spoke up.

"Good," he said. "Maybe he can straighten you out."

I made the appointment the following day.

⁂

I heard the door open on the other side of the room and a soft voice said "*Buenas tardes, señora.*"

The doctor looked to be my age—fortyish. I thought he must be six feet tall. He smiled pointing to his inner office and the chair in front of his desk. He waited until I had taken a seat before he sat down himself, leaned forward and asked what he could do for me. I had rehearsed the answer.

"I can't continue in my marriage without some kind of help."

The doctor's next words stunned me.

"No matter what happens, *señora,*" he said. "I'm on your side."

"You don't know what the other side is, doctor. Maybe I am a terrible person."

"But you are the one who is asking for help. That is reason enough for me," he said.

I spent the next hour talking about my life, describing Alberto and answering the doctor's questions. I felt completely at ease. When he mentioned alcohol, I told the doctor that I drank. I enjoyed wine with meals and an occasional martini before dinner.

"And your husband?"

Yes, he drank too—in fact he never stopped. However, I had never seen him drunk. He asked if I thought Alberto had or was having an affair. I had never seen any outward signs of infidelity—lipstick stains on the shirt collar, a perfume that wasn't mine on his suit jacket, mysterious phone calls, or late nights at the office. If he was having an affair, he was discreet about it. I don't know why I never thought to mention the visits to the pharmacist. I wasn't even sure there was anything beyond his vitamin shots.

The doctor said he would need to know me better before he could make any suggestions, and we set another appointment. He wanted to know if Alberto would see him at some later date, I said I would find out. I really didn't know. The session had ended, but before I stood up, I opened my purse.

"Do you speak English, Doctor?"

"A little," he said. "I read better."

I took the *Seven Steps to a Happy Marriage* from my purse, placed it on his desk, and spoke slowly.

"These are the problems, doctor. I think you will understand." He nodded. I wished I hadn't underlined the problems in red.

Alberto had taken the position that if the psychiatric profession could pound some sense into my head, all would be well. He showed some disappointment when I told him, after the first appointment, that I might need a couple of follow-up visits and that the doctor was interested in talking with him too—alone.

"Would you go?"

"Of course," Alberto said. "I don't have anything to hide."

For two people who had nothing to hide, we had made a mess of things.

A week later I sat with the doctor again. He apologized for his lack of familiarity with the emotional framework of American women. However, he thought being married to a German woman had provided him some insights that he might not otherwise have had— at least a heightened consciousness of cultural differences. He would always be aware that I was not Spanish. It was my nationality, he said, that had made him cautious during our first talk. He looked at the little book lying on his desk.

"And nobody ever put all their cards on the table as you have done."

I laughed—a reaction to the relief I felt. "Doctor," I said, "I don't think I have much time."

If the doctor knew little about American women, he knew everything about Spanish men—he knew them by age, class, education, and profession and how they had been affected by the Civil War. He told me things about my husband that I thought only someone very close to him could have seen. When I expressed surprise, he said, "It's my job." Without having met Alberto, he said he was an alcoholic. My notion of an alcoholic came from the movies and from a poor drunk I had seen sleeping (I didn't know the difference between sleeping and passed-out) in a doorway in Manhattan, or from bleary-eyed, staggering men who wandered the streets begging for money to buy their next drink. None of that described my husband. In fact, he had just published his second book. But I remembered something he said a few weeks earlier.

Alberto always exaggerated even his slightest health or physical problem. One day, as he was lighting a cigarette, a packet of matches exploded in his hand and burned his palm. Of course, it hurt, but the production he made went on for days. Every evening he brought a supply of bandages and ointments from the bathroom and spread them on the coffee table. *For crying out loud—in the middle of the living room!* I fussed to no avail, but the thing that bothered me most was that he drafted Ana as his nurse. Why would anyone in his right mind subject a little girl to peeling skin and sticky gauzes? He ignored my complaints. So, the day he told me about his shaking hands, I thought it was just more hyperbole.

"I don't know what the matter with me is lately," he said. We were crossing *Padre Damian* on our way to a new shop in the neighborhood, where he had ordered a jacket.

"Why? What's wrong?"

"My hands shake." He held them out. I could see the slight tremor.

"Well, you should probably see a doctor if it doesn't go away."

"The thing is it stops if I have a little beer in the morning."

Alberto made sure there were always a few bottles in the fridge—little bottles half the size of regular ones. I knew that's what he had for breakfast—a glass of *Tang*, a cup of coffee and a little beer. Still, I had never seen him drunk, and when the psychiatrist told me he thought alcohol was a problem, I wasn't convinced. I was eager to hear his opinion after he had actually met my husband.

Alberto kept the appointment with Dr. Calderon. He insisted I go with him even though the doctor had specified that he wanted to speak with him alone.

"You can wait for me at the coffee shop and drop me at the office later."

He showed no signs of apprehension. I could almost hear him thinking, *Naturally, I will do my part. I'll tell the doctor what her problem is, and then he can take care of it.*

At four o'clock on a Wednesday, I left Alberto at the doctor's door and a few minutes later slid onto a stool at the counter of the cafe and ordered a coffee and *una tarta de manzana,* the Spanish version of apple pie. Usually I didn't care for Spanish desserts, but the slivers of apple painted with apricot jam and baked on a thin open crust, well … that was different. Besides, I had an hour to wait, and one of the delights of eating in a Spanish restaurant is being left alone until one asks for the check. I ate the *tarta* and wondered about the conversation taking place next door. When Alberto came through the door a few minutes before five, I couldn't read anything in his expression.

He sauntered—slower than his usual measured gait—to the counter and signaled the waiter. *"Un café solo y un coñac."* I waited. He lit a cigarette. His movements seemed calculated. He took a sip of coffee then lifted the brandy to his lips.

"Well? What do you think? What did the doctor say?"

"I'll tell you what he said." Alberto took another sip from the little glass. "He said my wife was a very good, very intelligent woman."

I shrugged. I don't know what I had expected—not that. But before I could ask anything else, Alberto said, "And I am telling *you,* I will never go back."

"But—"

He signaled for the waiter again. "Check, please." Then he drained his glass and dropped some coins on the counter. "I need to get to the office."

I tried again. "I have another appointment scheduled for next week."

"Go ahead. Just don't count on me. I wonder how much all this is going to cost," he said. Money had not been an issue before.

⁂

Dr. Calderon never revealed the details of his conversation with Alberto. He only confirmed his initial diagnosis. I was married to an alcoholic. Other women had learned to live with an alcoholic husband, he told me—I remembered Conchita—and he could help me do the same. For that he needed at least one willing participant, but Alberto had refused to see Dr. Calderon again and I no longer cared. Alcohol might explain some of Alberto's actions, but not all. I didn't know the cause of Alberto's insidious behavior, and I had no inclination to find out. The admiration and affection I once felt had turned to fear and disgust.

"What is it you would like to do?" the doctor said.

What did I want? I felt the woman at the back of my head stir.

*"Say it!"* the voice said.

"I want to take my daughters away!"

No, that wasn't quite accurate. I didn't want to leave Spain—I just wanted to leave my husband. I knew, however, that Alberto would never agree to my leaving the house with the girls even if we stayed in Madrid. The law was on his side. A woman could end up in prison if she tried. If I left, I would have to put an ocean between us.

"What stops you?" the doctor said.

Maybe I could secretly stash enough money for tickets to the States but that would take years and I was afraid I wouldn't be able to take care of my children once I got there. I could manage for myself, but could I find a job that would support three people? Who would take care of my daughters while I worked? I was terrified of ending up destitute on a curb with two little girls asking for something to eat. The doctor shook his head.

"That will *never* happen to you."

On what, I wondered, did he base this assumption? How could he know? The voice in my head would not keep quiet. *"Take his word for it,"* she said. *"Just take his word for it."*

I took a deep breath, "I hope you're right."

# Chapter 31

I wrote to my parents that I couldn't take the girls to the States that summer and gave the same reason my husband had given me; we couldn't afford the trip this year. But I knew that wasn't true.

I never knew how much money was in our bank account. I had no need to know. Alberto had paid off the ten-year mortgage and had paid cash for a second car. He gave me an envelope of peseta notes periodically or wrote a check to me for household expenses. We didn't have extravagant tastes. We discussed out of the ordinary expenses such as a vacation or Aurora's salary. Once, when I was considering a new suit for a cousin's wedding, I asked if he thought it was too expensive.

"For heaven's sake, Diana, if you like it, buy it. You don't have to check with me."

I didn't think we were wealthy, but money had never been an issue or the subject of disagreement between us. Now, to keep us from going to the States, Alberto made the excuse we couldn't afford it. I knew that wasn't the reason.

I couldn't put that shocking information in a letter. My parents didn't know about our problems, or so I thought.

I expected my mother to write back expressing their disappointment. *We understand,* she would say, *maybe next year.* It hadn't occurred to me they might come to Spain instead. They had recently moved from the desert to what mother called a more civilized environment in Sun City, a retirement community. They hadn't planned a trip to Europe. Mother's note surprised me. If we didn't have other plans, they would arrive the second week of August and stay for fifteen days or until the girls started school. We only made long distance calls for special occasions in those days—the births of our daughters or the New Year—but that night I phoned. *By all means, come. We don't have any plans.*

Ana and Alicia were excited to see their *Granpis* again. Alberto said they were welcome any time. He enjoyed talking with my father; everybody did. My mother was another matter. Mother saw things that other people missed. I think my husband knew that.

⁂

"Brilliant!" Jan said when I told her my parents were coming. "My mum and dad will be here too."

Jan knew my parents and I knew hers from previous visits but the parents themselves had never met. We planned an evening together—a cocktail at my house followed by dinner in a restaurant that had once been a palace. The "mums" and dads found things in common. We were an affable group, except for Alberto, who acted bored one minute and uttered inappropriate comments the next. Why didn't I want more children? He looked pointedly at Jan's mother when he said this (Jan was an only child). And why was it that John took so easily to the Spanish language while Jan seemed to struggle? When the rest of us fell silent, he appeared not to notice or laughed as though he had made a joke. One moment he was cutting and the next he was oozing an exaggerated charm. When we said goodbye that evening, Jan's mother held me in a longer than usual hug. Her father patted my hand. I felt what the Spaniards call *vergüenza ajena,* a kind of shame for someone else. But the person who ignited the feeling was utterly untouchable. Alberto lived in his own world, ever more careless and reckless. My parents said nothing.

A few days later, prompted by Ana's report card from the previous term, Alberto made another remark.

My mother and I had put the girls to bed and were sitting on the sofa. My father sat in the brown armchair. I had turned over the cushion so the hole Alberto had burned in it didn't show. Perhaps the cushion, like the artificial Christmas tree, was symptomatic. My normal self would have sent the cushion for repair within days of the incident, but months later it still lay face down emitting a periodic whiff of burnt upholstery.

Alberto stood by the bar. I was expressing my concern about Ana's grades. Her previous year-end report card lay on the coffee table as I reiterated her teachers' recommendation that she repeat the year. School would begin in a few weeks and we should make a decision soon. My parents sympathized but didn't express a strong opinion either way. Abruptly, Alberto picked up the card, appeared to read it, then threw it down.

"Those teachers are a bunch of whores!"

I felt my mother flinch; my father stared at Alberto, motionless.

"*Rise above it,*" the voice in my head whispered. *"Rise above it."*

For a moment I felt curiously lighter.

Oh, Alberto," I said, "surely you don't mean that."

I didn't raise my voice. I might have been telling the girls to pull up their socks or finish their peas. I didn't feel shock or anger. I sensed the love of my parents and the afterglow of my visits with Dr. Calderon. And in that moment, I felt a slight weakening of my husband's power to hurt me.

*"It's a start,"* the voice said.

Alberto mumbled something, picked up the ice bucket and went to the kitchen. Two days later, my parents and I took the girls to Portugal.

No one planned the trip—it just happened. By chance at dinner one evening I had mentioned a friend's recent visit to Lisbon. My father said he would like to see Portugal, mother said a change of scenery might be nice. At that point my mother probably thought Hell, itself, might be an improvement. I looked at Alberto. School for the girls wouldn't start for another ten days.

"Good idea," Alberto said. "I can't take time away from the office, but you can take my car."

Before we had finished our coffee, I was on the phone making hotel reservations and my father had spread a map on the table.

"It's a little over 600 kilometers," he said. "How long do you think that will take?"

*Who cares?* the voice said.

Aurora, though she now came only in the mornings, would be on vacation at the same time, but Alberto said he could manage on his own. By lunchtime the following day we were 400 kilometers from Madrid in Evora, a Portuguese town with a temple dedicated to Diana, goddess of the hunt and the moon, to whom Roman women prayed for the gift of a happy marriage. Maybe I'd been going to the wrong church.

It was late afternoon when we crossed the Tagus River and entered Lisbon on a mile-and-a-half-long suspension bridge that reminded us of San Francisco's Golden Gate. Originally, the bridge was named for Portugal's right-wing leader, Antonio Salazar, whose 40 years in power closely paralleled those of Franco. Now the bridge was called *Ponte 25 de Abril*, marking the day a military coup deposed Salazar's authoritarian regime. The first half of the 1970s saw the death of two dictators; Salazar in 1970 and Franco in 1975. Their respective countries, that had once raised arms in salute or cringed in fear, tried to bury the past. Like Salazar's name on the bridge, Franco's image, too, disappeared, albeit gradually. Destroyed or stored in some dark vault, the statues and portraits of Francisco Franco Bahamonde, *Caudillo de España*, moldered out of sight. The memories, however, remained. Four decades after Franco's death, Spain would still struggle with the aftermath of Civil War. The afternoon we crossed the bridge that struggle had just begun.

⁂

Bright and fresh, Lisbon faced west overlooking the ocean. The hills and cable cars, like the bridge, reminded me of San Francisco. Other than a visit to the Gulbenkian Museum, we had no fixed agenda. Ana and Alicia soon tired of my calling their attention to this or that bit of art or architecture. The highlight of Lisbon for my daughters was a colony of ants near the hotel door. The girls, dressed in blue sundresses, sat on the sidewalk absorbed in the activity of the tiny black dots. Aged six and nine, they had no interest in Prince Henry the Navigator and less, if that's possible, in the Sé Cathedral. I, on the other hand, felt an urgency to cram our excursion with as much culture as possible. Who knew when we would pass this way again—or if? As we left Lisbon two days later, I was still at it.

"Look for watchtowers on the hills," I said. "The Moors made them 800 years ago."

In the back seat the girls slouched against my mother, who sat between them. I looked in the rearview mirror and met Ana's eyes.

"Can you tell us how we know the Moors built the towers?" I said.

Ana straightened up. "Because they're square! *Papá* said the Christians built round ones."

"Thank you, Ana," my father said. "I didn't know that."

"And, Grandpa, Gothic things are pointy. Did you know that?"

My father turned to me and winked. "Your *Papá* has a lot of information," he said.

"Yes, but *Mamá* told me about the Gothic things. Right, *Mamá?*"

"Right," I said. Hoping to maintain her interest, I added, "Soon you can start to look for the pretty chimneys."

We were headed south to the Algarve, where fanciful painted chimneys, typical of that area, outline the roof tops of white-washed houses. At that moment, however, we traveled a narrow road bordered by groves of cork trees. Many of the trees had been harvested, their trunks peeled of the bark that would make its way to everything from flooring to bottle stoppers.

When my father said he would like a closer look, I stopped beside a low stone wall. He pulled a pen knife from his pants pocket, intending to slice a sliver of bark to show his friends at home. No sooner had he cleared the wall than a wrinkled character whose face might have been made of cork, too, stepped from the shadow of a tree. He wore a brown leather vest and a red knit cap. Cradling a long-barreled gun in his arms, he appraised my father in silence. My father inched the knife back into his pocket.

"Don't move," I said to my backseat passengers, and got out of the car.

*Bonne di? Boun joor? How the heck do you say good afternoon in Portuguese?* Before I could compose a greeting, the cork grove guard grinned and in measured English said, "Do you speak French?" *French?*

I shook my head. My father backed over the wall. There seemed nothing malicious in the guard's grin, but there was still the matter of his firearm. We smiled and bowed repeatedly and, not wanting to raise any suspicions, slunk back to the car where my mother sat wide-eyed with a restraining hand on each granddaughter's arm. Later, when the car had reached 40 mph and we once again breathed normally, my father said, "I wonder why we didn't think to tell the man we spoke *English.*"

⁂

My life, at least my marriage, was well on the road to Hades, but the pleasure of those days cleared my mind—at least temporarily. I remember an amber-colored consommé as clear as crystal served in a white, wide-mouthed, double-handled cup with a tissue-thin strip of carrot floating on the shimmering surface. I remember the platter of grilled hake drizzled with olive oil and bits of toasted garlic resting beside three small boiled potatoes. Just before serving, the potatoes had been seasoned and lightly browned in a very hot oven which gave them a delicate salty crust.

I remember my father's laugh as he splashed with my daughters in the pool at the *parador* in Córdoba, and the scent of eucalyptus from the groves nearby.

I remember the *Monasterio de la Rábida* at Palos where Columbus stayed while negotiating his voyage of 1492. Across the *Rio Tinto* on a little spit of land, stood a colossal monument to the discovery of America, the work of the American sculptor, Gertrude Vanderbilt Whitney.

And I remember skirting Huelva, the town where teen-aged Alberto spent the final years of the Civil War. I mentioned this to my parents but otherwise my husband's name was conspicuously absent from our conversations. We had all felt the tension in Madrid. Even so, no one raised the subject. We wouldn't speak of it in front of the children. And on the few occasions they were out of earshot, well, it just didn't seem the right time. Why ruin a lovely holiday? There would be time later, I thought, when I could be alone with my parents.

After five days on the road, we turned north to the plateau of *Castilla* and suddenly, or so it seemed, we were home again.

# Chapter 32

Alberto was still at the office when we arrived. I turned the key, opened the door to our front hall and stepped into shadows. Ahead of me, at the end of the corridor, lay the dim entrance to the living room. The doorway on my right led to the kitchen where a bank of windows faced the street. The kitchen, the brightest room in the house, normally flooded the front hall with light. But that day, the windows were closed, the awning lowered, and the house trapped in a haze of stale cigarette smoke. I set down my suitcase, walked toward the windows, unlatched the panes and cranked up the green canvass awning. Gritty grains of *Tang* and *Nescafe* crunched under my feet. On the stove, a skillet held the remains of an omelet, or the attempt of an omelet. A spill of tomato sauce had congealed around the front burner. I groaned. A dirty plate, a cup half filled with coffee, a stale baguette and an issue of *Time* littered the glass table. My parents said nothing, but I could feel them watching me.

"You can unpack your suitcase in your room," I said to my daughters as I led the way to the living room. Here too, the windows were dark.

I raised the awnings on the balcony and momentarily wished I hadn't. The afternoon sun exposed the room where every surface was strewn with overflowing ashtrays and empty glasses. The ice bucket held three inches of lukewarm water and had left rings on the coffee table. A film of cigarette ash covered the parquet floor by the bar. A pile of unopened mail sat on the bookcase.

I crossed to the bedroom where the door stood open. My husband's soiled shirts lay in a heap at the foot of the unmade bed along with his new tailored slacks. Automatically, I bent to retrieve them but the voice of the woman in the base of my skull stilled my hand.

*Leave them! Dammit! Just leave them!* Her hot breath filled my head.

I had to start cleaning somewhere, somehow. I'd start in the kitchen. Between the bedroom and the hall, I felt the first tears. I didn't want to cry. The tears came anyway, hot and sharp like shards of glass. By the time I reached the kitchen, my face was wet. For all I knew I was crying blood, and the woman in my head was shouting.

*Get out! Get out!*

I didn't know how to answer.

I stood by the kitchen window thumping the sill with my fist. Strange sounds came from the back of my throat. My chest hurt. Then, I felt my mother's hand on my shoulder. I couldn't speak. I looked toward the hall. My daughters shouldn't see me like this. Mother read my thoughts.

"I told your father to take the girls for a walk," she said. "They've been cooped up in the car most of the day."

She pulled a chair from the glass-topped table and motioned for me to sit. I couldn't. *Tell her,* said the voice. *Tell her!*

So I stood with one hand on the window sill, the other on the back of the chair and, my eyes fixed on the empty bottles on the counter behind her, I told my mother why I hadn't taken Ana and Alicia to the States that year: that Alberto wouldn't allow me to leave with both girls; that I had gone to a psychiatrist; what he told me; and what Alberto said after meeting with the doctor alone, that he'd never see that man again.

"I don't know what happened," I said.

When I fell silent, my mother said slowly, "Your father is worried—that if you stay here like this, something … something will happen."

I didn't ask what that "something" was.

"You know we can't tell you what to do," she said. "But—"

"But?"

"We would try to help you."

"If I leave?"

She nodded.

I wiped my nose with the back of my hand, turned the chair and sat. "What made you come to Madrid?" I said.

Mother handed me a paper napkin. "Something about your last letter," she said. "It didn't sound right. We thought we should come to see what was going on."

"And have you seen?"

"I don't see how you can go on like this," she said.

"The problem is I don't have any savings in my own name. I couldn't pay for plane tickets. And I think Alberto senses that if I left, I wouldn't come back. But even if I did leave, I don't know how I could support myself and two little girls. The psychiatrist seemed to think that wouldn't be a problem. But how could he know?"

"Your father will lend you the money for the air fare," mother said. "He can charge it before we leave. You decide the date. As for a job, well, you worked for I. Magnin in San Francisco and they have a branch in Phoenix. Maybe you could work for them again."

"Really?"

"And, of course, you could stay with us for a while," Mother said. She stressed the word *while.*

My parents had sold the desert house and now lived in a restricted retirement complex—no children. But we could stay as guests until I found a job and a place to live.

"I'll have to leave everything here," I said.

From where I sat, I could see the hall. A brass cross that my brother-in-law brought me from Galicia hung over the door. Along the wall, a cantaloupe-sized piece of white coral and an ivory carving of Guanyin—wedding gifts from the days those things were legal—sat on a shelf I'd given so many coats of black paint and wax that it shone like enamel. By the front door lay a hooked rug I had made. Ana used to sit there and brush the red and black fringe until all the strands lay in a straight line. And there was the *Sargadelos* plate I found in an antique shop in *Santillana del Mar* and bought even though it was cracked. And the black and white lithographs and … *Stop it!* Now the voice sounded annoyed.

"At least I can take your silverware," mother said.

How like her. Mother had added to my sterling place settings since I first chose the pattern when I was sixteen. There was no way she would allow that to remain behind. My pragmatic mother had worked out an evacuation plan in less time than it had taken to decide on the trip to Portugal. Only this time Alberto must not know about the plan.

"Mom, did you ever think I should not have married Alberto?"

She paused a second. "Well, we didn't think he was right for you."

"But you never said anything."

This time she didn't hesitate. "Would it have made any difference?"

⁂

By the time Alberto came home that evening Mother had taken the silver wrapped in felt covers and stowed it at the bottom of her carry-on suitcase.

I don't know how we managed to make small talk that evening. I imagine we told Alberto more about Portugal than he wanted to know. Meanwhile I could see *The Plan* sitting on the arm of the sofa or leaning against the bookcase. I knew it would remain invisible to everyone else so long as there was chatter. But I was terrified that if the conversation faltered, Alberto would see *The Plan* in the silence.

The next morning my father and I went to a travel agency in the Eurobuilding Hotel. As we drove down *Paseo de la Habana*, I told him about the insurance check I was expecting. On my twentieth birthday I had bought a twenty-year endowment from the Prudential Insurance Company. In July (I had turned forty in June), they had contacted me to say I had a choice of reinvesting the money or cashing it out. I chose the latter though at the time I had thought only about saving it toward a vacation to the States. I told my father that I hoped the check arrived before I left Spain. That way I could repay him for the tickets. "Don't worry about that now," he said.

The travel agent smiled and put out her cigarette. She may have been getting ready to sell us a cruise but my father wasted no time. "One adult, two children to Phoenix, Arizona, ten days from today. One way."

I chose the date to coincide with Alberto's three-day business trip to Barcelona.

The agent checked the airlines, suggested an itinerary and calculated the cost. Fine. My father gave her his only credit card. My parents were not of a card carrying generation, and he had only recently acquired one to travel in Spain. The agent went behind a partition and returned a few minutes later. "Unfortunately, sir," she said. "Your card has been declined."

Of course, there was a reason. My father had used the card for their own plane fares and for some of the expenses in Portugal. He had simply forgotten about a credit limit.

"I'm sorry," he said, holding the door for me as we left the office.

When I looked up I saw the pain on his face.

⁂

My parents returned to the States, leaving me as much cash as they could spare. I prayed for a speedy arrival of the check and said a Hail Mary every time I saw Pedro the *portero* sorting the mail. If it arrived in time, I would take advantage of Alberto's absence and leave while he was in Barcelona. But what if the check lost its way between Newark and Madrid? That check was my only way out and that period of time was my only option. Four days before my husband's scheduled departure, I opened the mailbox and found the envelope from Prudential. I wanted to purchase our tickets immediately, but I waited. Everything depended on secrecy. If Alberto cancelled his business trip, I didn't see how I could coordinate our exodus. The day before Alberto was to leave, when he had his own ticket to Barcelona, I went to the travel agent, who told me she would do her best but she wasn't sure she could find three seats to Phoenix on such short notice. Could I leave on a later date? I could not. I told her I was responding to a family emergency.

"Very well," she said. "I'll phone you later."

"No!" I couldn't risk that Alberto would answer the phone. "I'll call you."

"*Muy bien,*" she said, hearing the panic in my voice "*no se preocupe.*" Don't worry. I clenched my teeth.

*No se preocupe* was a frequent expression among Spaniards. Everyone said it—from your dentist to your mechanic. "Don't worry" was the most worrisome phrase in the Spanish language.

It wasn't until late afternoon the following day that I was able to call the agent and learned that she had secured the tickets. All I could think was *What if he finds out? Oh Lord, what then?* When I went to the travel agency, I took the girls with me, but I didn't tell them what I was doing.

"You can play here by the fountain in the patio while I talk to the lady inside," I said, "and then we'll go for a *Fanta y patatas fritas.*"

As she handed me the envelope that contained our tickets, I gushed my thanks to the agent for her efforts on our behalf. She said she hoped my family emergency would soon be resolved.

"Yes," I said, "I hope so too."

⁂

Alberto left for Barcelona in the morning. Aurora was still on vacation, so instead of driving him to the airport as I usually did, I stayed home with the girls. I watched from the kitchen window as he got into the waiting taxi. There was nothing remarkable about it. He dipped his head, hunched his shoulders and pulled his briefcase in after him. He didn't wave or raise his eyes to the window and, as the cab moved away from the curb, the voice in my head said *You'll never see him again.*

I looked around the kitchen: a strand of garlic and peppers woven from straw that we found in a village somewhere hung by the window. The ceramic plate with a painted rooster, a gift from Ana, sat on a wicker shelf with my cookbooks and the recipe translations I had made for Aurora. Was there nothing I could rescue as my home went up in flames?

The woman at the base of my skull rose once more. *Photographs,* she said. *Then take the children and run.*

I spent the day planning what I would pack—not much—and shuffled clothes around in the closets so it wouldn't look as though anything were missing. I made a folder for my old résumés and found my social security card. Once the girls were in bed, I filled the suitcases with summer clothes. We wouldn't need winter ones in Arizona. I stuffed a manila envelope— report cards, vaccination certificates, a drawing by Alicia that had won a $10 prize at the club, and family photos. I chose ones of my in-laws and of the girls when they were babies, of their baptisms and with Aurora at her wedding. I found a few from Christmas and from a birthday party, and compressed my children's brief history into a 9" by 12" packet. I didn't wish to deny them their past; I only wanted to change their future. I took my wedding album too. I put that in my suitcase. At the last minute I layered between some shirts two pieces of art that my brother-in-law had made for me—bright paper collages of pears and a watermelon—happy colors. To make them lighter, I had removed the glass and frames and stuck them behind the sofa.

Later that night, when I thought none of the neighbors would see me, and after Pedro the *portero* had retired, I took the service elevator to the garage and stowed the suitcases in the trunk of my car. There would be no farewells. I had never told anyone I was leaving. I couldn't put my friends and dear Julina and Luis in an awkward position when Alberto confronted them later, as he surely would, to ask if they had known what I planned. The only other thing I had to do was return Jan's gift.

For Christmas Jan had given me a sewing basket. She had made it herself—painted and lined a large wicker basket and filled it with all the sewing accessories she thought I needed. It was a perfect gift, typical of her talent and thoughtfulness. But it wouldn't fit in a suitcase and I couldn't bear the thought of leaving it behind—not in that place. I would take it to her in the morning on our way to the airport. Much as I wanted to, I had never even told Jan.

I woke my daughters early. I hadn't told them we were going to take a trip. I didn't want to face the questions. *Are we going to see the Granpis? They were just here. Why are we going now? What about school?* And worse, *But I didn't say goodbye to Papá!*

Alicia, who was six, asked if she could take a favorite doll. Of course, she could. She was easily distracted when I told her we would have lunch in the sky.

"Like Mary Poppins?" she wanted to know.

"Almost," I said.

Nine-year old Ana worried that I had not yet bought her school supplies.

"When are you going to buy *los anillos?*" she said.

The *anillos* were loose, individual metal rings used to make notebooks. My daughter was obsessed with them.

"Don't worry," I said. "You will have all your school supplies on time." She didn't look convinced.

I could take only one step at a time.

First, we would go to my parents. Later I would tell the girls we were going to stay an extra long time in Phoenix and that they could go to a nice new school; Mamá would get a job, and we would find a place to live. Somehow I would work out the rest of the story. But I wasn't sure how I was going to do any of that when I pulled up in front of Jan's house.

"I'll just be a minute," I said to the girls. "You wait here in the car."

I rang Jan's doorbell and when she opened the door, I handed her the basket. For a moment she looked puzzled.

"I'm leaving," I said, "but I'll be damned if I'll leave this with Alberto. He doesn't know. And you won't say anything, will you?"

"Of course not," she said. "We wondered how much longer…" She put her arms around me for a moment. John came to the door and I tried to smile when I said we were on our way to the airport—it was either smile or cry. He didn't smile back.

"You haven't heard the news," he said.

"What news?" In the past two years the Prime Minister had been assassinated, Basque separatists had set off bombs and robbed a series of banks, and Franco, who had ruled with an iron first for forty years, had died.

"What now?" I asked.

"Jan's parents were scheduled to leave early this morning. We took them to the airport but had to come back. The ground crews are on strike, and all the flights have been cancelled."

*You can't turn back now,* said the voice.

I hugged Jan again. "I'm going anyway." I said. "I've got to try."

⁂

I had my choice of parking spaces. Airport porters were hanging around with nothing to do. I directed one of them to take our luggage to the TWA counter. If the flight was cancelled, I would find out soon enough. But the man at the desk only verified our tickets, checked our bags and waved us toward the departure gate.

I gripped my passport as we neared the control booth. All three of us held Spanish passports; small red booklets that I thought didn't really look official. Because my husband was Spanish and my daughters were born in Madrid, the paternalistic authorities had automatically bestowed Spanish citizenship upon us. However, I had registered the girls with the American Consulate shortly after their births and my own renewed US passport included their photos. I had all the passports in my purse. When we reached the booth, I held out the familiar green one with the American eagle on the cover.

So far so good.

I paced the waiting area, dreading the moment a voice might crackle over the intercom to say that our flight had been cancelled. If the ground crews were on strike, Trans World Airlines managed without them. As soon as our flight began to board, I motioned to one of the lounging porters. With a sizable tip, I asked him to mail the envelope I had addressed to Alberto. It contained the car keys and the parking receipt, nothing else.

A few minutes later we sat on a plane bound for New York, looking very patriotic in our red, white and blue outfits. The girls wore white blouses and navy jumpers trimmed in red; I wore a blue denim dress that I had made myself and had tied a red bandana at my neck. It was 1976. Even the Club in Madrid was celebrating America's bicentennial. Independence. What a thought!

One of the flight attendants asked Ana to help distribute packets of peanuts—an activity that thrilled my daughter, who loved to play hostess at any time. Timid Alicia hugged her doll and looked out the window. I prayed.

*St. Christopher, guide us. St. Joseph, guard us. Our Father, who art in Heaven … Our Father who art in heaven…*

Never entirely at ease with air travel, I always said a prayer before take-off. But this time was different. I wasn't worried about a plane crash—I was afraid of the long arm of Alberto Benitez reaching across the Atlantic. I imagined him returning early from his business trip. When he grasped what had happened, he would contact some ministry or other where he had a friend. Our names would be sent to Interpol or whatever agency is in charge of fugitive wives, and when we arrived at New York immigration, the agent at passport control would say, "Mrs. Benitez, you are under arrest for kidnapping." My daughters would see me taken away in handcuffs while a woman in a dark suit ushered them off to a child protection agency. I was still praying when we landed at JFK. *Please, God, just get us through passport control. I'll take it from there.* I didn't have all the details worked out, but I had no doubts about my decision. *Please, God, just get us past passport control!*

⁂

God was having a busy day. He sat on a high swivel stool wearing a light blue shirt and looking too young for such a responsible job. Something about his eyes, however, suggested that he had already seen a great deal of life in the faces of the people who filed before him. He lifted his gaze periodically to scan the long silent queues, and then returned his attention to the person in front of him and the document in his hand. I waited.

*Twelve more steps.*

*Nine more steps.*

I inched forward.

The sound of God's voice grew louder. He spoke with a distinct New York accent I could hear clearly when he questioned the old man in front of me. "Where have you been, sir? And the nature of your business?" Then it was my turn. I opened our passport and extended it to the Almighty with a sweating hand. He took an eternity to scrutinize our faces, comparing them to the photo. He asked me to lift Alicia's chin so he could get a better look. Finally, he seemed satisfied. He stamped the page, smiled and said, "Welcome home, Mrs. Benitez."

# *Epilogue*

My parents met us at the Phoenix airport with smiles that barely masked their concern, and I felt surges of relief mixed with anxiety and guilt. Alicia, then six, leaned against me, tired and quiet. Nine year-old Ana, in spite of her excitement to see her grandparents, wore an expression that seemed to say there's something funny going on here.

After the girls were asleep that night in my parents' home in their retirement community, I sat with my mother and father at the kitchen table trying to work out what to do next. I needed a job, a car, a place to live and a school for my daughters—more or less in that order. And when Alberto called, which he was bound to do, I had to stay calm.

My mother answered when the phone rang at noon the next day. After a curt, "Fine, thank you. Yes, she's here," she handed me the receiver. My hand shook but the voice that came over the line was cold and deliberate.

"So, you decided to visit your parents?"

"Yes."

"And how long do you plan to stay."

"I don't know. Indefinitely"

"But you'll send the girls back."

"No."

"I see."

That is all I recall of that conversation.

⁂

My mother was right when she told me the company I worked for in San Francisco had a branch in Phoenix. I got a job. I withdrew the $3000 that Alberto had put in a US joint account years earlier, bought a car for $2500 and used the rest for a deposit on an unfurnished apartment. My parents agreed to pay the tuition ($25 a month) to a Catholic elementary school nearby. I had been horrified when the principal at the public school told me I didn't need to worry about drugs on her campus. Drugs? In an elementary school? Why had she even mentioned such a thing? That particular problem had not yet reached Spain. I had a lot to learn about this country from which I had been absent for over a decade. Things had changed. In the meantime, I looked for what I thought was the safest place for my children.

⁂

And I wrote to my in-laws and friends in Spain. I was sorry about the way I had left and hoped they would understand that I had my reasons. If they chose to blame me, I would understand, I said. Julina was the first to reply; understanding, loving, and grateful that I had not put her in the position of having to lie when Alberto asked if she knew what had happened. Everyone I knew sent best wishes and a desire to keep in touch. Except for Alberto who raged and insulted, all the while promising that if the girls returned to Spain he would provide the best education money could buy. If they remained in the States he would not contribute a penny to their well-being. In that respect he kept his word. I asked in the only letter I ever wrote to him for help with Alicia's dental work. He refused. He made no attempt to talk through our differences and offered no solutions. I wasn't surprised.

⁕

I felt no urgency to file for divorce until the incident on the school playground. I never told the girls they should not communicate with their father. I gave Ana his letters unopened and didn't ask what they contained. I didn't tell her to hang up when he called even though both things upset her. And I never said they could not return to Spain someday. On the contrary, I hoped they could spend vacations there at some point, maintaining their fluent Spanish and developing strong ties with their Spanish family. But I needed to know they would be safe when they went. Instead of filing for divorce immediately, I took one day at a time wanting only a calm, stable, healthful environment—until Ana told me about the man and woman in the black car.

Alicia seemed able to take things in stride and to shrug off any unpleasantness. "I just don't buy into all that high drama stuff," she told me years later. But Ana was clearly upset when she described what had happened at school that particular day.

A woman who identified herself as a "friend of Papa's" approached her with a letter. In it Alberto, convinced that I was intercepting her mail, asked Ana to obtain a post office box where he could write to her in secret. She was nine years old! And who were these mysterious people? How did he know them? I immediately filed for divorce and legal custody of my daughters. When the attorney asked what amount he should list for child support, I told him not to waste his time. He insisted and came up with a figure I don't remember. I obtained the divorce but Alberto ignored the court's instructions There seemed little I could do to secure funds from an ocean away and, frankly, I was glad for the Atlantic between us.

⁂

I watched the girls thrive. From a struggling student in Spain, Ana went to the top of her class. Alicia had a talent for sports that I hadn't noticed before. When the time came, both girls were awarded scholarships to a Catholic High School. Alberto came twice to the States on business. I made no objection to his seeing the girls so long as I was present. On one occasion I took the girls to visit him in San Francisco. The trip had all the makings of a beautiful weekend but like the previous reunion in Phoenix, it was a disaster. He diminished the girls' accomplishments, ridiculed their behavior, insulted their appearance and tried to pick a fight with me. When I asked about Julina and Luis or any of our old friends, he denied any knowledge. I found out later that was true because he no longer had contact with the friends and rarely saw his sister since their parents had passed away. Long gone were those Sunday family lunches at Paseo de Prado, 24.

In spite of everything, the girls tried to have a relationship with their father. The year Ana turned twenty-one Alberto invited both girls to Madrid. I had no objections. By that time, I had already returned twice myself. My job came with a little bonus and I spent it as fast as it took me to get to the American Express office. I stayed with Julina and Luis and spent evenings with old friends. Aurora invited me to her house. I wanted to take her to lunch but she insisted on making a paella and her famous *croquetas*. "I know how much you like them," she said. Alberto never knew I was in Madrid. No one ever told him.

In contrast to my lovely visits Ana and Alicia endured a sad repeat of their father's trips to the States and eventually went to stay with Julina. Alicia came home on schedule with a look on her face that said, "Ain't doin that again." But Ana stayed another six weeks. She had always studied linguistics and language teaching. When she told her father she wanted to follow a summer course related to the Spanish language, he agreed to pay for it. The university's location came as a bonus and she spent the remainder of her days in Santander in the north of Spain as far from Alberto as she could get.

*

As I write the final lines of this memoir, my daughters and I have just returned from walking a section of the Camino de Santiago in northwest Spain. Return, returned, returning. The word gathers meaning. I mean we have returned to Arizona where we live. But we had also returned to Spain. In fact, the past years have been a series of returnings that seemed unlikely the morning my girls and I boarded a plane and departed Madrid in 1976.

*

In 2009, we returned and went in search of the church by the sea. I had never told Alberto about it, but I wanted to see it again. To make sure it was real.

As we drove, I strained to see something familiar along the shore. I couldn't. What did I expect after all this time? All I knew for certain was that we were headed in the right direction following a road, twisty as an eel, that overlooked the sea. Several meters below, the waves roiled against the rocks, just as they had a lifetime earlier.

I remembered the first time I saw the waves glinting between patches of fog—a chilly evening when I drove, anxious and alone. But on this morning, the world shimmered in sunlight, and Ana was driving, acting as chief chauffeur during a nine-day vacation in Spain.

"If we don't find it in the next five kilometers," I said, "we'll just turn around and go back. Maybe I dreamed the whole thing anyway."

"Oh, we're going to find it!" Ana's voice held no hint of doubt. "You've been talking about the church in Galicia for thirty years. Besides, the concierge at the *parador* told you it wasn't far, right?"

"Right." I didn't add that the concierge also said the church was no longer open to the public. That wasn't the point anyway. I just wanted to know it was still there. And for a reason I couldn't explain, I needed to show it to Ana. I wished Alicia could be with us. I wanted her to see the ancient church, too—the one where I heard the fishermen sing Mass in Galician dialect. And I wanted to show both my daughters the town of Bayona where we spent the month of August when Ana was three years old and Alicia was a howling infant in diapers. But at the moment, with a husband, three children under the age of ten, a dog and a demanding teaching position, Alicia had little time for travel.

"I can't believe you ever drove on this road," Ana interrupted my musings.

"Neither can I."

Ana knew how I reacted to heights. On a previous trip to Paris, we had climbed to the top of the Arc de Triumph and I had nearly passed out. We had to use an *Employees Only* elevator because I panicked at the sight of the descending steps. Now, with Ana driving, the sheer drop-off to the Atlantic only made me shaky. She slowed the car to take another curve and then, just like on that evening all those years ago, I saw the iron cross on the church belfry.

"That's it! Oh, my gosh! Ana, do you see it?"

She nodded. A moment later we saw the sign. *Santa Maria de Oia.*

We left the main highway and followed a dirt road that led toward the ocean. The road hadn't changed, and the weathered granite church stood on a slope facing the sea as it had since the twelfth century. Ana drove through an opening in the low stone wall that defined the church precinct, separating it from the rocky shore. She parked on gravel by the gate. A bleached blue fishing boat lay on its side, tied to a stake several feet from the water. Another one, little more than a skeleton now, looked as though it might have been there as long as the church, or at least since my last visit. There was no one else in sight. Ana pulled a camera from her purse, but neither of us spoke as we left the car. I walked to the front of the church, hoping the hotel concierge had been mistaken, but the door was locked. Maybe there would be another time to study the frescos I knew to be inside; I hoped so. I'd had only a glimpse of them a long time ago.

I pressed my palm against the wood door where other hands had worn a smooth patch above the rusting lock. I wanted tactile confirmation of my connection to this place where years earlier I had stood for a brief time, overwhelmed by the ancient setting and the voices singing in a mysterious language. I had felt a bond, a primal recognition, although I don't know why. I shivered now at the evocative beauty around me—and at the memory of a crushing loneliness.

A moment later Ana turned from taking photos of waves and walked toward me.

"Is it the way you remembered?" she said. "Happy now?"

I nodded but the tears rolled down my face.

⁂

After many disappointments, Ana had tried one last time to find peace with her father; the result was the same. She left his house in tears. When she entered it again six months later it was to settle the estate after his death.

⁂

We sat at the kitchen table; this time Ana's. After weeks in Madrid she had finally made order from the chaos Alberto left behind. She poured me a glass of wine and handed me an envelope.

"What's this?" I said extracting a check made out to me for more money than I had ever seen.

"I figure that's about what he owed you in back child support." She grinned.

I could barely speak.

"But … what about you … what about your sister?"

"We're fine," she said. "I've worked everything out. I'll keep the flat in Madrid, at least for the time being. Maybe I'll teach in Spain for a while, and when I get the place cleaned up, you can come and stay for as long as you like."

⁂

Ana did teach in Spain and in Paris for five years. Eventually, she sold the flat and returned to the States where, in the strange way the fates deal with us, she met a Frenchman right here in Arizona. Francois, a pilot, has a family home in Biarritz. I've visited several times—a beautiful place on the coast in Basque country. Ana has been a successful realtor for the past few years.

Alicia has been an elementary teacher in bi-lingual and gifted programs for twenty-five years and married to Barry for twenty-four. They have a son, two daughters and a dog.

Two years ago we made a pilgrimage to Spain and France: Ana, Alicia, Emmie age 16, Sarah, age 13 and me, age depends on who is asking.

Now my granddaughters have the travel itch, too.

Lately they have mentioned destinations as disparate as the Cannes Film Festival, Greece, and Portland, Oregon. I'm pleased, though if they say they want us to return to Spain to see more of its beauty, to learn more of the culture and history that still excites me, well ... I'll jump at that without a second thought.

⁂

# Acknowledgements

I am deeply grateful for the many encouraging voices I heard while writing this memoir. Some spoke and moved on, others speak to me still. Here, in order of their appearance in my life, I give my heartfelt thanks to those voices that spoke the loudest and were the most consistent: Karla Elling, Manager of Arizona State University's Creative Writing Program roped me into her class in Italy where I had gone only to study art in Florence. "You should write a book," she said. Paul Morris, Director of Liberal Studies and creative writing instructor at ASU found time even after class was over to sit with me and nudge my project along. I met Bonnie Pike and Jan Murra, both published authors, in one of Paul Morris's classes. We have been meeting periodically for years, each with a different project but always learning from each other. In a writing workshop at the Piper Center at ASU, I met Carolyn Allport and Judith Starkston. The same thing happened. My dining table became an ad hoc classroom. Finally, when I had a completed manuscript (and almost by chance,) I met the writing coach, Susan Pohlman. She helped remove the bumps. To all of these wise and generous helpers, *un millón de gracias de todo corazón*.

# About the Author

Diane Lorz Benitez grew up in the 1950s in Meadville, PA. Perhaps singing the Mass responses in Latin or the sound of her grandfather's German accent awakened her interest in language—or the visit from an uncle who had lived in Paris and spoke French. Maybe following her Army captain father from post to post during WWII created an appetite for travel.

Although encouraged by her parents toward a teaching career, she left college to work in a high-end retail store in Cleveland, Ohio. Her classroom was a salon of imported fashions and colleagues with accents. She wanted the story behind any voice that didn't sound like hers. But the accented voice that changed her life belonged to a Spaniard.

At the age of twenty-four, Lorz Benitez resigned from a hard-earned position, drained her bank account and sailed away with a civil engineer from Madrid ten years her senior. This is the inside story of a Spanish/American marriage during the final decade of the Franco dictatorship, and of an ongoing love for Spain.

After nearly twelve years in Madrid, Lorz Benitez returned to the United States and now lives in Scottsdale, Arizona.